WHAT MOGUL SKIERS ARE SAYING ABOUT MICHAEL MEAD...

"The *Invincible Mogul Skier* is full of great insights and very specific knowledge. If someone wants to learn to mogul ski, this book is a great resource! Michael and I share a passion for mogul skiing and it was fun sharing my experiences with him. It was a pleasure working with him!"

-Bryon Wilson
(Olympic Bronze Medalist, Team USA)

"There are three major details I remember from my time skiing with Mike, among many more intricacies. First, Mike's hands-on method of isolating body parts (shoulders, elbows, hips, quads, knees, etc.) on the hill, to put the skier in the ideal aggressive body position, is a method I still use today in my own skiing, as well as when teaching others. Second, the importance of intensity and confidence in jump takeoffs that Mike instilled in me. I'm reminded of a day at A-Basin, in the spring, I finally nailed a takeoff for my "cork 7." And lastly, the push it sometimes takes from an external source to innovate, try something new, and ultimately progress, even if it scares you. Example: Mike pushed us all to try a new trick on the spot... the only front flip I've done in a true mogul course to date. Good memories thinking back on our days ripping (Breckenridge) together. Thank you Mike for your influence and help in my career all those years ago."

-Dylan Walczyk
(World Cup Medalist, Team USA)

"You (are) still one of my favorite coaches. I miss seeing you around. I have wanted this all my life and now I'm ready to secure my spot at this month's World Cup!"

-Bruce Perry Jr.
(World Cup Skier, Team USA)

"Mike Mead was more than just a coach to me... He inspired me to find freedom and happiness on and off the slopes. He always encouraged a positive outlook on things... He inspired me to push myself, and to celebrate even the smallest of victories. He was a very fast, aggressive skier and he gave me the secret to not only speed, but to the right attitude as well."

-Lindsey Eckhoff
(Nor-Am Skier, Ranked 11th place in USA, 2015)

"Life begins at the end of your comfort zone, and this could not hold any truer to the teachings of Coach Mike Mead. For me, the most influential step from his process was easily to "scare myself." This is one of the most difficult things to do consciously, but once accomplished, opened me up to a world of possibilities. It taught me that not every crash is season ending and that every victory tastes sweeter when you knew you gave everything you had and a little more. Whether you set out to better a personal best or conquer the skier next to you, the first step is to scare yourself. Mike was the most inspirational yet frustrating coaches I have ever encountered in my time as a Mogul skier. He consistently demanded more of me than I thought physically possible, but I always knew that he would never ask me to attempt anything he didn't think I was capable of. With most coaches they ask you to perform a task they themselves could not complete. However, Mike was not only able to display the skills he was teaching but could break down his process in depth to the point where a basic knowledge of physics would be necessary to fully grasp the lesson. One of which was the concept of the glass plate. It took me years to fully understand what he was asking me to do but once I felt myself getting set on it, I knew I needed to stay stacked and relax my mind and body. Without his coaching I never would have been able to ski at the level I obtained."

-Matt Didonato
(Holiday Valley Freestyle Team, USA)

"The biggest thing about Mike is that he knew exactly what he was talking about. His complex systems were broken down for me so I could understand even at a very young age. He had developed his 5-step method and not only told me what it could do for my skiing, but he showed me as well. (To say he is a great skier is an understatement!) His idea of the glass plate was something I wrestled with for years but once I learned to get on it I never skied the same again! A few other huge things he taught me was to relax in the moguls and use my ski to make the turn instead of muscling the turn around. All of this and more, I certainly would not have achieved what I did without him being on the hill with me in rain, wind, and snow. Because of him I was able to work my way to ski at Nationals and even place as high as 24th."

-Nick Didonato
(Holiday Valley Freestyle Team, USA)

"Mike is a bit of a Renaissance man."

-David Colturi
(Youngest Diver Ever to Win a Red Bull Cliff Diving World Series Event, USA)

THE INVINCIBLE MOGUL SKIER

THE INVINCIBLE MOGUL SK1ER

A HIGHLY-DETAILED TECHNICAL MANUAL
for the Advancement of Competitive Mogul Skiers

By Michael Mead, PE

The Invincible Mogul Skier is published by Michael L Mead

Copyright © 2018 by Michael L Mead

Reproduction or other use, in whole or in part, of the contents without permission of the publisher is strictly prohibited.

ISBN-13: 978-1-7328355-2-8

Dedicated to all mogul skiers everywhere.
May challenges and successes
come in equal measures,
surpassed only by your passion.

TABLE OF CONTENTS

PREFACE	i
INTRODUCTION	v
DEFINITIONS	viii

PART 1 : THE BOOK OF FIRE : MECHANICS OF MOGUL SKIING
THE NEW MOGUL METHOD — 1

CHAPTER 1: THE EVOLUTION OF MOGUL SKIING — 3
- HISTORY OF MOGUL SKIING — 3
- TRADITIONAL MOGUL SKIING METHODOLOGY — 5
- AUGMENTED MOGUL SKIING METHODOLOGY — 7

CHAPTER 2: THE FIRE THAT BURNS WITHIN — 14

CHAPTER 3: THE BATTLE FOR THE FRONT SEAT — 18

CHAPTER 4: THE MECHANICS OF MOGUL SKIING — 21
- FROM AVERAGE TO GREAT, IN ONE DAY FLAT — 21
- EFFICIENCY SECTION — 22
- THE NITTY-GRITTY — 27
- SUSTAINABILITY SECTION — 31
- BALANCE AND FLUIDITY SECTION — 39
- FINE-TUNING SECTION — 51
- VISUALIZATION SECTION — 54
- PUTTING IT ALL TOGETHER — 54

CHAPTER 5: THE NEW MOGUL METHOD — 58

CHAPTER 6: THE GLASS PLATE — 70

PART 2 : THE BOOK OF WIND : APPLIED MOGUL SKIING
STRATEGY, PREPARATION, AND COMPETITION — 77

CHAPTER 7: OBSTACLES AND OPPORTUNITIES	79
OBSTACLES	79
OPPORTUNITIES	84
CHAPTER 8: COMPETITION	90
THE ATHLETE'S ADVANTAGE	92
TRAINING	93
SINGLES	103
DUALS	104
CONSISTENCY	106
CHAPTER 9: VISUALIZATION	108
CHAPTER 10: PRACTICING GOOD MOGUL SKIING POSTURE	112
THE PROGRESSION	112
CHAPTER 11: IMPACT, INJURIES, AND HOW BEST TO DEAL WITH THEM	147

PART 3 : THE BOOK OF ICE : PSYCHOLOGY OF MOGUL SKIING
HOW TO NOT GET BURNED BY YOUR OWN MIND — 173

CHAPTER 12: THE CAVE OF THE MIND	175
CHAPTER 13: MEDITATION	185
HOW TO MEDITATE	185
PRACTICAL MEDITATION	192
PRACTICING PRACTICAL MEDITATION	194
CHAPTER 14: TAP YOUR INNER STRENGTH	197

CHAPTER 15: THE LEARNING PROCESS	202
CHAPTER 16: SUPERHEROES AND JUGGERNAUTS	214
JUGGERNAUTS	217
SUPERHEROES	227
CHAPTER 17: LEGENDS, FLOW, AND DOING THE IMPOSSIBLE	248
FLOW	248
DOING THE IMPOSSIBLE	251
LEGENDS	259
CHAPTER 18: MENTAL WARCRAFT	269
FEAR AND INTIMIDATION	270
HEAD GAMES	272
THE LOOKING GLASS	274
CHAPTER 19: YOUR OPINION BETRAYS YOU	278
WHERE OPINIONS EVOLVED FROM	282
THE HUMAN BRAIN	285
CHAPTER 20: HOW TO LEARN	288
LEARN HOW YOU LEARN	292
LEARN HOW TO TEACH YOURSELF	294
LOCK & KEY	296
CHAPTER 21: LIFELONG LEARNING	313
THE PLATEAU TRAP	313
A FINAL WORD	316
BIBLIOGRAPHY	319
APPENDIX: PHOTO EXPERIENCE LESSONS	323
PHOTO EXPERIENCE 1: WHEN TO INITIATE UPHILL HIP DRIVE	325
PHOTO EXPERIENCE 2: HOW TO FIX MISTAKES IN REAL TIME	327
PHOTO EXPERIENCE 3: THE POWER STORED IN YOUR SKIS	328

PREFACE

I have always been a bit of a hellion, both on and off the mogul course. Probably the first time my parents realized that they were going to have their hands full with me, I was three. My mother is the one that tells the story best, but I also remember this happenstance myself. My mom was driving on an icy road in our pickup truck one afternoon, and she lost control of the truck. As our truck sped towards an icy snow bank, my mom told me to put my head between my legs and hold on. Without questioning, I said, "Okay mommy," and did just that. We slammed through the snow bank and tumbled in our truck over and over again down the bank, eventually coming to a stop upside down. The crash blew out the windshield and both side windows. There was glass everywhere. It was a bad accident. My mom was trembling and banged up pretty bad. She turned and asked me if I was alright, and instantly I shouted: "Let's do that again!"

When I was a little bit older, about eight, my ski-instructor father thought that I was finally a good enough skier to take me to the "steep hills" at Killington, VT. Killington was quite a step up from the hills I grew up skiing on at my home mountain of Holiday Valley. On our very first run, my dad took my brother and I to Ovation, which is Killington's steepest run. Ovation is so steep, it often has difficulty holding snow. Additionally, when it does have snow, it is usually covered in moguls because it is too steep to groom. Well, after tucking down the catwalk and jumping off the headwall, then navigating the moguls, I got the bottom of the hill unencumbered and utterly unimpressed. I was so far ahead of the pack that I had to wait for my dad and everyone to catch up. As soon as they did, I asked my dad, "Can we go to the steep hills now?" In my eight-year-old mind, I was picturing the razor-sharp, treeless mountaintops of the Alps that I saw in the movies. I remembered being so disappointed by Killington's "steeps."

Innumerable other occasions throughout my life separated me from what other people thought was scary, or ill-advised. For example, I remember going to Darien Lake with my friends, and we were all very excited to ride the new Superman roller coaster with the new 205 ft. initial drop:

Superman: Ride of Steel, Initial drop: 205 ft. Darien Lake, NY

As we were going up the "clunk-a-clunk-a-clunk" chain-elevator of the roller coaster, I remember turning and talking to my friend about something. I don't remember what, but all I remember is that as I was talking to him, his eyes got real big, and I saw the blood run out of his face. I kept on talking anyways, but I do remember that it struck me as odd. Suddenly, my body was jarred forward, and I had to catch myself before I slammed right into him. We were spinning round and round on the lower part of the roller coaster before I realized that I had completely missed the main drop off point of the roller coaster. The scare… the thrill. All of it. I had talked right through it. I never even got to feel the "rise in my stomach" feeling or anything. That was the first time I realized that I was pathologically different than most people when it came to these types of things. I was, and still am, mostly unaffected by such amusements.

PREFACE

Despite being on skis since I could walk, and despite the fact that my father was a skiing instructor, my mogul skills evolved slowly at first, because I did not join an actual mogul skiing team until I was thirteen years old. However, I took to it like a fish to water. I learned quickly and took third place in my first mogul skiing competition, but I won my second mogul competition. I won the New York State Upright Areal Championship shortly after that. I even managed to squeak out an appearance at the Junior National Freestyle Olympics in Whitefish, MT. I won many events through my mogul skiing career, including Holiday Valley's infamous "Bump 'n' burn," A-basin's "Lando's MoJo" competition, and open mogul competitions at Winter Park, Killington, and Aspen. My mogul skiing style could only be described as "full throttle." I was as intense in the start gate as a bull in a professional rodeo. My attitude was "win or die trying." Usually, I did the former, but other than that, I fell hard, and spectacularly. I was completely fearless when it came to speed. Possibly because I was pathologically different, but more likely because my Mogul Method was just so effective.

I had appearances in several Pro-Mogul events, at Killington, VT, Steamboat, CO, and Sunday River, ME. I've been on TV stations such as ESPN, OLN, and many local channels due to coverage of larger events, one of which was an 8th place finish at the United States Freestyle Grand National in Heavenly Valley, CA. I continued to improve drastically for two more years after my top-ten finish at nationals. It was the character building and the skill fortification that happened during those last few years that are the largest influence on my Mogul Method. During my final years as a competitive mogul skier, I developed a method of skiing moguls that not only made me one of the fastest mogul skiers in the country, it also made me remarkably consistent. At the end of my career, I posted the fastest time in 40 consecutive competitive runs I skied. According to the legendary United States mogul coach, John Dowling, who has put more athletes on the USA World Cup team than any other coach, I was indeed the fastest mogul skier in the country at that time.

After I retired from competitive mogul skiing, I got into coaching. During my nearly ten-year career as a mogul coach, I have had the honor of coaching some of the country's best athletes, including World Cup mogul skiers Bruce Perry Jr. and Dylan Walczyk, Nor-Am Skiers Brayden Pawlik and Lindsey Eckhoff, and a multitude of national and junior national level athletes.

I think my different way of thinking was what ultimately helped me discover my Mogul Method. But that doesn't mean you have to be pathologically different to use it. It is just something that helped me develop my method through trial and error. This book is built around my Mogul Method, which is an easy-to-digest five-step formula. Furthermore, the book will walk you through the process of getting you to the point where the method can be easily applied. It covers everything from the simple mechanics of good mogul skiing form, to specific ways you can strengthen your most important muscle groups, to how to improve your competitive edge psychologically.

I want to thank you and congratulate you on your decision to invest in your future mogul skiing success! It is my hope and passion that the information in this book will help answer all those lingering questions that you have about mogul skiing. It is my promise to you that if you dedicate yourself to my Mogul Method, it will help you to improve your skills beyond your wildest dreams. My name is Michael Mead, and this is the Invincible Mogul Skier.

INTRODUCTION

They always used to tell me: "You think too much," or "You're too much of a perfectionist." Many times, I attempted to think less and be less of a perfectionist to align with my coaches' wishes. But that just wasn't me. Over time, I began to realize that it was futile to go against my very nature. I had to embrace who I was. To do so, I had to identify my problems. Overthinking did, in fact, become a problem for me in competition. I could never seem to satisfactorily boil down all of the details of my upcoming competition run the way I wanted to, so on and on my mind would race, predicting outcome after outcome. For years, I tried clearing my mind before my run by listening to music and "chillin' out." That seemed to work for many people, but it actually worked worse for me. I needed to find a process that worked for me in a beneficial and repeatable way. It needed to be detailed enough to satisfy my racing mind's many questions, broad enough to work in all mogul skiing situations, and simple enough to be easily remembered.

"The New Mogul Method" that you will read about in this book is the process that evolved from that desire. It has been solidified, honed, sharpened and tested for the last 15 years. I used this method myself as a competitor and now as a coach. It's simplicity and perfectly cyclical nature is easy to understand and put into practice. From novice to expert, it works for everyone. No method exists that produces more rapid improvement or solutions to more mogul skiing problems than the New Mogul Method. The rest of this book dives deeply into all of the peripheral aspects of mogul skiing, their difficulties, and the solutions to them. This book is a compilation of 21 years of competitive mogul skiing application and coaching experience. It is the most all-encompassing book of its kind at the time of its writing.

This book provides a range of pure mechanical skills and techniques, but it also covers abstract thought patterns and mental skills that give one the advantage to win at mogul skiing. It contains powerful strategies that I have learned, developed, and applied successfully in my own life. I start and end each chapter with insightful quotes to offer some interesting perspectives on the topic of that particular chapter. This provides the additional benefit of putting you into the most beneficial state of mind for you to absorb the information in the chapter. Then I do it again at the end of the chapter so that you may better retain the chapter's essence. I also make use of "Keys" in a similar way at the end of my drills sections to make the main takeaway points easier to remember, as well as easier to find when you need to reference them again in the future. I use many personal stories as a means to best demonstrate the skills that I wish to teach you. I also use analogies quite extensively to help better explain my points. Everything in this book is the result of one or more of the very best skills that I have developed, propagated, evolved, and cultivated throughout my life, and have proven themselves to be the most effective. I hope for nothing more than to expand the awareness and skills that any mogul skier already has by reading this book.

Mogul skiing is all physics. Everything can be dissected and explained via physics, but it gets real complicated, real fast. Additionally, it is really more of an art than a science, meaning that it is a study of how your body specifically reacts to skiing moguls, more so than a strict matrix of dynamic formulas. Due to natural variations in all variables of the equations, everyone will experience the same mogul line differently. This is because everyone's body is different and every mogul is different every time you ski it. However, there are some keys to the physics that are fairly consistent between all athletes. I will focus on those areas to help you hone your mogul skiing skills.

This book is divided into three parts. Part 1: "The Book of Fire: Mechanics of Mogul Skiing," is dedicated to teaching and explaining the necessary skills and mechanics of mogul skiing. Part 2: "The Book of Wind: Applied Mogul Skiing," is dedicated to how to utilize those skills in a competition or other high-intensity settings. Part 3: "The Book of Ice: Psychology of Mo-

INTRODUCTION

gul Skiing," is dedicated to psychological techniques and tools that you can use to give yourself an advantage over your competitors, as well as tools to help you focus and improve the application of your current skill set with more consistency. Additionally, it will aid you in your mental toughness and lifelong learning process. I employ as many visual aids (pictures, charts, graphs, etc.) as possible to help clarify the concepts outlined in the text. They contain as much information as possible, in a simple to understand way. Pictures of actual techniques are utilized to help in their explanation. I have interviewed and conversed with many experts, both inside and outside of mogul skiing, to bring you the best set of skills possible for you to draw upon. I have had in-depth conversations with many elite athletes about their theories, art, and application of all types of skills. From those conversations, I distilled the applicable and suitable skills for mogul skiing.

Now you can have all that knowledge here in one place, inside this book. There is a downloadable PDF in which I transcribed several interviews in their entirety that I had with Olympians, World Champions, Head Coaches, and other top performers. The rest I draw from personal experience and my own unique way of thinking about the sport, which is largely a cross between an expert-elite mogul skier, an engineer's thoughtful perspective, and the ability to analyze and manage risk from my days as a stunt man. I am so grateful for everyone who helped contribute to this book. I want to especially thank my brother Nathaniel Mead, currently a member of the PSIA demonstration team (one of Ski Instructing's highest honors), who helped me pull this book together into its final form. He helped me make sure that the concepts in this book are coherent, easy to understand, and add yet another layer of quality to this book.

DEFINITIONS

In this book, I use specialized jargon fairly liberally. It is intended to be read by competitive mogul skiers who are already accustomed to the lingo, but some of the more important terms that you will hear about are defined below as these tend to be the most important and emotionally charged for mogul skiers:

BACK SEAT - When one's center of mass is further uphill than the heels of one's feet while skiing.

BLACK VEIL OF IGNORANCE - A psychological barrier that separates us from knowing that which we do not know. It can be a difficult psychological barrier to break through, because in order to do so, we must first admit to ourselves that we are less significant than we are programmed to believe. To admit that others are better than us can be the most painful step in the learning process, but a necessary one for us to go through in order to be able to find a mentor, coach, etc., and to reach our ultimate potential. Only you can lift your black veil of ignorance. All of us have one at some point in our lives.

BOBBLE - Any small mistake one makes that causes one to lose balance temporarily and break from a good "stacked position."

BOOT - Not like a boot that you wear on your foot. "Boot" in this book usually refers to the amount of "up" that a jump has; that is, how inclined against the slope it is. Jumps that have a lot of "boot" will send you higher into the air than jumps with little "boot." However, jumps with "too much" boot" present their own set of problems.

CROSS-RUT - Skiing the mogul across its given rut. For example: skiing from the backside of the mogul on the right side, to the top of the mogul on the left side, is skiing "cross-rut." Usually, better mogul skiers chose to ski slightly "cross-rut" by skiing the mogul line more directly or dynamically than the given shape of the line.

DEATH COOKIES - Chunks of hardened snow or ice that usually occur in groups. They are usually too heavy to push out of the way with a turn. If you try, they can knock you off balance. If you hit several of them, they can cause unpredictable results. Sometimes hitting a patch of death cookies can result in a nasty fall including serious injuries like torn ACLs, or a broken collarbone. This is because although they appear free and separate from the hill, they can at times still be frozen in the snow underneath. They also make for an uneven landing. Most skiers instinctively avoid them. There is no reason to try to ski death cookies. In the moguls, death cookies can be created from the chopping of the landings and pushed off the landing hill and further down the course. Sometimes, one or more death cookies can congregate in one or more ruts of the mogul course. Try to step out of the death cookies that are in your line before the competition starts, or do your best to avoid them.

FALL LINE - The line down the hill that is most directly downhill. In other words, if you pushed a bowling ball down the hill, it is the path that the bowling ball would take.

FLYING OVER THE HANDLEBARS - A type of crash or fall that is started by your feet drastically stopping or slowing down abruptly and without warning, which has the result of your upper body getting thrown suddenly forward, usually resulting in a crashing front flip.

FOUR-POINT LANDING - Each one of your pole plants and feet is considered one point, so a four-point landing refers to landing from an aerial maneuver with both of one's poles (two points) planted next to each foot (two points). It is generally accepted to be good form to have a four-point landing because it forces both the hips and the shoulders to be square down the fall line upon landing.

FRAME CONTROL - The level of emotional conviction in your beliefs, which helps to influence or control the outcome of a situation to how you see fit. Sometimes, two or more opposing sides will get in a "frame" battle, which is really just an argument of opinions. The one with the strongest ability to frame control will win the battle.

GLASS PLATE - A high plane in the moguls where—regardless of a mogul's size, depth, or spacing—the point of impact is never any lower than the tops of one's boots from the highest plane as drawn across the tops of the moguls. It is where all speed control needs to happen laterally. "Breaking through the glass plate" is when one puts their feet too far down into the rut in an attempt to control the speed, but it usually backfires and the skier gets bucked hard. This is difficult to recover from.

GRABBY SNOW - Snow that has a mixture of different coefficients of frictions, usually intermittent patches of snow with extraordinarily high coefficients of friction. These patches can "grab" your skies, slowing you down unexpectedly.

GROOMER - A large, industrial-scale piece of heavy machinery used to "groom" or "flatten" the trails at the end of every day at a ski resort. It has a large tread on it like a tank to propel it in the snow. It has a snowplow at one end, and tiller at the other. The tiller is used to "chew up" uneven spots on the hill and spits out nice corduroy strips of snow as it passes. Commonly referred to as a "**CAT**." It may or may not have a winch on it; if it does, it is called a "winch **CAT**."

GROOMER-MADE MOGULS or CAT-MADE MOGULS - Moguls made by a groomer or a winch **CAT**, by manually placing offset "waves" of snow next to each other. The final product of which is stepped out and skied in by the skiers to give them their final shape.

HOLLOW POSITION - A slightly concave position of the front part of the body that unifies all the frontal body muscles by getting one's hips into the "Mogul Skier Hips Up Position." This hip position straightens out the spine, most notably the lower back, which has the beneficial result of giving us more range of motion in the moguls. Additionally, it is a fundamental body position for doing almost all athletic maneuver, such as aerial tricks.

KEY - The knowledge, the opinion, or the explanation that paves the road for you to acquire a desired skill, trait, or advantage.

KNEE ANGLE - The angulation that your shins make in regard to the vertical position as seen from downhill. Knee angle occurs when we absorb a mogul across our body to the opposite shoulder.

KNEE POCKET - That place on the side of your knee directly behind the inside ball of your knee, that when that knee is bent and you put your legs together, your other knee rests and fits nicely behind it. It is a very important knee position in mogul skiing.

LEAD CHANGE - When we make a turn, the tip of our downhill ski is always slightly behind our uphill ski. Therefore, when we transition into the next turn, we need to switch which ski is out in front, in order to keep the downhill ski behind the uphill ski. The process of switching which ski is out in front happens at the inflection point (middle point) between the turns. This switching process is what is known as a "lead change."

LINE - A pathway of least resistance through the moguls, i.e., the most direct and rhythmic way through the moguls to the bottom of the hill. A pathway through the moguls that has consecutively alternating left-right turns without interruption.

LOCKBOX - A skill, trait, or an advantage that you seek to acquire, when no one is willing or able to teach you.

MAN-MADE MOGUL COURSE - Also known as a "groomer-made course." Which is any modern day professional mogul course, where a qualified CAT operator uses a groomer to create piles of snow in the exact spots needed to create the mogul course. The exact spot of the moguls is usually measured out and tagged by hand by the mountain's Chief of Course. After the snow "mounds" are pushed into the right spot, the local mogul team accompanied by its coaches will usually "step out" the course several times, because it usually has a lot of death cookies in it. After the course is "stepped out," then the mogul course is "skied in" by the skiers, which is usually a very slow process, and sometimes takes several days.

MOGUL SKIER HIPS UP - The process of rocking your pelvis downward and forward in order to remove the curvature out of your lower back. Closely related to the Hollow Position.

MOON DROP - A type of failure to do an aerial trick that causes one to abandon the trick and land on one's back. Usually associated with falling from a great height.

OBSTACLES - Those difficult sections of the mogul course that we need to create a Plan of Action for. Obstacles are given a difficulty rating on the "Obstacle Rating Scale," a scale of 1-10, with 10 being the most difficult. Obstacles rate 4 or above on this scale. If it is below a 4, it is not considered an obstacle.

OPPORTUNITIES - Line, Love, and Landings. The three L's of Advantage.

PIKE POSITION - The fully bent-over position where one tries to place one's face between one's legs while keeping their knees locked, legs squeezed tightly together, and toes pointed (if applicable). Usually accompanied by grabbing one's ankles with one's hands.

PRE-ABSORB - The act of rocking the weight back to the tail of the skis in an attempt to unload the weight from the front of the skis, so that the front of the skis do not take as much force upon impact. Usually accompanied with pulling one's feet up before one hits the mogul as well. This is also done to decrease the impact receive from the mogul when making contact with it.

PUMPING - Pre-absorbing (see previous), combined with pushing down hard on the backside of the mogul. It is used to increase or generate speed.

PUNCHY SNOW - Snow that tends to be more dense on the outermost layer than on the inner layers. If you turn too abruptly or land on punchy snow, you run the risk of "punching through" the outermost layer and deep into the inner layer. This often has the affect of causing one to fall.

RAZZLE-DAZZLE - The manual action of throwing extra turns in a mogul course, which are not inspired, nor influenced, nor assisted by the course conditions or actual mogul locations. This is considered one of the highest displays of skill that a mogul skier can make.

SKIED IN - The act of many skiers skiing the same line over and over again. Usually, this is done to manually create a mogul rut line wherever you might want one. An alternate meaning can be the manual smoothing out of a freshly groomer-made course.

SLIP THE COURSE - The act of sliding as much snow as possible from the back side of the previous mogul, on the same turn side into the rut of the next turn. Slipping the course is best done in pairs where one person does one side of the turns, and the other person does the other side.

SNOW SNAKES - Small, densely packed veins of grabby snow will get mixed into the natural snow, creating differences in texture in the snow, varying its consistency. These buried little "grabby veins" are known as "snow snakes," and they have been known to take down even the best skiers, because of their unpredictable nature. **Note:** The term "Snow Snake" is commonly used as a scapegoat when no other apparent cause of a fall is present. They also refer to tangible hidden dangers such as sticks, branches, and roots buried in the snow.

SPOT - Where one looks and keeps the majority of his visual focus during an aerial trick.

STEPPED - The act of stepping on a jump face or landing pad repeatedly with tiny steps in order to smooth it out and remove any inconsistencies.

STRAIGHT RUN - An anomaly where a mogul skier stops the majority of his side-to-side turning action while skiing. Often resulting in increased speed and decreased control.

(TO GET) STUFFED - Any hard impact one makes with a mogul or a landing that stops her forward momentum so much her upper body collapses like a book onto her lower body, often resulting in a large bobble, severely decreased speed, and loss of balance.

DEFINITIONS

SWEET SPOT (OF THE SKI) - Point on the ski where impact with a mogul will create the most flexure in the ski, which will, in turn, store the most energy. This energy can be harvested to help us make our turns more easily. Every ski is a little bit different, but it generally starts at the bottom of the curved part of your ski tip, and extends back on the ski anywhere from 6 to 8 inches.

T2B ("T-to-B" or "Top-to-Bottom") - This is one of the most emotionally charged phrases to mogul skiers because of how important it is for a skier's score combined with how difficult it can be to achieve. It is categorically the single most important thing in a mogul skiing run. Jumps don't matter, turns don't matter, even speed doesn't matter if you can't make it to the bottom. Any independently well-performed sections or parcels in a mogul run matter little to nothing if they are not woven into a solid T2B. If one can't put all the mogul skiing sections together in their competition run, the run won't matter much to the judges, and one's score will be negligible when compared to others who had complete T2Bs. Almost all of the best mogul skiers in the world train with T2Bs in mind, and set a goal for themselves or have a number in mind of exactly how many T2Bs they need to have under their belt on any given mogul course before the competition starts. T2Bs are also emotionally charged because they are proof in-and-of-themselves that a skier did not give up on any part of their run (or themselves); that they fought through it all, no matter what might have happened. Therefore, the term is not only linked directly and proportionally to one's skill level (as mentioned above), but also linked directly to determination, fortitude, and resolve, all of which are highly coveted (and practiced) personality traits of any mogul skier. There are few professions in the world that foster as much resolve and determination as mogul skiing. Mogul skiing can, is, and should be practiced in sections, parcels, or in specialties much of the time, but the overall goal is making it all the way to the bottom, to put all of the pieces together in a T2B. Once mogul skiers are consistently making T2Bs, they can then work on limiting their mistakes or "polishing" their runs, such as straightening out their landings or calming their hand position.

TIMING - Refers to when we place our feet on the mogul, as well as when we make our pole plant. If our timing is too late, we will get bucked. If our timing is too early, we will get backseat. Additionally, when our timing is off, the moguls will feel more abrupt and difficult to ski. It will also mess up our rhythm.

TRIUNE ATHLETE - An athlete that is refining not only the physical, but also the mental and emotional parts of themselves.

UPHILL HIP DRIVE - The act of driving our uphill hip forward in order to re-engage the hollow position or "Mogul Skier Hips Up Position." And to initiate the lead change with the uphill hip.

WASHING OUT (ONE'S TAILS) - The act of over-finishing one's turn. Usually followed by slapping one's tails into the mogul before, or at the same time as the feet hit the mogul.

THE INVINCIBLE MOGUL SK1ER
PART 1
THE BOOK OF FIRE
MECHANICS OF MOGUL SKIING
The New Mogul Method

Artwork courtesy of John Dowling

CHAPTER 1
THE EVOLUTION OF MOGUL SKIING

"Almost every advance in art, cooking, medicine, agriculture, engineering, marketing, politics, education, and design has occurred when someone challenged the rules and tried another approach."
-Roger von Oech

HISTORY OF MOGUL SKIING

When someone makes a turn, a small amount of snow is scraped off a relatively large area and pushed to and deposited where the turn is completed. These small deposits are created all over the ski slope by all the skiers on the hill. The initial deposits of snow are small and easily dispersed. Eventually, small deposits are pushed into and consolidated with other small deposits, making slightly larger piles, which are likewise consolidated into even larger deposits elsewhere. This consolidation and relocation process happens all over the hill. Eventually, the piles get so large that a single skier cannot move it anymore; at this point, it becomes a mogul.

Moguls keep emerging and multiplying by this same process until the entire run is covered in them. It is a natural process of skiing and cannot be avoided. If it weren't for the large industrial groomers used by modern-day ski resorts, every single run on the mountain would eventually become a mogul run, if it had enough traffic on it. The groomers usually chew up and spit out fledgling moguls into fine, flat corduroy-shaped snow at the end or beginning of every ski day. Most ski resorts groom the vast majority (if not all) of their terrain every night. They do this because it makes the terrain easier to ski. This is beneficial to the resort because the majority of skiers don't have enough skill to ski moguls and prefer the easier terrain.

There was a time, however, before groomers, where moguls were a natural part of skiing. Therefore, being able to ski moguls was an essential skiing skill to have. Moguls grow anywhere there are skiers. They happen naturally and are an inextricable part of skiing. Massive modern machinery known as "CATs," or "winch CATs" if they have a winch, are deployed all over the world to keep moguls from developing on ski runs with high traffic. It seems that most people and ski resorts prefer fighting against this natural part of skiing rather than simply learning to dance with these intrinsic skiing remnants.

There were a few people, though, who diverged from the masses and actually embraced this more difficult aspect of skiing. By the 1960s, skiing technology had advanced to the point where it was possible to consistently ski in the moguls. This made way for the evolution of competitive mogul skiing and led to the hey-day of mogul skiing, where skiing radicals known as "hot-dogs" used the sport as a version of freedom of expression, and began skiing natural moguls with consistency and skill. At first, the natural competitiveness of these people led to haphazard competitions.

The first freestyle skiing competition was a mix of alpine skiing and acrobatics, and was held in Attitash, New Hampshire in 1966 (wiki.fis-ski.com, 2016). The FIS Freestyle World Cup started in 1978, and the 1st FIS Freestyle World Championships were held in 1986 in Tignes, France. Freestyle Moguls became an Olympic sport in 1992 in Albertville, Canada (wiki.fis-ski.com, 2016).

At first, mogul skiing competitions occurred on natural moguls. The advent of airs was encouraged, but the airs had to be spontaneous, and so were the landings. In those days, one could try to shape their "air bump" with their skis before the competition, but there was no guarantee that someone else wouldn't use that same bump as a landing pad, destroying it as an effective air bump. In an effort to create more consistency and fairness for all athletes, man-made "air bumps" were introduced into the sport so that everyone would have the same equal opportunity to do their aerial maneuvers. Two airs, per mogul run, have always been the norm, and remained the norm when man-made airs got a foothold in the sport. Shortly after the incorporation of manmade air bumps, a flat or semi-flat "landing pad" was pushed out and even chopped for safety and consistency. Eventually, more consistency was desired, and thus the man-made course was born.

A "man-made course" is a mogul course in which the moguls are systematically created by a groomer, the landings are groomed flat, the airs are built by hand, and the landings are chopped. Groomer, or "CAT-made," courses are common nowadays, but mogul competitions are still held on skier-made moguls as well. Skier-made moguls are different from natural moguls because they are created intentionally by dozens of athletes, all turning systematically in the same spots in order to create it. It is a much faster and more consistent method to create mogul lines, as opposed to allowing them to happen naturally. Now let's discuss the original "natural" mogul skiing methodology that worked so well for those free-spirited athletes back in the day.

TRADITIONAL MOGUL SKIING METHODOLOGY

Traditional mogul skiing methodology consists of three main phases of the mogul skiing turn. These are:

- PRE-IMPACT
    - Aligning one's self to their chosen line, being careful not to deviate too far from the line while still checking to make sure they can make the next turn
    - Pre-absorption - Works to lessen the impact of the mogul, reducing shock and hinging

- IMPACT
    - Standing up tall
    - "Edging" or "carving" the turn
    - Pole plant on the backside of the mogul

- POST-IMPACT
    - Maintaining contact with the back side of the mogul
    - Lead-changing to the next turn
    - Segue into Pre-Impact phase

Much of this methodology still exists in today's mogul skiing, with some slight variations that we will get into later. Just remember, the takeaway from this methodology is what happens, or what is "supposed to happen," between the moguls. This method evolved to make skiing moguls look smoother, with a lot of emphasis on being able to align yourself with your "line." This strategy rewarded the higher level of skill of carving down the backside, rather than just hopping from mogul to mogul.

The problem here is that this method was developed by athletes who skied organic moguls. Organic moguls were much less rhythmic than today's artificial mogul courses. The increase in rhythmic consistency in the mogul courses has opened up a superhighway for speeds never seen before in natural moguls. Mogul skiing has rapidly been evolving every few years to make fast skiing both more important and more feasible. Just take for example that in 2015, a mogul course was shortened on average from 16 moguls in the top section, 32 moguls in the middle section, and 16 moguls in the bottom section to 6, 40, and 6 respectively, according to former US Mogul Team Head Coach Garth Hager. That's a decrease from 64 moguls to 52 moguls, which is an 18.75% decrease in length of an actual mogul course. This increased the amount of time a mogul skier has to slow down before the bottom air, while simultaneously decreasing the amount of time he or she would have to "hold on" to get across the finish line if they are less than perfectly stable. If that wasn't enough, it also decreases the overall amount of time a typical mogul skier would need to keep focused, due to the shorter course length, therefore decreasing the risk for higher speeds even further. Truly, it's becoming a fast mogul skier's playground after all.

So what does all this mean? It means that the traditional mogul skiing strategy had to evolve. The faster mogul skiers, therefore, were the ones who spurred the augmentation of the original methodology.

AUGMENTED MOGUL SKIING METHODOLOGY

The biggest change in the mogul skiing methodology was what took place between the turns. The rule of thumb that required maintaining contact with the snow down the backside to increase fluidity, and demonstrate skill, more or less went out the window. The reason for this was because the increased rhythmic nature of the man-made moguls didn't require a skier to keep in contact with the snow to ski smoothly. The method of skiing by "contact" gave way to skiing by "contour," where one follows the general curvature of the back side of the mogul, but rarely makes actual contact with it. Because of this, a new step in the mogul skiing methodology was needed, and some of the phases were revised. The augmented mogul skiing methodology consists of four main parts:

- PRE-IMPACT
    - Pre-absorption - Works to lessen the impact of the mogul, reducing impact shock and limiting hinging

- IMPACT
    - Standing up tall
    - "Edging" or "carving" the turn
    - Pole plant on the backside of the mogul

- POST-IMPACT
    - Contouring down the backside of the mogul
    - Lead-changing to the next turn

- HOLLOW POSITION
    - Requires a "contour" method of skiing moguls
    - Gives us an opportunity to "re-stack" our form (mogul skiing posture)
    - Centering of one's center of mass, while squaring off the hips to one's line
    - Provides a neutral position from which to initiate one's lead change

The advent of the hollow position occurred because mogul skiers can now belay some of the cognitive supercomputing required by skiing organic moguls with a somewhat predictive mogul skiing strategy. Skiing groomer-made moguls is so much more systematic and straight than skiing natural moguls. This systemization of the mogul course is what allows present-day mogul skiers to ski so much faster than the original "Hot-doggers." Modern day groomer-made courses do not require as much lateral, forward, or aft deviation, allowing skiers to retain a constant neutral center of mass between the moguls. This strategy is "predictive" because it requires, or "predicts," that the lateral movements that we will need to make will be minimal. In other words, since we now feel comfortable knowing that the moguls are more or less a consistent depth, width, and rhythm down the course, we can ski them at unprecedented speed when compared to skiing natural moguls. No matter how limited the lateral deviation in a mogul course is nowadays, the depth of the moguls can still push the limits of our absorption. With our lateral range minimized and the need for deep absorption still of great importance to us, the hollow position is the perfect solution. It allows us to re-stack our posture, while centering and squaring away our hips between every mogul turn. It is a more "direct" (straight-line) trajectory of one's center of mass through the moguls, due to the nature of the hollow position.

The hollow position was being used by mogul skiers long before anyone knew what it was or why they were doing it. They just did it because that was the only way it worked. The hollow position was, at first, only known to be of use in aerial maneuvers. Even then, however, most people didn't really know what it was called or even knew it had a name. Take for example, a conversation I had with Olympic silver medalist Travis Mayer many years ago. In our conversation, we were talking about jumping and how to stabilize oneself at great heights while doing tricks. Travis had a solution that he affectionately called "the table top." The "table top" was little more than a feeling he had at the apex of an air while being balanced—otherwise known to many athletes simply as that weightlessness feeling when you run out of upward momentum, and before you start to feel the acceleration of falling. The only trick was that you had to be stacked, and slightly tense, while you were on the "table top" in order for it to work effectively. Travis went on to point out that the better you take off and "pop" off the jump, the longer you will be able to extend the duration of this weightless feeling. In his immensely talented mind, he knew all these things were connected somehow, and they just "worked" for him.

The takeaway here is that Travis alluded to the ability to not only feel the "table top" part of the jump, but to being able to physically extend its duration, increasing his efficiency to do tricks. With little practice, most mogul skiers know instinctively that the apex of the jump is the best part to do tricks and really stall them. But it is also the part of the jump that is the most efficient to do your tricks in because you are not fighting the feeling of acceleration, either up to the peak of the jump, or down from it. This gives us a good goal and location to do the majority of our tricks, because the apex feeling of weightlessness is extendable, and the hollow position is the key.

As mogul skiing and aerials merged, many aerial coaches began teaching the hollow position for what it was in mogul airs. However, since the "contour" method of skiing moguls is essentially an aerial position, I knew that the hollow position had to have some applicability there as well. Many years ago, I had a hunch that this position went much deeper than air tricks, and that it can and should be used in the moguls as well. Eventually, I found the answer I was looking for, and from a very unexpected source.

By and large the hollow position is an advanced skill that still doesn't usually get the attention it deserves in most mogul skiing programs, especially when trying to apply it in the moguls themselves. With precious little information on the topic inside the fledgling sport of mogul skiing, I turned to one of the oldest sports known to man: diving. In order to uproot a deeper meaning to this advanced technique, I discussed it with a co-worker of mine during my stunt-man days. Since my enlightening series of conversations with this athlete, he has since gone on to become one of the biggest names in the world of cliff diving. This kind, easy-going, and unassuming individual's name is David Colturi. In case you aren't familiar, cliff diving is one of the most spectacular forms of diving, where the world's best, most highly-trained diving professionals compete against each other in picturesque locations at near bone-breaking heights.

David Colturi: Professional Cliff Diver

Balazs Gardi/Red Bull Content Pool
David Colturi hits his hollow position right on takeoff

David is the one who finally explained the true meaning and versatility of the hollow position to me, in enough detail to make it applicable to skiing moguls. Not too long after our conversation, this seven-time NCAA All American became the youngest person ever to win a Red Bull World Series event, so we can all rest assured that he truly knows what he is talking about. All I did was apply the same concepts to mogul skiing. In fact, it was already there. People were already using it. They just didn't know they were using it, or that what they were doing even had a name. Therefore,

Dean Treml/Red Bull Content Pool
David Colturi in an apex hollow position

the hollow position never stood a chance of getting improved upon. Until now.

The hollow position is best described in person, as it can be very difficult to understand, do correctly, and more importantly, it can be hard to FEEL correctly. If done correctly, it locates one's center of gravity in such a way that optimizes body movement in all directions. It is an advanced skill that can be difficult to learn.

THE HOLLOW POSITION

Essentially, it is a slightly **piked** position, which pulls one's center of mass to just about the navel. It is most easily felt and practiced by laying on the floor on your back in a slightly piked position, with your arms tucked tightly into your "center cord" or "centroid," which runs parallel to your body from your feet to your toes.

In physics, the hollow position most closely represents the neutral axis of a solid body, but more importantly, the hollow position is what gives us athletes complete control of our body by allowing us to dictate the location of single point (for flipping) or single cord (for spinning). This allows us to spin, flip, twist and fly through the air with remarkable precision. The neutral axis is not only well known to athletes, but it is also one of the fundamentals in structural engineering applications that relate to anything tangible that has mass. The neutral axis as defined for structural analysis in Wikipedia is:

The Hollow Position

Romina Amato/Red Bull Content Pool

David Colturi in the hollow position

MichaelPiniewski/FrostHollow.photo

Michael Mead in the hollow position

*The **neutral axis** is an axis in the cross-section of a **beam** (a member resisting bending) or shaft, along which there are no longitudinal stresses or strains. If the section is symmetric, isotropic and is not curved before a bend occurs, then the neutral axis is at the geometric **centroid**. All fibers on one side of the neutral axis are in a state of **tension**, while those on the opposite side are in **compression**. Since the beam is undergoing uniform bending, a plane on the beam remains plane. That is:*

$$\gamma_{xy} = \gamma_{zx} = \tau_{xy} = \tau_{xz} = 0_{li}$$

*Where γ is the **shear strain** and τ is the **shear stress**. There is a compressive (negative) strain at the top of the beam, and a tensile (positive or "tension") strain at the bottom of the beam. Therefore, by the* **Intermediate Value Theorem**, *there must be some point in between the top and the bottom that has no strain, since the strain in a beam is a* **continuous function**.

If you don't understand this, that is perfectly okay and you are not alone. In general this means that any ridged slim body (like a human body) that is supported at both ends and has some external force exerted on it will bend slightly. This makes the side in contact with the force be in compression, while the opposite side of the object will be in tension. Logically, there has to be some point in between that is neither in compression nor

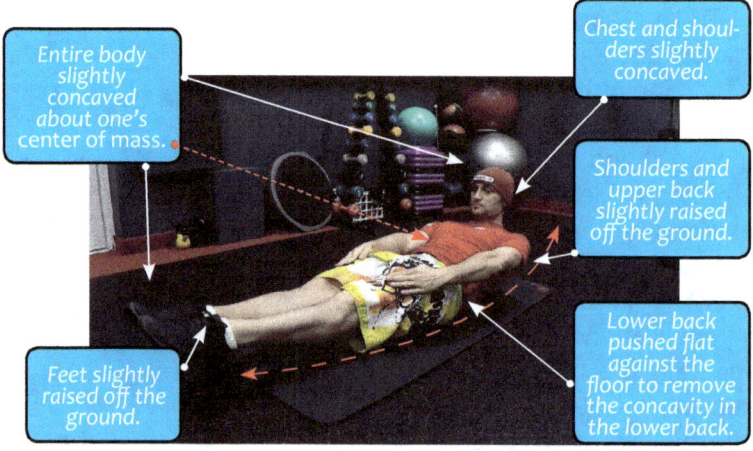

The Hollow Position - *It can be practiced on any flat surface.*

tension, hence the "neutral axis." So, basically, the hollow position exercise that I explained above is simply a means to bend your body slightly so that your abs act as the side in compression, and your back acts as the side in tension, and in doing so, you "feel" for your neutral axis or "hollow position." Since you are a human and not a beam, you can act as your own supports as you lift your head and feet with your muscles to simulate an artificial neutral axis or hollow position.

Pretty cool, huh? But it doesn't stop there! Kinematically (mathematically), any dynamic force, gyration or trajectory of any object, no matter how amorphous, can always be simplified to the trajectory of the center of mass. Since the hollow position gives us the ability to "feel" our center of mass, it also gives us the ability to "feel" our trajectory, no matter how many flips or twists or off-axis tricks we are doing. Ever wonder how elite athletes seem to have a sixth sense about where the ground is at all times? Or how they seem to posses an uncanny ability to put their feet down for a blind landing at the last possible second? The hollow position is the key to that sixth sense. It gives us unparalleled control over our bodies by tying together all of our extremities in a posture of perfect balance. Therefore, all you have to worry about to do the tricks of your wildest dreams is to control your center of mass and your neutral axis. Constantly controlling and always feeling your hollow position allows you to do both simultaneously, while only focusing on one thing: the hollow position. This is well known to most elite athletes because they practice it extensively every day due to its monolithic importance.

Did you know that the hollow position is probably one of the biggest secrets of elite athletes? It allows us to coordinate all of the strength of all of the muscles of the front of the body together. Oppositely, the "Arch Position" does the same to coordinate the strength of all of the muscles in the back of the body.

"Evolution is a process of constant branching and expansion."
-Steven Jay Gould

CHAPTER 2
THE F1RE THAT BURNS WITHIN

*"There are two great days in a persons life:
the day you were born,
and the day you discovered why."*
-John C. Maxwell

Men and women are not born perfect, and they do not mature by age alone. They are scorched by the fire of their life's chosen challenges, forged on the anvil of their own resolve, by the hammering of their training. One can choose an infinite number of paths in this life. Most people choose paths of security and safety, paths with low risk and high reward. It is only natural, after all. However, it is a special breed of people that see past the brutal, unforgiving obstacles that reside in the sport of mogul skiing, and focus on its hidden rewards. They must be able to see beyond the 90% severe injury statistics that mogul skiers must endure, the hefty financial burden, the rigorous day-in and day-out training, and all the sacrifices of one's personal life, to see the greater beauty in mogul skiing. The beauty I am speaking of is the chance to work with a great teacher of life and all its challenges.

There are few better teachers of life than mogul skiing. Mogul skiing will force any mogul skier, for however long they chose to pursue this sport, to learn the value of dedicated training. It will teach them to be ambitious, yet humble; dragon-hearted, yet tempered. It will force them to lean into their boundaries, face their fears, learn, grow and achieve things that they never thought possible. I firmly believe that the sport of mogul skiing is one of life's greatest teachers, and like most great teachers, it comes at a high cost. Not just high financial costs, either—some are physical, and some are mental. Most are difficult lessons that every mogul skier learns during their training. These lessons are generally hard won, but not just applicable in mogul skiing. They usually have an application in the real world. Lessons like dedication, persistence, and getting back up when you get knocked down. They are also lessons that the students will never forget for as long as they live. Yet sooner or later, all of the monolithic challenges that go along with mogul skiing are finally conquered. At that time, all of the other, everyday challenges in the world seem to become easy in contrast. So much so, that they seem to smooth themselves out. That's what makes a great teacher after all, isn't it?

The lessons that mogul skiing teaches are so hard won, that when you do finally learn them, you never forget them. Contrary to what you may be thinking, I am not suggesting that those teachers who throw you to the wolves are the best—that's not what I am saying at all. However, the teachers that throw you to the juvenile wolves might just be geniuses. Likewise, mogul skiers play the risk of severe injury very close to the chest, so to speak, on a daily basis. However, they do have some degree of control over that risk, but nowhere near total control, which adds to the beauty of the sport as a life teacher that has the ability to evolve one into a great man or woman. Mogul skiers are rarely in actual mortal danger, although it does feel like it sometimes. We as mogul skiers are fortunate enough to be able to constantly temper our risk level by our skill level. This is not to say that it is ever exactly proportional, though. This is because we constantly have the choice of how much risk we want to take on, and we bet that risk on the collateral of the sum total of our available skills. This checks and balance system of risk vs. skill allows us to gradually increase our tolerance, for fear, risk, and peril vastly beyond what most people would consider adequate. The risk vs. skill balancing act is what develops our fortitude as skiers and as human beings.

In mogul skiing, "bigger and faster" tends to win competitions. The problem is that "bigger and faster" come at a higher risk factor because they are more dangerous. This plots danger and success in the same type of balancing act as risk vs. skill. Therefore, in mogul skiing, danger is proportional to success. Most other professions shy away from success that is laden with danger. This is not to say that danger in mogul skiing is a good thing, however. Danger is still bad. But with greater risk, there is a greater reward. In mogul skiing, danger and success are inseparable, but danger can be diluted with high levels of skill, which minimizes the risk. That is another reason it is such a beautiful sport, and usually why only the bold and talented will pursue it.

The takeaway from this is that the more danger there is, the more potential for success. The more fear there is, the more potential for success as well. This makes sense, because if you ever watched a mogul skier ski, that was scared out of his mind, but still managed to finish his run successfully, what happened? The crowd goes nuts! They get HUGE points. They had a dangerous run, managed to pull through it because of their high skill level, and managed to keep enough control to keep it together. In further explanation:

$$\text{Skill Level} = \frac{\text{Aptitude of the Athlete * Quality of the Coach * \# of Times Trained}}{\text{Difficulty of the Skill}}$$

$$\text{\# of Times Trained} = \frac{\text{Need or Desire to Learn the Skill * Availability of Training Resources}}{\text{Fear * Social obligations}^2}$$

Where:

CONTROL = The degree to which you can turn, stop, jump, and land on command.

FEAR =

    1. INHERITED FEARS - Fears you are born with. Generally primal fears, fear of snakes, spiders, wolves, water, the dark, the unknown, etc.

    2. LEARNED FEARS - Fears you have because of something you have done, seen, or encountered in your life.

    3. IMPRESSED FEARS - Fears that someone in your family (usually parents) has that are then impressed or imprinted onto you. These types of fears are distinguished from learned fears because they have no activating incident, no experience that caused them. You merely are afraid because someone else is afraid. After all, fear IS contagious. Sometimes these types of fears are difficult to distinguish from the inherited fears, but they are the most easily corrected. For the most part, all you need to do is distance yourself from the person(s) who have the impressing fears, and then realize that they were never your fears to begin with.

In summary, I put all of this into a simple mathematical formula below based on inverse and proportional relationships.

RISK MANAGEMENT:

DEGREE OF DIFFICULTY + FEAR - SKILL - CONTROL = RISK

That is part of the beauty of mogul skiing. Mogul skiers can actually push themselves and their danger tolerance by balancing it against their ever-increasing skill level and control as they train. Using a gradually increasing system of checks and balances, they can cultivate their risk capacity very close to the chest. The fire in a mogul skier's heart burns with such voracity because of the constant forging of the athlete by the sport itself and all of its inherent difficulties. It is the noble pursuit of the perfect mogul run that is so nearly intangible that drives us. The constant training, improving, learning, testing of our limits, suppressing of our fears, and pushing through injuries and failures—they all make it such a worth-while pursuit. Every single mogul run is both a test and a lesson. That is why it can never be perfected. And that is beautiful. There are simply too many variables constrained to too many other variables. Just like life, every challenge, every difficulty, is both a test and a lesson.

We must try our best and learn from both our successes and our failures. Most mogul skiers know this by heart. They come off the mountain and into the real world with a much clearer understanding of what life truly is, and how to succeed at it. This rare method of honing one's life skills gives mogul skiers access to an ingrained pattern in their personal experiences that furnishes them with the formula to succeed in anything they put their mind to. Explicitly or implicitly, all mogul skiers know this, and most high-level athletes do as well.

It is this formula, this method that gives this book its title, that places the mogul skier firmly on the path to invincibility. The invincible mogul skier is not one that is invulnerable, but one that is masterful at the art of balancing danger and success, learning from mistakes, and cultivating an indomitable resolve. It is our vulnerability, after all, that gives us the emotions that make life worth living, and the things worth accomplishing feel worthwhile. This book makes no false pretense about how unattainable invincibility is. This book stands as a salute to the mogul skiers who, by nature, are the ones who pursue such a notoriously difficult and un-perfectible sport. It is a tribute to all of the skills I inherited along my pursuit of this beautiful sport and my attempt to give back to a sport that has furnished me with so many secrets to success in my own life.

> *"There is definitely a connection between finding your passion and reaching your potential."*
> *-John C. Maxwell*

CHAPTER 3
THE BATTLE FOR THE FRONT SEAT

"Time is not a line, but a series of now points."
-Taiisen Deshimaru

    We start this journey with the most prevalent problem in mogul skiing: the battle for the front seat. The one critical rule is that nothing... nothing, matters so much as this: Great hips. Beginners can barely comprehend its complexity, and experts are exhausted by its maintenance. Snow conditions, the type of moguls, and the speed of the skier all contribute to the intricacy of mastering this skill. A mogul skier with good hips will consistently out-perform those who are fast, or fantastic aerialists. It is a common misconception that great turns are what win a mogul competition. They don't. Great hips do! This is because they transcend the mogul turns themselves. Great hips link turns to speed, speed to takeoffs, and landings to turns. They help us spin better, jump higher, and perform better tricks. Hips are everything! Just about everything related to the mechanics of mogul skiing in this book is based on this principle.

    Great hips are what will win the battle for the front seat. When an athlete finally gets out of the back seat, the moguls seem less abrupt, and the hill feels less steep. You may even feel more relaxed and able to ski faster than you ever have before. Great hips are marvelous when you have them working for you, not against you. This is the greatest battle for a mogul skier. Great hips make you feel unencumbered, able to do anything. On the contrary, when you have bad hips, you are, by definition, in the back seat. It is as black and white as mogul skiing gets. Your hip position wins or loses the battle for the front seat. It's as simple as that. Winning the battle provides us the ultimate reward, which is doing more with less, skiing better, looking better, feeling better, skiing faster, and being more efficient in the process. One of the most important things to learn about mogul skiing is understanding what great hips are, and what they look like. I cover this topic in much more depth in the next chapter. For now, it is sufficient to understand that they are a crucial part of what makes up the "Stacked Position" and how to maintain it. To be able to keep your hips in the "Mogul Skier Hips Up Position" and realize the hollow position between each turn. Ultimately, they are what keep us in the "front seat," and on balance.

There are all degrees of skill levels in mogul skiing. Everyone may think that they are the best, and that is why we compete—to establish a pecking order of who really is the best all the way down to the least skilled. Even so, it is generally agreed what the best mogul skier should ski like, even if it is only conceptual. The best mogul skier should be faster, have better turns, and take bigger air than everyone else. All of these things are not only achievable, but augmented with a good hip position. I have coined the highest degree of perfection of great hips as "The Glass Plate." The pinnacle of mogul skiing performance is rooted solely to perfect hip placement. This pinnacle of hip position allows the competitor to be the fastest, lightest of foot, and biggest jumper of them all. However, it can be incredibly hard to do, and even harder to maintain. Without proper training, that is. A great deal of this book is dedicated to teaching you the right building blocks so that you can not only ski on the Glass Plate, but do it consistently. We will learn all about the Glass Plate in Chapter 6.

Proper hip placement makes moguls smooth out and feel almost slippery, which can be a little scary at first. By the application of my Mogul Method, it becomes second nature. After that, you will need a great deal of repetition under the highly tuned eye of the best mogul skiing coach available to help you practice this method. At the very least, after reading this book, you will finally know how to win the battle of the front seat.

Above, I gave you the basic understanding of why great hips are so important, as well as all the potential bonuses it provides. I developed my Mogul Method exactly as described in this book for my own personal benefit in my skiing career. I also continued to hone and refine it for 10 years after I retired from competitive mogul skiing for the athletes that I coached, several of which have made it to the World Cup. Although my method may be new to some people, it is as tried and true as it gets. It has never failed me, nor any of my athletes. It is both a strategy for skiing moguls properly, and a remedy for when things go wrong. It is perfectly cyclical in nature and can be implemented at any and all points on the mogul course at any time. It's validity is race-proven, not race "tested." It is as "watertight" as it gets. That is why it is called the "New Mogul Method." You will learn all about this method in Chapter 5.

The crown jewel of my Mogul Method, The Glass Plate (Chapter 6), was created for the sole purpose of defeating the world's best mogul skiers, and it never failed me until my secret leaked out. However, no one has had the whole story until now. You, my readers, are an elite group that will have The Story, The Method, The Secret, and The Explanation of how to use them properly, direct from their creator. I am about to explain my process to you, in painstaking detail, which only a handful of the best skiers in the entire world know how to utilize. It serves as their secret weapon, but I will reveal it to you in the pages of this book. Now, I have already told you WHY to use my method, next I am going to tell you HOW and WHEN to use it.

*"When the student is ready,
the Master appears."
-Mabel Collins*

CHAPTER 4
THE MECHANICS OF MOGUL SKIING

*"Is it not one of the hardest tasks of life
to separate precious pebbles of truth
from out of the quarry of profession?
Yet it is our supreme task to separate them,
by our enlightenment,
forsaking the shadows with light
that will banish the shadows."*
-F. Beck

FROM AVERAGE TO GREAT, IN ONE DAY FLAT

Over the past decade of coaching mogul skiing, I have had the opportunity to work with all levels of skiing athletes. My favorite types of athletes to work with are the average mogul skiers. Average mogul skiers have already put in lots of miles in the moguls but just seem to hit a plateau. Over the years, I have gotten by far and away the biggest improvements from this category of competitors. Time and time again, I have coached skiers from merely an average mogul skier at the start of the day to moments of sheer brilliance by the end of the day. The best examples of this tend to be athletes who, for whatever reason, are unable to accomplish all of the complexities needed to get them over that hump. Athletes with slightly better than average mogul skiing skills, moderate to little fears, and an athletic background have truly enormous potential in their mogul skiing ability. That is why they are so exciting to work with!

The reason most struggle at this average level is because they were never taught the proper cause and effects of mogul skiing. Almost all of the mogul skiers that I coached here in the United States and Canada don't teach mogul skiing mechanics the same way as I do. There is a good reason for that. My method was developed as I was training to be an engineer, while coaching active mogul skiing athletes at the same time. Prior to that, I acquired a decade of competitive mogul skiing experience up to the international level. As I learned about vectors and forces in my engineering classes, I could transcribe them accurately into the world of mogul skiing through the filter of my experience and expertise in the sport. I've had nearly a decade of coaching experience to test my new ways of explaining things on actual competitive mogul skiers, and let me tell you—the results have been really exciting! In the next section, you will hear not only how you are supposed to ski moguls, but why we do the things we do. Why they work so well, and in which order to do them.

Mogul skiing is a freestyle sport, which means that there are many different styles that you can choose from to ski the moguls well. Most people have a certain style that they learned or developed by trial and error, or by the traditional mogul skiing school of knowledge, complete with all of the default and traditional flaws in their skills. My way of teaching good mogul skiing form comes purely from the physics of the sport. The theory is simple. Mogul skiing has two parts: efficiency and sustainability. Move only the parts of your body that you need to move to get through the moguls (efficiency), while keeping all the parts of the body that would cause you to have problems, if you moved them, still (sustainability). In general, our lower body is the efficiency engine, and our upper body is the sustainability section. This is because our lower body needs to move, act, and react dynamically with the moguls as we move through them. To stabilize all those dynamic movements, our upper body is used as a dampener to lessen the effects our lower body has on our overall center of mass.

EFFICIENCY SECTION
WHAT TO DO WITH YOUR SKIS AND FEET—AND WHY

> *"Perfection is not when there is no more to add,*
> *But no more to take away."*
> *-Antoine de Saint-Exupery*
> *(Pioneer of international postal flight)*

This section deals entirely with the efficiency aspects of mogul skiing. Hands down, one of the most powerful things that helps transform an average mogul skier into a great skier is changing the line they take in the moguls. With everything else being equal, changing your line in the moguls to a more dynamic (more direct) line makes the largest visual (and technical) improvement. Notice how in this picture to the right, Brayden Pawlik is taking a more direct/dynamic line because his ski path trajectory is more straight down the fall line than the actual shape of the rut. To achieve a straighter trajectory down the fall line than the mogul(s) are actually shaped for, one must "cut the corner" of the end of the mogul, as seen here. This makes for a huge advantage because most people ski the entire rut of the mogul, exactly as it is shaped. As competitive mogul skiers,

we don't do that. It is considered the wrong way to ski moguls for a number of reasons.

THE WRONG WAY

First, let me explain what I mean by, "'They ski the entire rut of the mogul." While skiing over the top of one crest of a mogul, they will immediately turn their skis the other direction, just after they pass the crest. Then they slide down the backside of the mogul with their skis across the hill, down into the rut of the next mogul. This is wrong because when they do this, their tails are actually the first thing to hit the next mogul. This is because the rut of the mogul is pointed more downhill than their skis are when their skis are all the way across the hill. When the tails of our skis hit the mogul first, it forces us into the back seat, even though we are trying to stay slow and in control. Not only that, but it knocks us off balance because the root of the problem (our tails impacting the mogul first) is actually occurring behind our field of vision, so we can't even see it happening. Because we can't see where the problem is coming from, we are prone to widen our stance in an attempt to stabilize our self more. Yet widening our stance in the moguls is also wrong and prone to its own set of challenges. The wider we spread our legs apart in the moguls, the more difference there is in the contour and texture of the moguls underneath our feet. We may have our uphill ski up on the carvable snow on the back side of the previous mogul, while our downhill ski is shooting down the icy part in the rut of the next mogul. It is better to have our feet close together so that your center of mass only has "one" contact point which we are able to follow much more easily.

You want to at least attempt to follow the direction of the rut. Slightly better mogul skiers will do this. Their entire ski hits the mogul all at the same time. However, this method is not as correct as it should be. Doing it this way still puts them at the mercy of the mogul's rut. When you try to follow the rut the entire length of the mogul, it tends to spit you out in off-balancing ways. People who make contact with their entire ski lengths at the same time will also have a tendency to ski with their feet apart, in an attempt to mitigate the unbalancing effect that comes along with skiing the entire mogul rut. Skiing moguls with your feet apart is like putting duct tape on a leak in a garden hose—it's "better," but looks horrible (remember mogul skiing is a judgment sport) and it makes a mess of things. Plus you don't really want your friends to see it. Better to solve the actual problem with the real solution.

THE CORRECT WAY

What you want to do is have the tips of your skis hit the mogul first, before your feet, and your feet before your tails. This has lots of benefits.

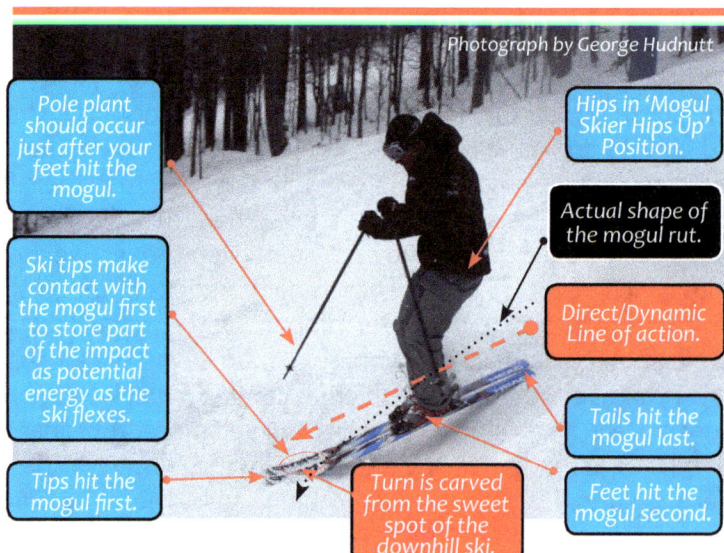

First, it causes your skies to flex as you are impacting the mogul. This flexion in the ski just before the feet hit is one of the best methods we have in mogul skiing for controlling our speed. Not only that, but if we store some of that energy in our skis, it lessens the impact that we take on our knees and our backs. If we want to speed up, we take a shallower angle of impact into the mogul, which causes less flexion in the ski than a steeper angle of impact into the mogul. Also, we hit the mogul with the stronger, thicker part of our ski closer to just in front of our toes. Therefore, it leaves more of our momentum moving forward, down the hill, and has less tendency to break our skis. That is why it is faster from a pure physics point of view. If we want less speed, one thing we can do is to simply increase our angle of impact with the moguls, which creates more flexion in the ski and thereby storing more of that forward-moving energy, slowing us down.

Obviously, there are limitations to just how much flex a ski can take, based on the length and stiffness of the ski, your size, and your speed. All skis have a different breaking point, so it is good to know what kind of ski is good for you. Softer ones will bend more easily, and therefore can't absorb as much of the impact of the mogul for you. However, they are the correct choice if you have little body mass and/or ski very slowly, and you want your skis to be very forgiving if you take the wrong path through the moguls. If you are more of a mogul skiing "heavy weight" and carry a lot of momentum through the moguls, you may benefit from a stiffer ski. The takeaway here is that there is considerable energy storing capacity in the heart of a good mogul ski. (See picture in the Appendix for calculation on just how much energy they can store!) You can choose to store as little or as much as you see fit. Anyone who doubts this just needs to remember a time that they, or someone they know, got "stuffed" in the moguls where it sent them flying over the handlebars. Getting "stuffed" in the moguls is a phenomenon where our skis hit an abrupt mogul or jump, which causes our skis to store so much forward momentum in the flexion that our feet actually stop, causing us to catapult head-over-heels down the mogul course. Usually, when this happens, our skis don't even break, so that will (hopefully) resolve any doubts as to whether or not skis can store enough of our forward moving momentum. They can store too much, in fact, so be careful.

It is necessary to point out here that this storing of energy in the ski is a factor of how new or beat up our skis are. If our skis can actually store too much energy, then that is a sign that you have a stiff young pair, which is good. If you cannot bend the skis enough, or are not able to control and utilize the stored energy in it, then those skis are too stiff for you. If your skis used to store a certain amount of energy that you were able to harvest, but now only hold a portion of that energy, or none at all, then your skis are considered "worn out" or "lifeless," and need to be replaced. Similarly, if you are unable to collect and store a meaningful amount of energy, yet they are new, then those skis are too soft for you. Generally, good mogul skiers should have a stiff, straight ski—although it is relative to how much they weigh and how fast they ski. Consult with your head mogul coach on a good pair of skis that suit you.

In order to control the amount of energy we store in our skis, we use two tactics: pre-absorption and touch. "Pre-absorption" is the act of pulling one's feet upwards and back as we make contact with the mogul. This lessens the impact the mogul has on our bodies. The more we are able to pull back, and up, the less energy there is available to store in the skis, because we are doing the work ourselves. To modulate how much energy actually gets stored is known as "touch." Touch is an advanced skill that you learn in order to know how much to pre-absorb on any given mogul to store the right amount of energy. Sometimes, you don't want to store any at all, like when you want to slow yourself down. And other times, you may want to store as much as possible, like when you are trying to increase your speed. Other times, it is not necessary to pre-absorb at all, like when you are on the Glass Plate. Using a combination of touch, feeling the sweet spot of the ski, understanding how much energy it takes to bend, and pre-absorption, we can control just how much energy is stored in the flexion of the ski.

Just storing forward moving energy in the flexion of the ski is not enough. We have to be able to do it while carving out a turn. We want to do that to set up the transfer of the stored energy, from a forward momentum impact to an upward and lateral motion across the body to make ready for the next turn. To do that, we use the flexion of the ski not only to store some of the energy of the mogul if we need to, but also to change the direction of that energy. Changing the direction of the energy from our forward impact with the mogul to a sideways motion helps us to speed up how quickly we can move our feet from side to side. Therefore, the ski tips and the shape of the mogul we are impacting actually act as a "cam," which is nothing more than an engineering term for a tool that changes the direction of a force. Here, we convert forward force into lateral (sideways) force. When you get good at this, you will find that you are able to use the energy created upon impact with the mogul to propel your feet across and underneath the body to the next mogul much faster than you can do manually.

Additionally, we are able to do it faster and more efficiently than we would be able to manually on dry land. When I was an athlete at the SSWSC (Steamboat Springs Winter Sports Club) in Steamboat Springs, CO, my lifting/strength training partner, Pep Fujas, and I were able to consistently do at least 120 sit-ups per minute during our regular training sessions. That is pretty fast, even for mogul skiers. It means that we could do about two sit-ups per second moving as fast as we could. However, a good mogul skier skis at a pace of three moguls per second or more, which requires us to move at a pace up to 50% faster during our absorptions than we could do on dry land! So where does that extra speed come from? Yep, you guessed it: it comes from the energy we harvest from the moguls themselves. That is the power of simply taking the correct line, and doing the right things with your feet in the moguls! Have you ever wondered why it is so difficult to turn when you are straight running in the moguls? It is because when skiers start to "straight run" in the moguls, there is less and less stored energy in the flexion of the ski to help propel the knees and feet from one side of the body to the other! So you see, there definitely are maximum and minimum amounts of flexion you want in your skis. This is why we always make the first impact with the mogul with the tips of our skis, and we do that by choosing a more direct (dynamic) line.

THE NITTY-GRITTY
FOR ADVANCED MOGUL SKIERS

In mogul skiing, we carve our turns from the "sweet spot" of the ski. The sweet spot of the ski is like the sweet spot on a baseball or softball bat. All skis are slightly different, but they all have one. It begins at the part near the tips that is still completely flat (at the base of the ski tip) and extends

THE SWEET SPOT

back usually about 6-8 inches. "To carve a turn" means to initially dig in the front of the ski (starting from the sweet spot), while placing the skis on edge. With forward momentum, this "digging in" of the downhill ski creates a track in the snow that the rest of the ski can follow. This is similar to how ice skates work, except skis bend or "flex" when we turn them. At any point in the carving of the turn, some or all of the back part of the ski can derail from the initial edge ("track") that we set at the beginning of the turn. When this happens, the entire back part of the ski breaks free from the carving edge, and in doing so, loses its traction in the snow. The entire back part of the ski can then come sliding down as far as being even with the tips of our skis, completely perpendicular to the fall line (across the hill). When the middle and back part of our skis break free from the initial edge set by the tips of our skis, releasing its grip on the snow and sliding partially or completely sideways, this is what is known as "washing out." However, when the entire middle and back part of the ski follow roughly the same track as you set initially with the front of your skis, that is what is known as carving the ski. Being consistent at carving a ski takes a great deal of skill and finesse. However, you will be much more consistent and in control if you start each carve with the sweet spot of the ski. Sometimes the sweet spot of the ski is a little longer or does not start right at the base. You should get familiar with it if you have never thought about it before. The previous two pictures are good representations of me carving with the sweet spot of the ski. And on the previous page, you can see two more pictures of me physically pointing out the beginning and end of the sweet spot of my ski in this layout.

The carving is done largely on the inside edge of the downhill ski, as I mentioned before, and the uphill leg is generally just following along, in

THE MECHANICS OF MOGUL SKIING

parallel, to help distribute our balance. Interestingly, the front of the ski of our uphill leg will actually extend further down the hill than our downhill ski that we are initiating the carve with. One ski further down the hill than the other, is known as the "leading ski." When we make a turn, the ski that is in the lead, switches. This is what is known as a "lead change." A lead change only ever happens at the inflection point between our turn as we transition from one to the next. This is why it is imperative to only have about 25% of our weight on our uphill leg, because if we put too much pressure on the uphill ski, it could cause that ski to create a track of its own for our uphill ski to follow. When this happens, our skis will usually create two different trajectories carved into the snow, which typically intersect. When our two skis—which are following two different paths in the snow—intersect, they get crossed. Most people have trouble with crossing their tips in the moguls and don't understand why or how it is happening. If you have ever been one of those people, you might consider reading this section again very carefully.

Here, my right ski is the uphill ski and it **leads** my downhill ski, which is doing all the carving.

Hips in '**Mogul Skiers Hips Up**' Position. Increases range of motion when absorbing the moguls.

Sweet Spot of the ski is used to initiate the carving of the turn. To do so, use the inside edge of downhill ski, near the tip.

Very little weight applied to the uphill ski. Only about 25% weight bearing upon impact.

We initiate our mogul turns with the sweet spot of the ski on the crest of each mogul. We make an impact with every mogul with our skis pointed slightly "cross-rut," with about 75-80% of our weight on our downhill foot. Moguls skiers put more weight than you would expect on the downhill foot for a number of good reasons other than the one previously mentioned. First, it takes the weight off of the foot that we need to do the uphill hip drive with. If we can't properly do the uphill hip drive because we have too much weight on the uphill foot, this is another reason which causes us to cross our tips in the moguls. Furthermore, it is really bad to initiate contact with the mogul with the uphill foot. We ensure this doesn't happen by putting so much emphasis on extra weight on our downhill ski. When we make first contact with the mogul with our uphill ski, it has a chain reaction of negative effects. First, it "tightens up" the uphill side of our body, bringing about what is roughly equivalent to an early uphill hip drive, which is really hard to recover from. By doing so, it creates an axis of rotation that is on the uphill side of the body that blocks the energy transfer from the downhill side of the body to the other downhill side of the body as we transition to the next turn. We don't want to block this energy transfer. We need it to keep up our rhythm. What's more, on that next sequential turn you will be forced to drive your uphill hip too early as well, in an attempt to compensate just enough to keep them square down the fall line. When this happens, you may feel a noticeable separation between your upper body rotation and your lower body rotation. This is because your reflexes no longer know which side of the body the next impact is coming from, so your core relaxes in order to prepare for the worst. This often results in negative results for you. Usually, before your third turn in this sequence, you will find yourself off of your timing, usually followed by "getting stuffed" seemingly out of nowhere. You may also experience a major bobble, blow out, or even fall. So don't make first contact with your uphill foot! The consequences might seem inconsequential at first, but they escalate quickly!

Next, it allows us to ski with our feet close together. Not to mention that it is nearly impossible to ski with 75% of your weight on your downhill foot and 25% on your uphill foot, while your feet are spread wide apart. That would not only be difficult to do, but it would be silly-looking as well. Additionally, the dynamic (direct) line we chose to take in the moguls is highly topographically dynamic. Meaning, if our feet are not close together, they will have different topographies to navigate at the same time. In other words, the farther our feet are apart from each other, the more different terrain each foot has to navigate simultaneously. Have you ever tried to do two different things with each of your hands at the same time, like patting your head and rubbing your tummy? It's difficult! The same principle applies here. Putting our feet right next to each other ensures the smallest difference in terrain for each foot. It simplifies things greatly because you can use both of your legs as a single shock absorber, both working to absorb the same impact at the same time. We take the brunt of

THE MECHANICS OF MOGUL SKIING

the force on the downhill leg while leaving the uphill leg in reserve in case we need it. This also gives each quad muscle a bit of a rest on every other turn, which helps us to reserve our energy.

In summary, the carving of the turn happens in the subtleties in how we choose to hit the mogul with the sweet spot of our skis, the direction of the feet on impact, and the weight distribution of our feet. The energy stored on impact is harvested to help slow us down, speed us up, and to increase the speed at which we are able to move our feet from one side to the other (from one turn to the other). Fine tuning how to carve on the sweet spot of the ski with the right amount of pressure on each foot, while harvesting just the right amount of energy from the impact, is one of the most intricate, artistic, and skillful aspects of mogul skiing. No amount of practice, training, or effort is wasted in pursuing this aspect of mogul skiing to its perfection.

SUSTAINABILITY SECTION
WHAT TO DO WITH YOUR HANDS, ELBOWS, AND POLE PLANTS—AND WHY

In the previous section, we talked about what to do with our feet and our skis. It is no coincidence that the feet and skis section dealt with the efficiency aspects of mogul skiing, like speed and control. Conversely, this section deals almost entirely with the sustainability aspects of skiing moguls. In fact, what we do with any part of our upper body has to deal with the sustainability aspects of mogul skiing, meaning that everything you do with your hands, arms, and poles either causes or relieves problems in your skiing style. There is really no "efficient" way to use your arms other than you shouldn't be moving them too much.

Your arms are your best asset to sustainability in the moguls. This is because they can be used to make pole plants anywhere you need, in order to sustain, or regain, your balance. Pole plants can also be made with great accuracy as well, which is why they are our best sustainability asset. However, we don't want to rely on our arms to correct our balance in the moguls all the time. They should be barely used, if we are skiing in a good "stacked position." (To get a good understanding of the "stacked position," see pictures and commentary in the Mogul Skier Hips Up Position 1 and Mogul Skier Hips Up Position 2 sections later in this chapter). In a good stacked position, our hands, elbows and pole plants are better left as motionless as possible, with as light of a pole plants as possible. If we have to use our pole plants all the time to regain our balance, then that would suggest there is something more seriously wrong going on (probably with our lower body not skiing efficiently). We want to use our arms, hands, and elbows in such a way where they are out of our way and don't cause any problems, while at the same time, have them exactly where we need without having to move them should a problem arise. This section explains how to do that. But first, I want to talk about the wrong ways to use your elbows and hands in the moguls.

THE WRONG WAY

Most people who are just learning to ski the moguls tend to ski with their hands spread wide apart, far away from their body. They do this because it "feels" more stable to spread their arms (and legs) wide (see picture to the right). Similar to boats, the wider and longer the hull, the more stable it will feel. However, skiing with our hands far away from our bodies is wrong for several reasons. In the act of trying to stabilize ourselves by widening our feet and our hands in the moguls, we actually make the situation much worse. We already talked about why separating the feet far apart from each other was the wrong thing to do in the previous section. Both wid-

ening the feet and hands are a form of reflex that we do to try to take control of the uneasy situation that mogul skiing puts us in. However, this is a sport that tends to require us to do just the opposite of what our reflexes want us to do. First of all, it is important to remember that the pole plants we make can have quite a bit of an impact on the rest of our body when we make them. This impact is usually in the form of "torque." In physics, torque is defined as the tendency of a given force to rotate an object around an axis.

It is essentially equivalent to the force multiplied by the radius (see illustrated definition to the right). For mogul skiers, the force is applied on the hand by the impact of the pole plant with the mogul. The radius is therefore equal to the distance our hand is from the center

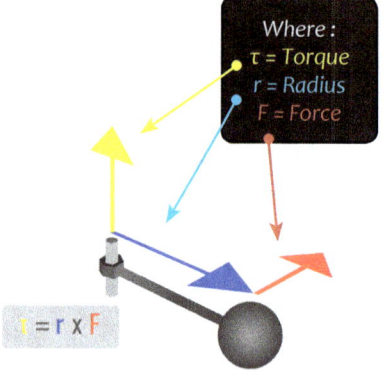

THE MECHANICS OF MOGUL SKIING

*Notice the farther away from the body the hand and pole plant get, the weaker your ability to keep it in place. This is due to the presence of high torque. Which creates a twisting motion in the upper body. Which can cause us to lose our balance.

Centerline (Axis of rotation) that torque acts on.

Effects of torque: Twisting of the upper body. (High torque is bad.)

of our body, where our body acts as the central axis about which the torque is applied. In other terms, torque is a turning or twisting force. Turning and twisting forces are bad for mogul skiers. Just remember that the farther away from the body that we have our hand upon impact of the pole plant (radius), the larger that impact (force) will have on the rest of our body (torque). In explanation, if you have a force of ½ your body weight acting on your hand, let's say it's 80 lbs., and you try to make a pole plant with your arm all the way out away from your body—let's say 3 ft. from the centerline of your body—the torque acting on your body (the force that will be working to twist you off axis) will be 240 lb-ft of torque (80 lbs. * 3 ft. = 240 lb-ft). Whereas if you pole plant with your hand directly next to your body (radius=1 ft. from your centerline of rotation), then the torque that will be acting on your body will be only 80 lb-ft of torque (80 lbs. * 1 ft. = 80 ft-lb). That is just some simple physics to explain why pole planting in the moguls with your hands far away from your body is a bad idea. The further away from your body that they get, any impact that you make with your pole plants will be amplified that much more on your body. Pole planting far away from your body in the moguls causes more problems than it solves, so pole plant close to your feet! Just look at the picture to the right: can you see how much stronger of a body position this is than the picture directly above it? It's a lot stronger and more sustainable!

THE CORRECT WAY

What you want to do is keep your elbows in line with your shoulders and your hands in line with your elbows, slightly above your waistline. One reason we do this is because there is much less torque on the body when we pole plant, which makes it easier for us to stay on balance (sustainability). Not only that, but by aligning our hands, elbows, and shoulders in this way, we have the added strength of our strong back muscles to "back us up" should that pole plant's impact get too aggressive. Think of this: If you were to stand up and put both hands way out to each side, and I came along and pushed one of your hands backwards, how much energy would I have to use to get you to rotate (due to the torque I just put on your body)? Not very much, right? You wouldn't be able to stop the rotation, even if you tried. Now try putting your hands in front of your body, making sure you align them with your elbows and your shoulders. Your elbows should be tight to your sides, and your hands should be in front

Hands in line with elbows, in line with shoulders. Elbows tight to the silhouette.

of them. On really tough impacts, we can use our lats muscles to help disperse the energy of the impact as well as the shoulder and upper back if we align them properly. How much more force would I need to push one of your hands backwards, as if to imitate a force "up the hill" like an impact with a mogul would give you, to knock you off balance or get you to rotate? A lot more, right? I might not even be able to knock you off balance or rotate you at all if you use good core strength! It is a more sustainable way to ski moguls because there is less of a chance for our pole plants to knock us off balance. The position is stronger the closer you have your elbows to your sides.

From a judge's perspective, they don't want to see your hands or elbows break too far away from your silhouette. If you have very light pole plants, you can choose to extend the hands and therefore plant your poles further down the hill, but you shouldn't get the elbows or hands away from your silhouette (as seen from downhill) in this position either.

Pole plants and their locations on the mogul has come under some debate in recent years. I hope to shed some light on the topic from a pure physics standpoint. The "old-school" style of coaching mogul skiing teaches potential skiers to "reach for the back side of the mogul with the basket of your pole." More "new-school" coaches don't even watch the actual pole plant basket location at all. What they do watch, however, is how quiet your hands are—although they may default to the traditional "accepted knowledge" to "reach for the backside of the moguls" as means to quiet your hands down, should they be prodded for an answer. However, they don't put much actual thought into the matter, if they do so.

There is a reason the "old-school" style of making your pole plants on the back side of the mogul used to be so effective. Many years ago, back when mogul skiing was just starting to evolve, the poles that skiers used were much longer than they are today. Many of them were just as long as current ski poles issued to the masses via rental shops. The standard convention is to have the poles come up to the hand at the point where the hand makes a 90-degree angle with the elbow. You were something of a radical, back in the day, if you choose to cut your poles down, yet some people did it anyways. These "hot dogs," as they were called, did, in fact, cut their poles down, but they were still longer than they are today. With longer poles, one was able to not only reach the backside of the mogul with ease, but it was also one of the best strategies for keeping the hands quiet. It worked well in those days when mogul skiing was still evolving. Those first mogul skiers taught it to the following generation of mogul skiers, and that generation taught it to the next generation, without much thought. And that is why it became the "status-quo" or the "proper way" to make your pole plants.

However, in recent years, we have put much more thought into rethinking the status quo. Nowadays, our mogul poles extend barely up to our waist, much shorter than ever in the history of mogul skiing. We do this be-

cause, on the odd chance that we need to pole plant right on the top of a mogul for some reason, it ensures us that we will still be able to reach the top of our pole without it lifting us off the ground while we are deep in the opposing rut. Taller poles would knock us completely off balance in that situation, or force us to drop that pole completely. In this way, short poles themselves act as a sustainability tool in mogul skiing.

Now the proper place to plant your pole with shorter poles is somewhere between the front of your front binding to the toe of your boot, right next to your downhill ski. It should be noted here that on flatter courses (courses below a 20° pitch or so), you can get away with planting further down the hill. On steeper courses (28° pitch or more) you should be planting closer to your foot. Placing the pole plant close to the foot ensures that the elbow is close to the body, should you need to reinforce a hard impact with your back or trapezius muscles.

Pole plant just in front of the toe part of the binding. Right on the crest of the mogul.

Additionally, keeping the pole plant close to the body, and not away, ensures that neither your hands nor your elbows are breaking the seams of your silhouette. However, it should only be used as a last resort, after all effort to keep the hand in front of your body has failed. It is preferable, then, to reduce the amount of time the pole is planted, if at all possible. This will help your turn scores. Sometimes, when we are skiing really fast in the moguls, we may not be able to keep our hands completely in front of our bodies. When this happens, the hand breaks away from our silhouette and shoots out to the side. This is bound to happen sooner or later to all mogul skiers. However, the strategy is to only break our hand away from our silhouette when we have no other choice, like when resisting the mogul anymore will knock us off balance. When this happens, it is okay to let the hand come behind the body. As this is preferable to getting "bucked."

We want to place the pole plant right on the crest of the mogul. This affords us the option to put pressure on it if we need to. This places our hand at its highest point on a lower part of a mogul closer to our foot, so that it will be lower than if placed on the summit of the mogul. This is because the mogul is lowest at the rut and gets higher the further away from the rut that you get, all the way up to the apex of the mogul, meaning that we won't be moving our hands up and down as much. Also, they will be much quieter as opposed to what would happen if we placed our hands farther out, away from the body, closer to the top of the mogul. Alternatively, placing the pole on the backside of the mogul can be troublesome because it is on a much steeper part of the mogul. Planting on the backside of the mogul is especially dangerous on steep courses, because it has the ability to "slide out" on you, causing you to miss a pole plant. Needless to say, this can and will knock you off balance, forcing you to bobble or even fall.

Pole plant just in front of the toe part of the binding, right on the crest of the mogul.

Conversely, it is also bad to plant your poles too far on the front side of the mogul as well. Doing so throws off your timing, and can cause you to "step through" your pole. "Stepping through your pole" is a phenomenon that we have when we break our poles just above their pole baskets. This is caused by planting the pole inside of where the downhill ski needs to be. When the downhill foot slams into the mogul to take its rightful spot, the force combined with the sharp edge of the ski is enough to make a clean cut right through the pole. If a clean break is made, you might not even realize you broke it until you're two more turns further down the hill when you need to make that pole plant again. If the pole doesn't make a clean break, you will stuff yourself on your pole causing a large bobble, or even a fall on impact. You can tell if your pole plant is too far forward on the face of the mogul if your elbow is next to, or actually behind, your torso, or if you plant at the heels of your feet or further back.

Planting the pole basket right next to the front of our toe piece is just about how far forward we can comfortably reach with our short poles without over-extending our arms (see photos above). We can reach the pole out about as far as the tip of our skis, but contact with the snow should be somewhere between the sweet spot of the ski and the toe piece. It will vary depending on your style of skiing and what you need to do at any given mogul to keep balance. The planted pole is released by the time it gets to the tailpiece of our bindings. The tighter our elbows are to our torso, the stronger impacts we can take with our pole plants and not get thrown off balance. Just don't keep constantly tense. It is just a quick power move. Keeping the pole plants next to your feet has the added bonus of preventing you from over-extending your elbow and shoulders as well. Sometimes, to appease our coaches, we will overreach too far with our little "T-Rex" style shorty-short poles and throw our turns out of whack. Doing so could cause a "C-turn." C-turns are bad because they can cause unnecessary movement to the upper body, as well as forcing your uphill hip too far across the hill. Getting your uphill hip too far across the hill will knock you off balance, or at the very least make it more difficult for the next turn. This will usually put you high into the rut of the next turn, where will leave you at its mercy.

All this is not to say that many great mogul skiers don't ski with their elbows away from their sides—they do. We see it all the time. It is just purely from a physics standpoint that I make the claim. It is more sustainable to ski with them close to the body. Personally, I ski with my elbows in close to the body and plant my poles somewhere between the sweet spot of my ski and the toe of my boot, and I prefer it that way. I very rarely get knocked off balance because of my pole plants. Nor do I get the tennis elbow that some mogul skiers get from a habit of planting away from their silhouette. I think it is the best way, and I wouldn't do it any other way. But the choice is up to you.

BALANCE AND FLUIDITY SECTION
FLOW LIKE A RIVER, STEADY LIKE A TOWER
WHAT TO DO WITH YOUR SHOULDERS, CHEST, AND HIPS— AND WHY

Our shoulders are a product of our hands, elbows, and pole plants. As such, they are a good indicator of our side-to-side (left-right) balance in the moguls. If we are on balance, our shoulders will move very little, if at all. If we are off balance, our shoulders can show considerable movement. Therefore, we want our shoulders to be as "quiet" as possible (i.e., as little movement as possible).

Our chest is an indicator of our front-to-back balance and our "timing." Front-to-back balance and "timing" are closely related. "Timing" is the word we use to describe whether or not we are making our turn on the right "part" of the mogul, or at the right "time." Turning too early or too late can be disastrous, therefore we must constantly be monitoring our timing. When our timing is late, our upper body will "hinge" forward all the way down to our knees, folding us over like a book. When our timing is too early, our chest can get too far behind, which puts us in the back seat. You can't have bad timing and good front-to-back balance. The difference with simple front-to-back balance is that it can be good or bad, regardless of your timing. For example, you can still get stuffed, bucked, or "snow snaked," which will throw off your front-to-back balance, even if your timing is good. We will delve deeper into that later on.

Your hips are a product of both your side-to-side balance and your front-to-back balance. This is because the hips are the closest part of our body to our center of mass. Our center of mass moves as a sum total of all the forces from all parts of our body as we move through the moguls. You can't have a good hip position if you have bad side-to-side and/or bad front-to-back balance. You cannot have a good hip position if your timing is off, you are in the back seat, hinged over, have too much weight on the uphill foot, or if your shoulders won't remain quiet. Exhausting, eh? This is why the hips are usually the last thing a mogul skier will learn to use correctly, because everything else in their mogul skiing has to be right before their hips can be. Most mogul skiers will continue to work on their hip position their entire careers. Incidentally, they are also the most important thing in our mogul skiing.

Author's Note: Many people have relayed to me how quickly and good my athletes get at mogul skiing. The reason I believe my athletes are so successful is because proper hip position is the first thing I teach them. Then I weed out all the different ways that they are blocking that good position from happening, and then I train them repetitively until they can do it unconsciously. The improvement that these athletes experience is large, strikingly fast, and sustainable.

THE WRONG WAY

Our shoulders usually only get off balance for three reasons. The first and most common reason is that something bad happened with our pole plant. If we stiff arm a pole plant it can create movement in our shoulders. If we leave the pole planted in the mogul too long, and/or plant far away from the body, it can create a twisting motion that can throw off our balance via our shoulder movement. Another major problem that comes along with leaving a pole planted too long or planting too far away from the body is that it causes uphill rotation in the hips. Uphill rotation in the

THE MECHANICS OF MOGUL SKIING

hips creates a series of related issues.

First, when our uphill hip is twisted and forced further uphill, it makes it more difficult for us to initiate our uphill hip drive. If we can even drive it at all! If the uphill hip gets driven back too far, then the uphill hip drive can become impossible to do. As a general rule, this happens when the uphill hip passes 45° from the trajectory (line) of the mogul skier. (The picture above is showing good hip rotation. Bad hip rotation is not shown.) Another way to think about it is anytime your hips are more than perpendicular to the natural trajectory of the rut of the mogul. If this happens, your

only option for making your next turn is to pivot on your downhill foot, which immediately results in all of your weight on your uphill foot after the pivot. I've already explained why having all of your weight on your uphill foot is bad.

Secondly, it will usually result in your initial contact with the following mogul to be with the tails of your skis. (We already discussed why that was bad in the Efficiency Section.)

The third reason mogul skiers get their side-to-side balance out of whack is that they are either reaching too far for the backside of the mogul with their pole plant, or they are trying to do a "C-turn," and it backfires. Both things result in the same set of problems, though.

The first problem is that both of these methods cause the downhill shoulder to drop. When we drop the downhill shoulder, it is very easy to overweight the downhill ski. Dropping the downhill shoulder and overweighting the downhill ski is wrong because it elongates the uphill hip, and takes pressure off the uphill foot. Taking all the pressure off the uphill foot makes our uphill hip drive nearly impossible, because it is already elongated prematurely. It also slows down the transition of the feet from one turn to the next. The reason the transition speed of the feet from one turn to the next is slowed down is because the downhill hip is over-weighted. We cannot unweight the downhill hip soon enough because our uphill foot has no pressure on it, and therefore it diminishes the quickness at which we can drive the uphill hip. We are thereby forced to simply wait for the mogul that we over-weighted our downhill foot on to pass underneath us before we can do anything about it. In doing so, we forfeit the energy we stored in our skis, and lose the benefit of the shape of the mogul because our timing was off. This is what slows down the transition from one turn to the next and also continues to mess up our "timing" for many more turns to come. These turns can make our legs feel like they are dragging through molasses—it can literally feel that slow. All this when the simple root of the problem was that we simply dropped our downhill shoulder!

THE CORRECT WAY

Our resistance to excessive side-to-side and front-to-back motion is all managed by our core. In most sports, "core" refers just to the abs. Although abs are massively important in mogul skiing, "core" refers to much more than just that. First of all, our lower back muscles are considered part of our core, as well as our abdomens. Our lower back works to lift our upper body back up if it ever hinges over (as it often does); it also works in unison with the abs to stabilize our forward-to-back balance should everything be going smoothly. Our abs work in unison with our quads and shin muscles as part of our "core" as well. Mainly, we do this to "pre-absorb" the mogul before it gets to us in a fine-tuned and preemptive manner, which is how we dictate to the mogul, and our skis, just how much energy from the impact we want stored in our skis.

Secondly, our upper back provides great strength to our core as a "backup" when we need it, like when we take a hard shot to our shoulder via one of our pole plants. Our side abs, or "oblique abdominal muscles," are also a crucially important part of our core. Obliques are highly used in mogul skiing. They control the twisting motion of our core, and our side-to-side balance as well. Additionally, they are the main driving force behind the uphill hip drive. Just make sure that when you drive your uphill hip, you are not simultaneously dropping your uphill shoulder, as this can sometimes happen automatically. If you do this, you are actually blocking your uphill hip drive. You want to keep your uphill shoulder raised as much as possible, and square down the fall line. This will give your uphill hip a "place to drive to," meaning that since your shoulders are square to the fall line, your uphill hip is approaching a position square to the fall line, and therefore your uphill hip trails it slightly. This is good. When you drive your uphill hip, you want to drive it forward so that it becomes re-aligned with the shoulders, and once again square to the fall line. All of this finely tuned technique is largely processed by our oblique muscles. They are hands-down the most important muscle group in the upper body of a mogul skier, so do your best to strengthen them as much as possible! (Refer to section "Uphill Hip Drive" in Chapter 10 for examples of exercises to strengthen obliques.)

You want to set up a good core position before you start mogul skiing. Most mogul coaches teach this. They will make you stand at the top of the hill before your run, and make you get into a good mogul skiing position. I do this with my athletes as well. Here is how I explain it.

First of all, you want to get your hips in the "Mogul Skier Hips Up" position. This position is very important to mogul skiing, yet is rarely taught properly, so I will explain it in depth now. To understand it completely, we must start with an explanation of good basic human posture. Then I will explain how to transform that posture into good mogul skiing posture.

GOOD "NORMAL" SPINAL POSTURE

Take a look at the sketch of the skeleton to the right. This is what is generally accepted as a good natural spinal posture. The shape of the human spine has four natural curves to it: the Cervical, Thoracic, Lumbar, and Sacral curve. When we are born, we have one C-shaped spinal curve to start with. In reality, both the Thoracic and Sacral curves are fully developed at birth. Since both of these curves face the same direction (see picture at right), it looks like one continuous curve at birth. This "double curve" is what gives babies the ability to put their feet in their mouth. Soon after, we begin to lift our heads and move them around. These actions are what help develop our Cervical curve, the third spinal curve that forms. We develop the fourth and (hopefully) final spinal curve when we begin to crawl, sit, and stand. The Lumbar curve, as it is known, is what gives us the ability to stand for long periods at a time. Also, notice the "locked" position of the knees, meaning they can't bend any further backwards. I will go into more depth as to why this is important later.

Each spinal curve serves an important function in allowing us to maintain balance while moving about, from sitting, to standing, to walking, to running, to jumping. Since the spine is integral to every movement we make, it is necessary to understand how to properly position and use it as efficiently as possible as we are skiing moguls.

The spine has all of these curves in it to help us distribute the external and internal forces exerted on us by mass and momentum. In essence, the spine is like a big spring that helps absorb the forces and cushions us as we make impacts on it, such as when we run and jump. Our spine is truly a miracle of evolution; however, it falls considerably short when it comes to mogul skiing. During mogul skiing, we subject our spine and the rest of our body to massive forces that it was never designed to endure. Free-runners are renowned for their ability to jump from heights as high as 30 ft. onto flat ground and come away unharmed. The secret to their skill is landing on all fours and rolling out of the jump to disperse that massive impact. It is a very impressive stunt to watch. However, as mogul skiers, we don't have the luxury of being able to "roll-out" of the massive impacts we make with every single mogul. We have to remain tall and take every consecutive impact in stride, without affecting our posture. So how do we do it?

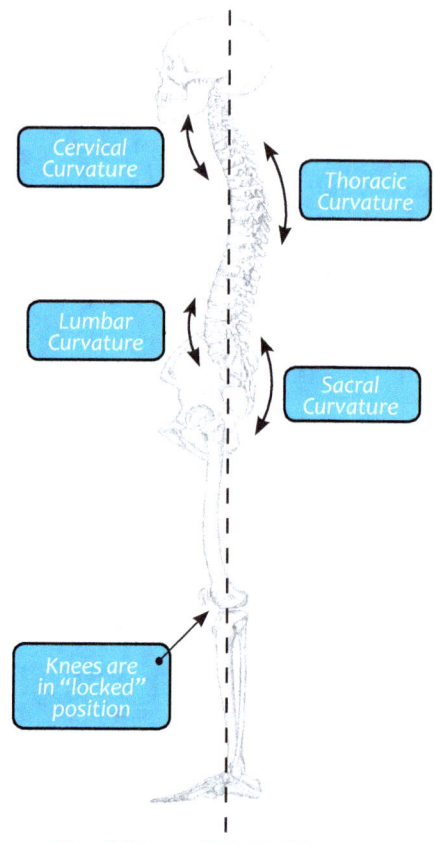

Good "Normal" Spinal Posture

MOGUL SKIER HIPS UP POSITION STEP 1

As a spring is compressed, the coils get closer together. The spring can no longer be compressed any further when the coils touch each other.

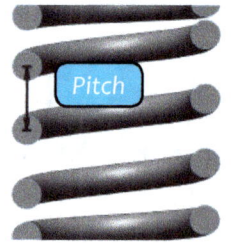

This is known as the maximum compression length of the spring.

As mentioned above, our spine is like a big spring designed to take large impacts. However, it falls far short on the amount of impact length it needs to take when one skis in the moguls. In the world of springs, when one needs a spring with a larger maximum com-

THE MECHANICS OF MOGUL SKIING

pression length, one would choose a spring that has the coils separated further apart. The gap between wire center to wire center of two adjacent coils is known as the "pitch" of the spring. The pitch is equal to the max compression distance of the spring.

As mogul skiers, we need to maximize the "pitch" of the "spring" that is our spine. This body position maximizes our ability to absorb large impacts from moguls. Since we can't elongate the pitch of our spinal curves, all we can do is combine those curves into one big curve. We do this by pushing our tailbone between our legs, and pulling our pelvis bone upward, which is what I coined as the "mogul skier hips up position." Notice the higher position of the pelvic bone and the rotated position of the hips in the picture below. By making this move, we are removing the Lumbar curve, which then combines the Thoracic and Sacral curves into a single large spinal curve, similar to when we were babies. This single larger spinal curve has twice the pitch (maximum compression length) of a normal spinal posture shape, which gives us more range of motion with which to ski moguls. We will see just how much this works in real life with photos in just a little bit.

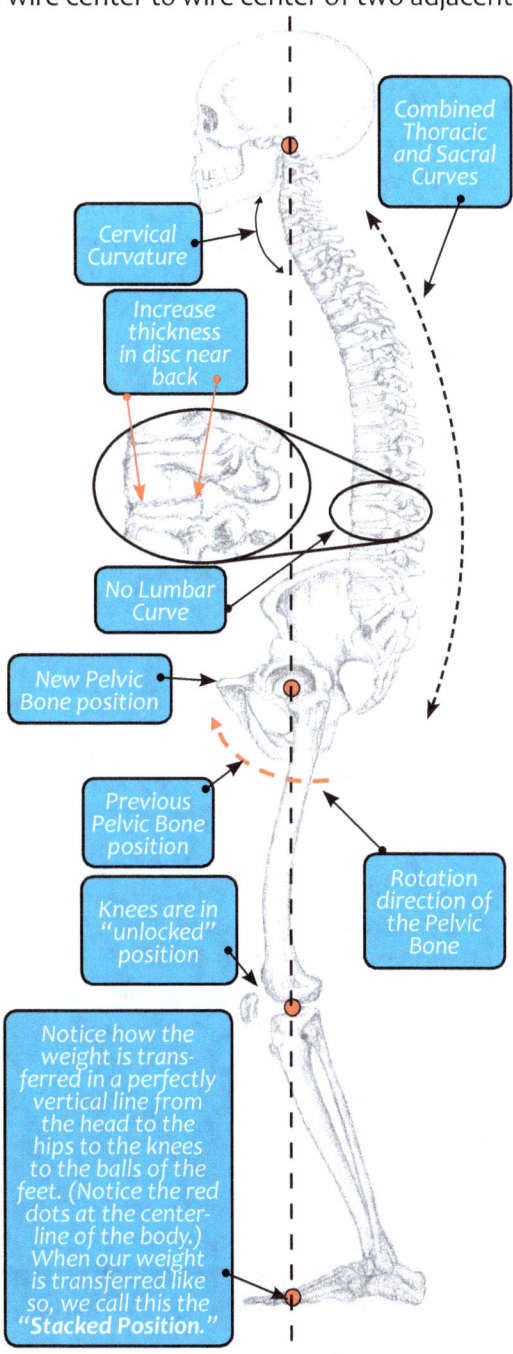

Combined Thoracic and Sacral Curves

But first, let me point out just how we are able to double our range on impact. Notice the position of the pelvic bone in the picture to the right. It is tilted forward and upward about 15°-20° by pushing the pelvic bone forward and upward between the legs in a pendulum-type motion. In addition to increasing our range of motion, this hip position has two main benefits. First, it increases the thickness of the cartilage in between each vertebra in the Lumbar part of the spine by compressing the front part of the cartilage (see enlarged detail to the right). This is good because the force of impact from moguls will exert itself hardest at the back part of the cartilage disc.

Secondly, this position of the hips has the added bonus of forcing us to "unlock" and bend our knees at all times while we are standing. This is good because you never want to take a mogul or any large impact with your knees in a "locked" position.

MOGUL SKIER HIPS UP POSITION STEP 2

With mogul skiers being the perfectionists that we tend to be, we cannot be satisfied with just a perfectly aligned body position. As you may have noticed by doing this hip move yourself, it makes you shorter. This is because it forces you to bend your knees and ankles. So in an effort to regain that lost height, we can attempt to straighten our spine out even more. We do this by getting rid of the last curve left in our spine, the Cervical curve. However, it is not easy to get rid of the Cervical curve. To do so, we must change our center of balance a little bit because straightening out our Cervical curve tends to push our head back off of the four-point centerline alignment that we

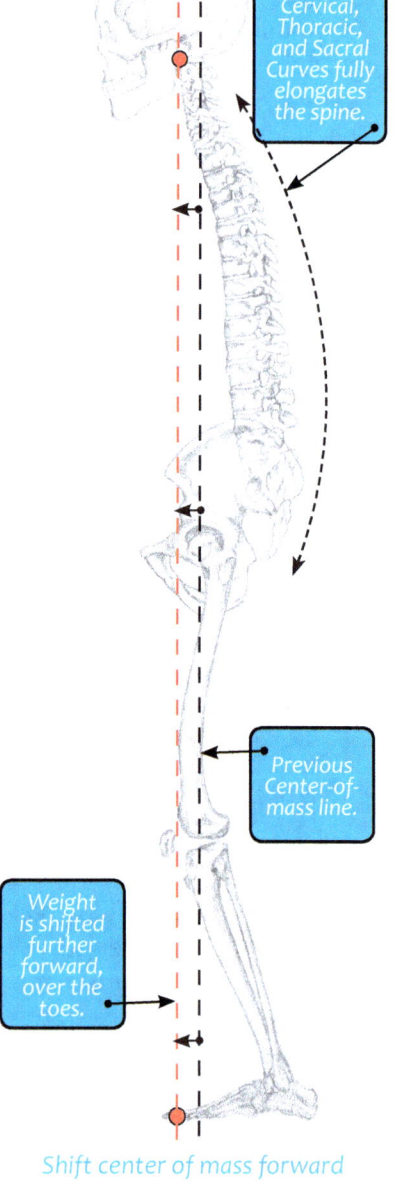

Shift center of mass forward

had in the previous illustration. This also straightens out our entire back so we must actually "tip" or lean forward, until the weight of our head comes (at least) back in line with our hips and the arch of our foot. This body position is considered the highest caliber of the "stacked position" because in addition to the benefits of the Mogul Skier Hips Up Position 1, it also adds height. However, it has some inherent difficulties.

First of all, it is more unstable than the previous position because of how unnatural a body position it is. To correct this, we must "tip" our entire upper body forward until our head is actually a little past the center line of our body (previous page). This places our weight uneasily far forward, onto our toes. This is actually desirable, since the extra far forward center of mass acts to combat the impact of the moguls which are constantly trying to knock us backwards. Hence, it is "off balance," yet we use that to our advantage.

The other problem that we are faced with when trying to get rid of the cervical curve is that it is nearly impossible to do without dropping your chin. Dropping your chin is akin to dropping your eyes, and most mogul skiing coaches will tell you that is a bad thing. However, I find that dropping my eyes tends to have very little effect on my turn scores, and the elongated spine helps my range of motion immensely, and tends to be where I am most comfortable. As one of the fastest skiers in the country, it certainly didn't slow me down any either. Ultimately, you should do what is best for you, but I prefer to have a longer spine than having my eyes a little further downhill when I am forced to choose. Just be sure to pick your eyes up before you get to the jump!

Think of this body position more as the "goal" of how we want to be stacked in the moguls. The reality will be closer to the previous picture. It looks good on paper and looks good in nice easy moguls, but it has its limitations in real-world mogul skiing. You can and should try to ski in this position as much as possible, because it is excellent training, but just be aware that you may never be able to hang onto this position for more than a brief second or two. However, practicing this position will train your muscles to hold yourself in a proper stacked position.

MOGUL SKIER HIPS UP POSITION STEP 3

The position of our hips in mogul skiing is important for several reasons. First of all, it allows us to disperse the force of impact with each mogul throughout our entire spine, rather than just the lower half. Second of all, it grants us more range of motion for absorbing the moguls—typically about six extra inches of range, which is very helpful in the moguls (see below).

Third, and most importantly, it prevents us from blocking our uphill hip drive. The uphill hip drive is the most important part of our mogul turn, which we learned all about earlier in this chapter. Once we notice that there is considerable concavity in the lower part of our backs in a traditional athletic stance (or even in a regular standing up straight position), and that it is bad for mogul skiing, we can easily make the correction that we need (see pictures on next page).

Cocking our hips forward by trying to push our tailbone between our legs is what gives us the advantage of about six extra inches of absorption that we didn't have access to before. Additionally, it makes driving the uphill hip that much easier because it is already that much farther forward, and therefore has less distance to travel.

THE MECHANICS OF MOGUL SKIING

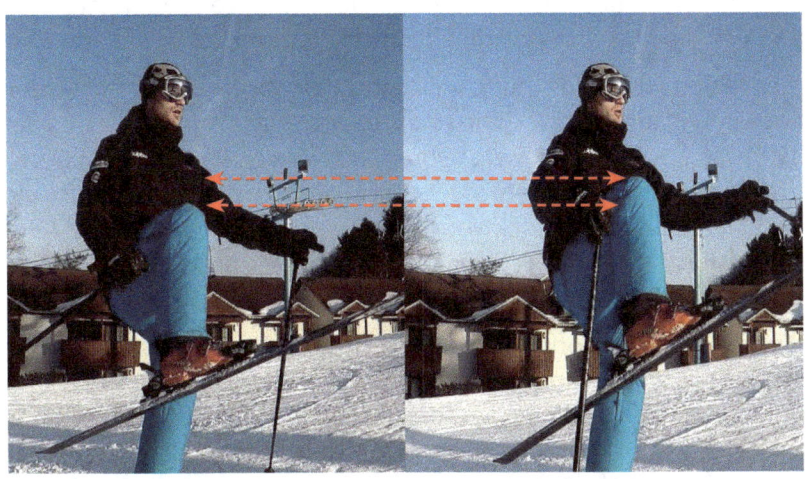

Traditional Athletic Stance — *Mogul Skier Hips Up Position*

We can see the complete hip movement by overlaying the skeletal sketches over top of each other. I did not make any changes to these two pictures except overlay them so that the hip movement is better depicted. If you look at the picture on the next page, you will notice that the starting position is shaded slightly darker, so it is easier to see where to start. Notice how the hip bone is cocked up, and forward between the legs. This is the movement that eliminates the Lumbar curve, which inhibits our range of motion. The only other difference in the "Mogul Skier Hips Up" position is the alignment of the spine into the stacked position which combines all of our spinal curves. In other words, the picture is showing you the complete difference between the

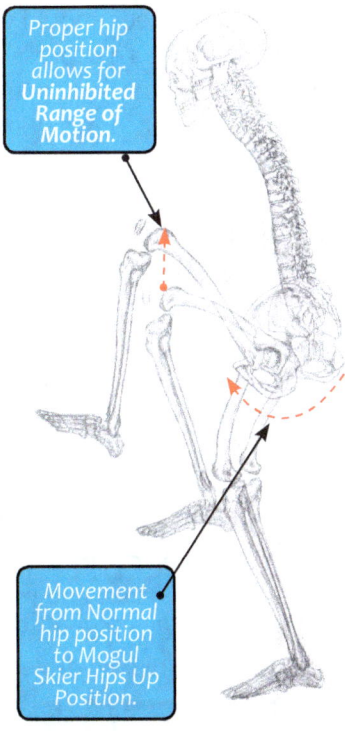

Proper hip position allows for Uninhibited Range of Motion.

Movement from Normal hip position to Mogul Skier Hips Up Position.

Uninhibited Range of Motion

normal athletic stance range of motion performance as compared to the Mogul Skier Hips Up final position. It is a big difference!

Leave your shoulders hunched slightly forward, yet tall and level with each other, because they are the rocks the impacts from the waves of moguls will crash over. Plus, it helps you realize the hollow position between our turns when our shoulders are left slightly concaved. If your shoulders are back, it is difficult to cock your hips forward like they should be. You should finish it off by raising your chin up so that you are looking straight ahead.

To finish off a good stacked position, align your hands and elbows with your shoulders, as described in the previous section, and keep them as tight to your silhouette as possible. It is okay if they drift a little bit from your sides as you make contact with your pole plant on the mogul due to the impact. It is very hard not to make any movement at all. But the goal is to make as little elbow-to-silhouette visual breaks as possible. It can be distracting to the judges to see the snow between your silhouette and your elbows, just like it is distracting for them to be able to see the snow behind you between your knees should your knees ever come apart. This can negatively impact your turn scores. Therefore, it is beneficial to wear baggy enough clothing so that not every little break will show the bright snow behind you. However, don't wear too baggy of clothes either. As mogul skiers, we must remain tactical at all times.

Standing tall like this gets you out of your own way by removing all of the obstacles from blocking your uphill hip drive and range of motion. All of the other stuff in this section was described in such a way to prevent your uphill hip drive from getting blocked. Also, all of the methods that I described above work together in unison to make your mogul skiing more efficient, easier, and more sustainable. We did all that work just to get to the uphill hip drive.

As we now know, the action of standing nice and tall in a good body

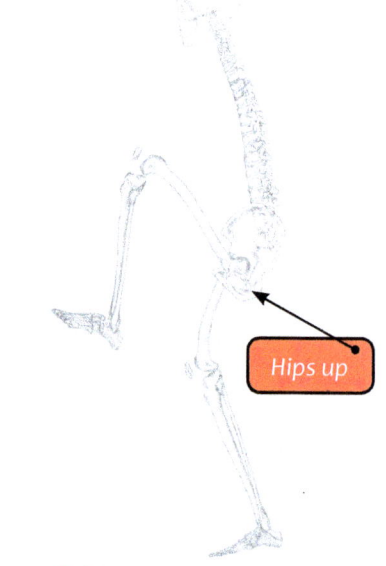

Mogul Skier Hips Up Final Position

position which is not restricted from movement is what is known as the "stacked position." In other words, the stacked position's sole purpose is to keep you from blocking your uphill hip drive and range of motion in any way, shape, or form. It is like the fence you put around the garden. It is the preventative pesticides you put down around it. It is also one of the most crucial steps in the New Mogul Method. See below for images of me using the Mogul Skier Hips Up Position in actual moguls.

"Mogul Skier Hips Up Position" in practice

FINE-TUNING SECTION
WHAT TO DO WITH YOUR KNEES—AND WHY

"Knee angle" is a term used to describe the degree at which we can get our shins horizontal across the hill as viewed from below. "Knee angulation" is considered impressive when the knees break the outer edges of our silhouette and/or our shins get to a 45° angle with the ground, with 0° being standing straight up and down, and a little shin angle being about 10°. Mogul judges like to see good knee angulation because it means that you are finishing your turns, and are in complete control. The reason they look for good knee angulation is because when we "straight run," our knee angulation tends to be very poor (~10° or less). However, other than the sort of "general consensus" in the mogul skiing community, "good knee angulation" (at or about 45°) is "ideal." Little is known about why exactly. Well, allow me to illuminate the reasons why.

Our knees are like rudders when we ski moguls. They are the lead point of our body, and have the greatest influence on the direction our center of mass takes. Knee angles exist for the purpose of aligning our center of mass between the turns that we need to make. At times, the moguls are far apart horizontally, so that we can't make a direct line successfully. Typically, we always try to keep the line at which our knees oscillate from side to side, parallel to the fall line, and therefore the same as the path which our center of mass follows. Sometimes, however, the left and right turns are so far apart that we have to drift our center of mass a little bit horizontally.

Knee angulation happens during the full absorption phase of the turn where they angle toward the opposite shoulder. In this photo, Brayden Pawlik's downhill foot is his right foot. He is bringing both of his knees up toward his left shoulder (opposite shoulder) while keeping his upper body tall and his shoulders square to the fall line.

Shoulders remain square to the fall line.

Knee angulation

There are two reasons for this. The first is that the mogul line that we are in physically dictates it. The other is we need to slow down. Either way, the point at which the knees hinge over, from left to right, and vice-versa, designates the center point that our center of mass will follow. This center point should be in line with the most direct path through the moguls. Our "knee angles" are the vehicle by which we initiate a new lateral center-line-point as they pass the uphill hip as viewed from a downhill vantage point. This is required when the turns are so wide that even a consistent center point that we tip our knees from side to side won't be possible.

When this happens, the center point we generate with our knees will be in "flux." In other words, it will have to be a "moving target." Moving target center points are the most difficult. Although great knee angles can look spectacular, and are required when moguls are laterally far apart, it should be pointed out that they create a bad uphill hip position. This is because when the knees are fully absorbed and pointed across the hill, the uphill hip is driven backwards from the lateral motion.

It will create a constant battle for you to "pull it out" of the backseat whenever this happens.

The best advice I can give is to be aware of the big lateral moguls before you get into them, and do your best to have the uphill hip as squarely down the hill as possible before, and during, each big lateral move. This will prevent you from getting twisted too far sideways, which can make the next turn back the other direction impossible at times. Like I stated previously, getting twisted too far sideways means getting your uphill hip more than 45° uphill. Therefore, it is best to limit your knee angle to a point at which they don't force the uphill hip more than 45° uphill. Just be aware that they are one of the biggest adversaries to the uphill hip drive, albeit a necessary one. These two conflicting aspects are one of the most delicate and respectable battles that makes great mogul skiing such a beautiful art form. When the mogul line we ski dictates severe knee angles just to make it work, many times it is best to choose another line. Even if you can ski the line well, at best it will severely limit your speed, and therefore your overall score. Luckily, nowadays, most manmade courses only have one or two laterally separated turns at most (usually out of the top air).

However, it is possible to make wide lines work for us, and to make them work well. It will require great knee angulations, but it can work. The great mogul skiers of old, those who ushered in the current mogul era, were masters of it, and we shouldn't abandon those archaic skills simply because we ski on consistently "groomer-made moguls." It is an advanced and very applicable skill to have. Not to mention if done skillfully, knee angulation is a beautiful thing to watch. This tends to add points to our turn scores. Anything that improves our turn scores is a good thing.

VISUALIZATION SECTION
WHAT TO DO WITH YOUR MIND

Repeat to yourself what you are going to do before each run, as well as why you are going to do it. Ask yourself what benefits it has so that you remember it during your run. Visualize every part of your run, turns, airs, etc., as many times as you need to until you are able to visualize three full, T2B (Top-to-Bottom) runs, without any mistakes. Once you can do that, you are ready. Upon the visualization of your third Top-to-Bottom run, you want to be sliding into the gate. Upon completion of the third T2B, open your eyes and smile. Go on the judges' command.

Always be positive. Talk in reassuring or positive statements, both to yourself and to others. It keeps negativity from creeping into your mind. Avoid asking yourself questions, especially "What if...?" questions. For more in-depth explanation and examples of how to use your mind to make you a better mogul skier, refer to Chapter 9: Visualization.

PUTTING IT ALL TOGETHER

Simply, take a more direct line in the moguls. To do so, you must be patient, and allow the mogul to come to you. Don't rush and throw your feet out at it. This is disastrous and will get you in the back seat quickly. Start by standing tall; with your chest up, hips up, and arms forward. Make

Pole plant is next to foot, no further than my rear binding as I pass over the crest of the mogul.

Photograph by George Hudnutt

THE MECHANICS OF MOGUL SKIING

contact with the moguls with the sweet spot of the skis at a more direct angle than the actual mogul. Doing so allows energy from the impact to get stored in the flexion of your skis. Meanwhile, you should plant your pole on the crest of the mogul just before your feet make impact, and after your ski tips have already made contact with the mogul. Your pole plant should be next to your foot as your feet pass over the crest of the mogul, and should be released as soon as your feet leave the mogul. Then use it to assist you in the transfer of the feet from one side of your body to the other. The energy stored in your skis, along with the sideways shape of the mogul (as a cam device), changes the direction of that energy with very little effort from you, allowing gravity and kinetic energy to do the work for you. Doing so makes the lead change much faster and effortless.

The key to the energy transfer is the uphill hip drive. We can't drive the uphill hip if we are hunched over, or in the back seat, so we must be standing tall in a good stacked position in order for it to work. When we stand tall, we also need to make sure we keep our chin up, and look several moguls ahead of us whenever possible. This allows us to identify problems, and gives us time to react to them before it is too late. Keeping our hips in the "Mogul Skier Hips Up" position allows us to have increased range of motion, but also makes driving the uphill hip easier because it has less distance to travel. Our downhill hip has most of our weight on it when we first impact the mogul. Our downhill hip also holds back the energy we stored in our skis from allowing it to transfer to the other side. To transition to the next turn, we need to unload the weight from our downhill hip and foot. The uphill hip drive allows us to "unweight" our downhill hip. As we unload our weight from the downhill hip, by driving our uphill hip forward, all of the energy stored within the flexion of our skis and in the deflecting shape of the mogul (that we use as a cam device) can be used to catapult our feet across our body in a brief unabated instant.

Note: *At this point, if you want to get up onto the Glass Plate, simply add an upward motion to your uphill hip drive. That way, some of the energy stored in your skis will then be transferred upward to help lift you up onto the Glass Plate. I will go into more detail about what the Glass Plate is in Chapter 6.*

It is here at the weightless transition in between turns that we can feel the hollow position. We can feel it only if our hips are in a Mogul Skier Hips Up position, and we are standing tall with our chest slightly concaved. It happens just as both of our hips become square to the fall line, and perpendicular to our trajectory. When we are skiing, only the very tops crests of the moguls while maintaining this position, then we are skiing on the Glass Plate.

It is a very cool feeling. When you get to the position where you are in the hollow position, it signifies the end of the previous turn and the beginning of the next. All you have to do is just repeat the process I described above on the following turn. As a benchmark for reference, an average competitive mogul skier skis about three moguls per second. Therefore, the entire process described above would take about 1/3 of a second, or less.

THE PERFECT TURN

In summary, is important to remember that the culmination of the perfect mogul turn is a good uphill hip drive. Everything else that we do to improve our mogul skiing form is mostly just to prevent the blocking of the uphill hip drive. I explain the uphill hip drive as flexing the oblique muscles. Olympic Medalist Bryon Wilson likes to think about it as weighting the downhill ski with the uphill hip. So you can think about it whichever way makes the most sense for you. Remember that we want about 75-80% of our weight on our downhill foot. This is the only way we are able to do that without knocking ourselves off balance.

"The difference between ordinary and extraordinary is that little extra."
-Jimmy Johnson

CHAPTER 5
THE NEW MOGUL METHOD

> *"Systems permit ordinary people to achieve extraordinary results predictably."*
> -Michael Gerber

THE NEW MOGUL METHOD IS BORN

> *"Everything should be made as simple as possible, but not simpler."*
> -Albert Einstein

That first day I decided to write this book, I wrote 21 pages straight. I extrapolated, interpolated, interpreted, induced, deduced, pondered and let marinate everything I had ever known about mogul skiing, and what made me good at it. Every concept was put through the filter of my engineering knowledge to make sure it had a sound place in reality before I put it on paper. Page after page poured out of me as I explained methods and reasons. As I was writing, I was also coaching my mogul skiing athletes as well. It helped me hone not only my mogul method, but my verbiage for explaining it. I developed my simple mogul skiing method long before I became a coach. However, I just never thought of it as a simple unified, cyclical method as I describe it here. At the time I was competing, all I knew was that certain things worked well in multiple circumstances, and that I knew instinctively when to use them. At the time, I never could have imagined how interrelated everything was. Nor did I know how universal some of my highly developed skills actually were.

It took many years of reflection and deduction to develop what worked for me into something that could work for everyone. I have been revising and coming up with better ways to explain the method, to make it as digestible as possible. I used, tested, and refined every single part of this method, and it is one of my greatest works. I offer it to all my athletes as a high-level mogul skiing coach, and now to you as my reader. There are dramatic improvements to be had, if you believe in and practice this method. Many mogul skiers have already realized some of these benefits for the past decade. What follows is the most distilled version of my method ever created. Not even my own athletes ever had access to as much detailed, descriptive, illustrative information as you have here at your fingertips.

Some skiers may not understand my method at first, which is understandable. After all, even I couldn't put it into words right away, because I didn't even fully understand it myself. For a long time, I only knew THAT it worked. I did not burden myself with HOW or WHY it worked. But rest assured I have used this exact method to consistently oust some of the world's best mogul skiers in head-to-head competition. I have also taught it to many high-level mogul skiing specialists who used it to climb the ranks of World Cup mogul skiing. This method is the real deal. When I have used it properly, it has never failed me. And when I failed to use it, I failed myself. It has worked for me, and every single person I ever taught it to. It took many years of coaching mogul skiers, years of professional stunts, a degree in engineering, and a great deal of inward self-reflection and self-analysis for me to boil down my most successful attributes as a mogul skier into a simple to digest, 5-step process. (Although it may seem simple, it is anything but. I expound on each of these topics in greater detail below.) So, without further ado:

THE NEW MOGUL METHOD

Step 1 : Scare yourself

Step 2 : Get stacked

Step 3 : Relax

Step 4 : Be patient

Step 5 : Smile, you are being judged

STEP 1 : SCARE YOURSELF

> *"Life begins at the end of your comfort zone."*
> *-Neale Donald Walsh*

To fear or not to fear, that is the question. "Scare yourself" is hands-down the most misunderstood step in my mogul skiing method. When most people think of "scaring yourself" in the context of mogul skiing, they conjure up vivid memories of losing control, leaning way back, pointing em' straight, and holding on for dear life. No. That is not the type of scaring yourself that we are talking about. Being scared like that is the result of bad technique, culminating an exponential loss of control. Essentially, there is little you can do when you completely lose control, which is unintentional. Therefore, you should and will be scared.

However, the key distinguishing factor in the type of scaring yourself that you do in the first step of my mogul skiing method is that scaring yourself is intentional—and comes at a point where your control is at its peak, near the top of the course. This is followed very closely by the best form that you will have in the entire run (see Step 2). The reason we scare ourselves in the moguls is to activate our mogul skiing reflexes. The best way to scare yourself is to get up to speed as fast as you can when you first start the course, then go a little bit "too fast" before you get to the top air. This will set the pace for the rest of the course and activate your mogul skiing reflexes that you wouldn't have access to otherwise.

There are several reasons for this. First, mogul skiing is a highly complex sport that involves so many variables that can make your head spin. Every mogul has a different shape, texture, contour, contrast in lighting, lateral distance, vertical distance, length, and not to mention, size. Not only that, but your speed and body position vary from mogul to mogul as well. With all that being said, an average mogul skier skis about three moguls per second. Simply put, there is too much to think about and not enough time to think about it. So we need a means to turn our thinking brain off, yet still be able to do this incredibly arduous task called mogul skiing.

Within all advanced mogul skiers, there lies good mogul skiing reflexes. Reflexes that happen so quick and so reliably you don't even have to think about them, you just know they are there. They just plain happen when you need them to. The trick is, however, to bring those same reflexes to the surface and leave them there for the entire run. Use those highly-tuned, highly-conditioned skills to be in control, and make all the decisions for you all the way down the course. "Scaring yourself," therefore, is the catalyst we use to bring those reflexes to the surface, and keep them there.

Beginner Mogul Skiers:	Advanced Mogul Skiers:	Expert Mogul Skiers:	Expert-Elite Mogul Skiers:
1. Get Stacked	1. Get Stacked	1. Scare Yourself	1. Scare Yourself
2. Be Patient	2. Relax	2. Get Stacked	2. Get Stacked
3. Smile	3. Be Patient	3. Relax	3. Relax
	4. Smile	4. Be Patient	4. Be Patient
		5. Smile, you are being judged	5. Glass Plate
			6. Smile, you probably just won

REASONS FOR SCARING YOURSELF

- Activates your "fight" reflexes
- Activates the primal part of your brain
- Prevents you from overthinking

STEP 2 : GET STACKED

> *"If you take control of your behavior,*
> *your emotions will fall into place."*
> *-John C. Maxwell*

"Getting stacked" is a simple phrase used in mogul skiing, which basically means getting yourself into the perfect mogul skiing position by getting perfectly balanced over your skis. As most mogul skiers know, "getting stacked" is anything but simple. It takes years of practice to be able to have a good stacked position, which has been practiced enough that you can call on it whenever you wish. Most mogul skiers struggle with a good stacked position well into their careers, and it may feel like a never-ending "work in progress" at times. You want to get to the point where you know when you are in a good stacked position just by how it feels. Ultimately, however, you want a good stacked position to be a cornerstone of your mogul skiing reflexes so that when you scare yourself, it naturally and immediately rises to the surface and roots you to the moguls underneath your feet. For a better understanding of the mechanics of a "Stacked Position," review the pictures in the sections on Mogul Skier Hips Up Position Step 1 and Mogul Skier Hips Up Position Step 2. However, I will go over the basics again as if you had skis on.

There are many characteristics that make up a good stacked position. To get in a good stacked position while on the hill, follow these steps:

1. Stand perpendicular to the pitch of the hill.
2. Place your hips in the "Mogul Skier Hips Up" position. This increases the range of motion.
3. Raise your hands in front of your center of mass and reach forward.
4. Get into the hollow position.
5. Stand as tall as you can by raising the upper chest and back.
6. Raise your eyes. Pretend you are looking three moguls ahead. Try to imagine you are seeing the moguls closest to you, only with the motion sensing parts of your eyes (your peripheral vision) not looking at them directly.

"Stacked" Position in Action

7. Lead change your feet so that the ball of your downhill foot is beside the instep of your uphill foot.
8. Press your legs firmly together, as you put your downhill knee into the knee pocket of the uphill leg.

Disciplining our bodies into a perfect predisposed stacked mogul skiing position can be difficult when we are scared, so see if you are able to convert that scared feeling into anger. It is surprisingly easy to get into a good stacked position when you're angry.

After I was to the point where I'd begin to realize that I should be scared, but wasn't, that was the time that I found the benefit in relaxing. ("Relaxing" actually has further significance above and beyond the scope of this book). My skill at relaxing in the moguls evolved over the years, and without knowing it at the time, I began practicing skiing on the Glass Plate. The rest of the run I was basically just subduing this very strong fear/anger with relaxation and patience. However, you must be careful not to relax too much, as this can prove to be disastrous. Always keep in mind: staying in your line is a choice, landing is a choice, staying relaxed in the presence of fear and peril is a choice, and actually hitting the air when you're at top speed is also a choice. Therefore, winning is a derivative of the choices one makes in a mogul course.

STEP 3 : RELAX

*"If you surrender to the wind,
you can ride it."*
-Toni Morrison

*"The less effort, the faster
and more powerful you will be."*
-Bruce Lee

Fundamentally, and universally, the most significant thing I ever learned about mogul skiing was to relax. Believe it or not, it is the same with most martial arts as well. But first, what does it mean to relax? Does it just mean to go limp fish, loosey-goosey down the mountainside? No. That form of relaxation has no place in the moguls. Mogul skiing at its very essence takes a great deal of discipline and a carefully structured body position, which is both strong, flexible, and incredibly quick at the same time. Now, the difficult thing here is that these basic mogul skiers' traits are all opposites, meaning that they shouldn't go together in the same body—or at least be happening at the same time. A body that is strong is not flexible, a body that is quick is not strong. A body that is flexible is not quick.

Yet mogul skiing requires all of these things simultaneously. First, let me explain the virtues of each attribute individually, and later I will show you how we can tie them together.

ONLY STRENGTH AS A VIRTUE = A mogul skier with overwhelming strength but no other traits will be too rigid. A rigid-bodied mogul skier will inevitably get bucked too hard and tossed out of his line, no matter how much he tries to "force it." Although he may be strong, he will use too much energy, too quickly, to fight this mogul and that. He will get tired more quickly, be more prone to injury and get frustrated, which only perpetuates his rigid skiing style.

ONLY FLEXIBILITY AS A VIRTUE = A flexible-bodied mogul skier invariably lets the course do too much of the dictating on what direction they let their body go. They will stay in the rut too long, often separating their upper body direction from their hip direction, washing out their tails this way and that. Their hands and pole plants will be undisciplined and sporadic. They will hinge every time they hit a mogul, which is bad. They will get stuffed and/or miss their pop on every air.

ONLY QUICKNESS AS A VIRTUE = A mogul skier that only focused on quickness will constantly overcorrect his lower body with his upper, his timing will be off (usually too soon), and his rhythm will be out of sync with the course. He will often pre-hop moguls as well (which is bad). He will invariably be inefficient with his efforts, wasting valuable energy where it is not needed and not utilizing spots where the course can actually do most of the work for him.

Which type of mogul skier are you? Do you see some things above that maybe you need to work on?

THE STATE OF RELAXATION—LEVEL 1

So how does one combine strength, flexibility, and quickness into one body, simultaneously? This is the greatest question an athlete can ever ask. The answer is surprisingly simple: relax.

Relaxation only acts as a medium to transfer from one form of action or reaction to another. The more relaxed a skier is, the smoother her transitions are. So at any beginning or ending of an action or reaction, there should only be relaxation. Yes, you do have to mix relaxation in between a mish-mash of opposing actions and reactions, which can become very complicated to think about. Every time you go through one of those transitional events, you just have to keep reminding yourself: "Relax, relax, relax." In fact, a more realistic sequence would be, "React, relax, act, relax, react, relax, act." Relaxation gives your body the means to "shift gears" from a power move, into a test of your flexibility, then into quick rapid-fire reactions. A relaxed state allows the body to produce any type of action that you want, but it has to be there at the beginning and end of every move you make.

Let's look at an example. Say something happens to you, like you get bucked in the moguls. What does getting bucked in the moguls mean in the terms listed above? Well, as a consequence of getting bucked in the moguls or "stuffed," you are in essence, maxing out your flexibility. Now if you are like most people and you max out your flexibility, you want to take control via strength, and you immediately get real strong and rigid. What happens to people who get strong and rigid (from **"Only Strength as a virtue"** above)? They get bucked harder and get tossed off the course. Not the result we are looking for, is it?

So what about the other virtue, **Quickness**? Well if we max out our flexibility and then follow it up with quickness, we will separate our upper body from our lower body, our timing will be off, and our rhythm will get "outta whack." So what can you do? Well, in this case, you would need to relax as the maximum flexibility is being reached, and then be patient and wait for the first reaction to finalize itself. The duration you need to wait, or not wait, is completely unique in every case. But relaxing and allowing our muscles the time to switch gears is what we need to remember. In this case, after getting bucked, getting stacked again should be at the top of the priority list, and what better state to try to get stacked from than a state of relaxation? After that, relax, be patient, reimplement the New Mogul Method cycle from there. The cyclical nature of this 5-step process is what makes it so beautifully effective. Being cyclical means that you can start at any point in the 5-step process and then just proceed with the following steps. For example, if you are in the middle of the course and you get bucked really hard, and you now know that you need to relax (Step #3), you should also know that your next step is to be patient (Step #4). Then the next logical action step would to be to get stacked (Step #2). We can assume that getting bucked will automatically satisfy Step #1, and we can discard Step #5: "Smile" from the remedy cycle because it only applies at the bottom of the course. But always remember, in the back of your mind, to relax after every action or reaction as much as possible. The greatest athletes of any given sport make it look easy because they are relaxed. Remember, relaxing is what allows us to tie together the three seemingly unrelated virtues. This leads us to the next level of relaxation...

THE STATE OF RELAXATION—LEVEL 2

The next level of relaxation is level 2. Level 2 Relaxation is the ability to "draw out" and prolong the individual inflection points between actions and reactions. These are the moments in which relaxation is supposed to be occurring. If we get good at it, we can sequence these moments between action and reaction to span the duration of the entire run. That way, there is an overall presence of relaxation without having to be relaxed the entire time. This encompasses our body as a whole, regardless of the fears (and sometimes in the face of them) we might be enduring. It looks and feels like a completely selfless feeling and an acknowledgement of a great fear, yet the utter dismissal of the related emotions. In essence, Level 2 Relaxation is a measure to which you are comfortable (relaxed) during great peril, at great speed, and under great pressure. It works to increase our efficiency of movement, to combine together strength, quickness, and flexibility in the face of our fears. It provides us with whatever athletic attribute is required at any given moment.

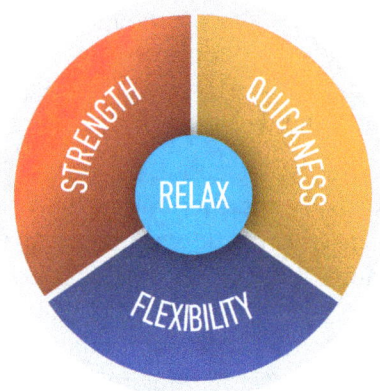

Relaxation Ties Together the Three Athletic Attributes

THE NEW MOGUL METHOD

STEP 4 : BE PATIENT

> *"There are things in life you have to work for,*
> *and there are things in life you have to wait for."*
> *-John C. Maxwell*

The process of being patient is easy to explain, but difficult to do in practice. The concept is this: be patient and wait for the moguls to come to you. This is difficult because when we get going too fast, we want to start throwing our feet at the moguls as fast as they come at us. This inevitably leads to us getting in the back seat and it makes it difficult to get stacked again.

In fact, the solution for getting stacked again—when you finds yourself in the back seat—is to be patient. Which if you did in the first place, you probably never would've gotten into the back seat to begin with. Nine

Be Patient: Wait for each mogul come to you.

times out of ten, when someone is in the back seat, it is because they got impatient (or scared). They start throwing their feet out ahead of them at the moguls too soon. Even after landing out of the top air, this is a problem. You have to be patient and let the moguls come to you! The goal is to remain stacked and keep your feet underneath you by being patient. Note, it helps to remember to be relaxed before you try to be patient. It solves more mogul skiing related glitches before they arise than all of the other of the Mogul Method steps combined. Hence, why this step follows the Relax step in the New Mogul Method.

STEP 5 : SMILE, YOU ARE BEING WATCHED

"Life isn't about waiting for the storm to pass,
it's about learning to dance in the rain."
-Vivian Greene

"Smile, you are being watched" is not overly complicated, but it is deep. It has three parts to it. First, it is a statement that I like to remind my athletes of as much as possible. Mogul skiing is a judgment sport, but it is also a dueling sport. People who judge you will inevitably judge you better if they like you. And people like people who smile more than people who don't. It's a simple, basic human characteristic. Like it or not, the more you smile, the more people will like you. It's better to have judges that like you judge your run.

The second part of this step is for the people that you are competing against. If you let them see you beat yourself up over this mistake or that, they will see that as a chink in your armor and do their best to get under your skin and intimidate you, or get into your brain and make you worry about things you normally wouldn't. So don't let them see when you are having a bad day. Do your best to smile, even in the worst of times. It keeps the vultures and scavengers at bay.

The last part of this step is for visualization purposes. As athletes, we are trained to visualize our runs, over and over again. It is almost a non-stop process. Go to any mogul course, anywhere in the world, and you will see athletes stopping to visualize their top air, their bottom air, their landings, their middle sections, everything—even at the start gate before their actual competition run. This is very helpful, but, what most people don't know is that the most important thing is to visualize you smiling, or being happy at the end of whatever you visualize.

The stronger you can make that smile/emotion feel in your visualization, the stronger your subconscious will try to make it a reality for you during your actual competition run. I always remind my athletes in the start gate to visualize themselves smiling when crossing the finish line, and it has had outstanding success. Smiling also releases endorphins and serotonin, brain chemicals that put you in a better state.

"The most complicated skill is to be simple."
-Dejan Stojanovic

"Tension is who you think you should be.
Relaxation is who you are."
-Chinese Proverb

CHAPTER 6
THE GLASS PLATE

"Confidence is like going after Moby Dick in a row boat, and taking the tartar sauce with you."
-Zig Ziglor

WHAT IS THE GLASS PLATE?

"Seeing it once is better than being told 100 times."
-Chinese Proverb

If you are an expert-elite mogul skier, you may recall a run that you had that was hands-down the fastest run of your life. Where your feet felt so light, even weightless, and the depth and spacing of the moguls was a complete non-issue. You may be able to remember that your balance was perfect, your body position was stacked perfectly, and the moguls went by effortlessly, with minimal impact, and yet you were energized. At the time, the moguls seemed to coast under your feet in droves of tens or twenties, rather than twos or threes. You felt a speed that can only be compared to as terminal velocity. Your skis barely touch the snow, and you rode on a plane in the moguls that felt slippery. It also felt fragile, like you could fall through it at any time.

It's the highest skiable plane in any given mogul line. It's fast, slippery, thin, and fragile. That's the Glass Plate.

Well, at least, that's how it feels. A skier might know what it feels like, deep down in their muscle memory, yet they may not be conscious of the exact mechanics that it takes to put them there onto the Glass Plate, or of its true potential. The nitty-gritty mechanics of the Glass Plate are what this chapter discusses. Later in this chapter, I provide you with both the exact formula that I used for getting up on and sustaining the Glass Plate, as well as a simplified formula.

It is not only the fastest way to ski moguls, it is also the most stable. The Glass Plate's front door is open only to those who are relaxed. Its lobby is paved with fear, and it is tamed by no one. It takes a great deal of courage and discipline to tango with it. However, its power is unmatched, and all these things are what makes it so coveted. With this chapter, I will lay out the basics so that you have the correct concepts and all of the basics to achieve and realize the benefits of the Glass Plate for yourself.

We now know that the Glass Plate is the subtle, fragile, and best plane that the hips can take while in the moguls. In other words, when the hips no longer oscillate with the rise and fall of the moguls, while only the feet and knees do. That is the Glass Plate. It is when the hips are at a sufficiently high plane that they are unimpeded by the moguls and all impacts with the moguls have only has a secondary effect on the hips. It usually coincides with the feet skiing on the crest of the mogul with little more than just the part of the ski directly under the boot making contact with each mogul. It is a very thin plane, set very high on the mogul. It is achieved only through the perfect use of one's hips. One should only attempt to control her speed in lateral motions (by turning higher and wider) while skiing on the Glass Plate. This is because it is incredibly easy to fall back into the bone-jarringly deep ruts of the mogul course. That is why it is called the Glass Plate. Attempting to slow down by pushing ones feet down to the face of the mogul can result in disaster. When this happens, it is known as "punching through the Glass Plate," or "falling through the Glass Plate." It often results in a major bobble or fall. A skier will lose almost all control and balance if she falls through the Glass Plate, so you have to be extra careful where you choose to put your feet once you are skiing on the Glass Plate. Be sure to only attempt to control your speed by going higher and wider with your feet placement and never punch through the Glass Plate!

Most of the time, even good mogul skiers are just too afraid to take all the speed they can generate from a mogul run, so they leave a lot of it on the table. The Glass Plate isn't for those skiers. The Glass Plate is for the skier who is familiar with skiing fast in the moguls, who has simply hit the ceiling for speed with her current mogul skiing mechanics, and yet, other people still manage to beat her to the bottom. It is also for those individuals who are already fast, but just want the next lesson to keep pushing themselves. (The Glass Plate is actually more applicable to this type of athlete.) The Glass Plate is for those athletes who do not let fear curb their speed, and any speed that gets left on the table is purely due to less efficient mechanics. Simply put, there are no mogul skiing mechanics as efficient or as fast as the Glass Plate.

BENEFITS OF THE GLASS PLATE

BALANCE

Lightness of foot. Increased agility. Easier to maintain a good stacked position.

STRENGTH

The elevated position your body is at relative to the bottom of the mogul (the rut) allows more force to be applied perpendicular or laterally on the top of the mogul, rather than on the face. This decreases the negative energy that the mogul is applying on you, and increases the positive energy that you are applying to the mogul. Therefore, it leverages your strength moves.

SPEED

The fastest way to ski moguls, hands down.

HOW TO GET UP ON THE GLASS PLATE

Anyone who remembers skiing on the Glass Plate may recall how effortless and light on his feet he was while on the Glass Plate. Other than the raw speed itself, this is the most persistent memory of how the Glass Plate "feels." Effortless and light. Therefore, it is only logical that the athlete will try to be light on his feet in order to attempt to get back up on the Glass Plate. However, this is wrong. Below, I list out easy-to-understand steps on how to get up on to the Glass Plate. There are two ways of explaining how to get up onto the Glass Plate. One is more detailed than the other:

THE AUTHOR'S METHOD

1. Initiate uphill hip drive slightly earlier than you would in your normal skiing speed (this is only a fraction of a second sooner).
2. Drive the uphill hip hard to a square hip position at the crest of the mogul.
3. Use the impact of the mogul to raise you higher than normal (relative to the bottom of the rut) onto the Glass Plate.

4. Relax.

5. Be patient. You're on the Glass Plate. The moguls will come at you so fast you will not be able to move your feet fast enough manually to keep up with them. If you listen to your reflexes and throw your feet out at the moguls before they get to you, it will likely spell disaster in about three moguls! You need to be patient and let the moguls come to you. And when they impact your feet, you need to let the energy of the mogul do most of the work for you. All you should be focused on (and all you will have time for) is to just guide the energy laterally across your body (this is possible because you are relaxed). This is very similar to the core principle of Jiu-jitsu. Use the energy of your opponent—in this case, that would be the moguls coming at you—against them by using their energy to empower superhuman speed in your legs. That is simply not possible, manually. (Refer to Chapter 5, the section on "What to do With Your Skis and Feet and Why" for more information on how to do this.)

THE SIMPLIFIED METHOD

1. In between Steps 3 & 4 of the New Mogul Method (see above), just before impact with any mogul, initiate the hollow position.

2. Be patient with your feet; wait for the moguls to come to your feet.

Explanation: Initiate uphill hip drive just before the ski tips hit the mogul, so that when you hit the mogul, the impact will come up as your hips are perfectly square to the fall line as you hit the crest of the mogul. Your uphill hip drive should be strong enough to counter the lateral force of your knee angulation due to the impact, resulting in a net force slightly upwards. This is the familiar feeling (for those who know it) of being lifted onto the Glass Plate. It is important to remember to relax up onto the Glass Plate, because the resulting net upward force is very small and can easily be negated by too rigid of a posture. This is the threshold and front door to the Glass Plate. Once you are up there, remember to be patient. This process is essentially repeated, mogul after mogul—although once a skier learns to maintain it, it is not a conscious task.

Your body will do it for you, as you will be moving too fast to comprehend all the movements you will be making. You must practice this until the effort goes away, only then can you be entirely relaxed. Only then, can you harness the benefits of the Glass Plate.

*"Be such a man that not only embraces,
but relies on things that he does not understand.
Calling upon a greater knowledge so that his mind is not
clouded with the burden of "How,"
but only with the purity of knowing it will work."*
-Unknown

*"It is a lot easier to give credit for something
that we can see with our eyes,
than something we have to see with our minds.
Although the latter may be of a greater accomplishment,
the former will receive the acknowledgement."*
-Unknown

*"Faith is trusting in advance what will only
make sense in reverse."*
-Philip Yancey

THE INVINCIBLE MOGUL SK1ER
PART 2
THE BOOK OF WIND

APPLIED MOGUL SKIING
Strategy, Preparation, and Competition

Artwork courtesy of John Dowling

CHAPTER 7
OBSTACLES AND OPPORTUN1TIES

*"You cannot win if you do not begin!
The people who get ahead in the world
are the ones who look for the circumstance they want,
and if they can't find them, they make them."*
-John C. Maxwell

Now that we have learned all about the mechanics of mogul skiing and how to implement them properly, I will teach you everything you need to know about strategy and preparation in competitive mogul skiing.

OBSTACLES

"Every problem introduces a person to himself."
-John McDonnell

The goal of any mogul skier, as they are surveying a mogul course, should be to break it down into mere obstacles and opportunities. Basically, what is good and what is bad about each line in the course. It is important to note that not every mogul is an obstacle as one may expect. Conversely, not every mogul is an opportunity either. Not all moguls were created equal, nor should you treat them that way. Every mogul will have a personality of its own, and every mogul will have distinct boundaries on how it will allow one to interact with it.

You should begin your analysis of any course by first attempting to identify all the obstacles in a course first; then you should rate it according to how much of a problem it is likely to be on a scale of 1-10, with 10 being the most difficult. You can use this method to help you choose a line as well. You want all obstacles to fall somewhere between 4 and 8 on a scale of 1-10. If it is below 4, it's not considered an obstacle. If it is a 9 or 10, see if you can find a better line. Keep track of all the obstacles in your head or use a teammate to help you rate them. When you've finished your course inspection, total all the obstacles together. For example, if you see a difficult transition coming into the top air, you might rate it a 6 in difficulty. Then, you rate the landing coming out of the top air as an 8, followed by two difficult moguls after that, that you rate as 5s each. Then, there is on oddly placed mogul in the middle section that you have to remember and you rate it a 4. Then you notice that there are death cookies in your bottom section that are not likely to go away, so you rate the entire bottom section as a 4. Totaling them, we get 6+8+5+5+4+4=32. Generally, you want to keep your total score for your obstacles 20 points or under, never to exceed 25 points.

I will go through this more difficult course as an example to you and how to create a plan of action for it. However, if you find yourself on a very difficult course, and all of the lines you rate at 25 points or above—or there is a tie—I sympathize. Then what you need to do is take the line with the lowest overall score, which you get by summing the category points and the obstacle points (see below). You can then at least be confident that you chose the easiest available line. If a tie between two lines occurs in the obstacle rating, and/or the overall score, and you still don't know which line to choose, analyze the opportunities of each line and choose the one with the best opportunities that suit your specific style of skiing best.

After you rate each obstacle in your chosen line, you should then categorize it by location, and develop a plan to deal with it. The categorization of its location should be one of seven locations only:

1. TOP SECTION - Moguls from the starting line to the top air transition.
2. TOP AIR TRANSITION - Extends three moguls before the top air.
3. TOP AIR EXIT - Extends three moguls after the top air landing pad.
4. MIDDLE SECTION - Section of moguls between the top air exit to the bottom air transition.
5. BOTTOM AIR TRANSITION - Three moguls before the bottom air.
6. BOTTOM AIR EXIT - Three or four moguls after the bottom air landing pad.
7. BOTTOM SECTION - Last section of moguls before the finish line.

After you have categorized the obstacles, record them in your head or write the number of the section (location) that each problem area (obstacle) occurred in, then sum up those numbers, just like before. Using the example from the previous page, the location totaled value would look like this: 2+3+3+3+4+7=22. Generally speaking, you should never choose a line that has a category total above 20, like this one does, but we will use it because it is a good example that requires strategy in order to deal with it. Ideally, you want your category total to be around 15 points, as this seems to be the sweet spot. Anything below 10 points would be considered an easy line (course). Now, you need to develop a plan to deal with them. A plan to deal with the same obstacles from the previous example might look like this:

LOCATION (CATEGORY)		OBSTACLE RATING		PLAN OF ACTION
Top Air Transition	2	Abrupt mogul in Transition	6	Be patient, wait to place your feet on the crest of the abrupt mogul.
Top Air Exit	3	Huge sideways mogul at end of the landing pad	8	Be patient, let the mogul come to you. Keep your feet underneath you.
Top Air Exit	3	Deep mogul	5	Relax. Let the energy of impact travel up and out of your body, while remaining stacked.
Top Air Exit	3	Quick mogul	5	Roll over into the knee pocket quickly! Re-stack on next mogul.
Middle Section	4	Mogul located Out of Fall Line	4	Aim low on the crest of the mogul or place a pseudo turn before (uphill of) the rut.
Bottom Section	7	Death Cookies	4	Get on the glass plate. Coast over low spots of moguls that contain death cookies. Avoid, if necessary.
Category Total	22	Obstacle Total:	32	Combined Score: 22+32=54 Likely max points: 1/54 = 18 points

Generally, it is better to have problem areas in the bottom section than in the middle section, and better to have problem areas in the top section than the middle section. This is because the bottom section is closest to the judges and your speed will generally be at its fastest. It is the last spot that you want to have hazards in your line. Gladly, however, due to the "blown out" nature of most bottom sections from everyone skiing that section at top speeds, major obstacles in the bottom section are rare at best. But they do pop up once in a while, so watch out! The middle section is where the majority of your turn points will come from. This is because it is not only the longest section of the course, but it is the only section that has an air exit (top air) and an air entrance (bottom air). All of that will be plainly visible to the judges. However, it is better to have problems in the middle section than the bottom section because it is longer, and you have more time (distance) to deal with, and sort through any problems spots.

The best place to have any obstacles in is the top section, the reason being is that it is not only the farthest away from the judges' view, but many times, judges aren't even able to see past the top air on many courses due to their perspective. Therefore, any potential bobbles or splitting of the knees due to an obstacle has a fairly good chance of going completely unnoticed. Additionally, this is the section of the course where you are moving your slowest. Sometimes advanced mogul skiers like to push and skate through much of the top section, and that goes largely unpunished by the judges because they understand that you are merely getting up to speed.

Basically, using the method of categorizing the obstacles on a mogul course numerically, according to difficulty and location, helps you simplify the problem areas of the course to an overall level of difficulty of a section, as well as the course as a whole. This is the same thing that happens naturally in the mind of a professional mogul skier whether she actually calculates any totals or not. They generalize the difficulty level of specific moguls into a broader perspective and range of territory that it would take to deal with each specific problem. For example, if you have a large difficult mogul coming out of the top air, you will need to generalize your take off strategy, landing location, the impact of said mogul all the way down to several or more moguls down the course to deal with that one problem area. It's never just you vs. that one specific obstacle; it's a broad strategy that spans 10 moguls or so to sort out. That's how professional mogul skiers think. They don't think about each specific mogul and how to deal with it, they identify the largest problems and then spread out its negative effects over several moguls; it is the art of making a difficult obstacle look easy.

An inexperienced mogul skier might try to identify the obstacle ratings, categorical location, and plan of action or strategies of how to deal with every single mogul. It can take up to 25% of the course to implement a method to deal with a difficult obstacle, but you want to limit it if possible. Your entire run needs to blend together in one seamless display of spectacle and skill. The greatest mogul skiers never let any difficult obstacles shatter the illusion of perfection. Spread the problem areas out over distance, that's the key. Besides, the collective personality of a group of seven or so moguls in a "small group" provides a better indicator of how to deal with a particularly difficult mogul, anyways. Consider dealing with it and its adjacent (3) moguls before and (3) moguls after (totaling seven, yay for math!). Studying a problem area as a group of (7) moguls will provide you just enough information so that you may pinpoint the problem, but not so overly specific where you miss the big picture.

If the obstacle is a very deep mogul, for example, then you must take 5-10 turns before it to gradually raise your center of mass to a plane and speed where you can gracefully pass over the massive mogul. For advanced elite mogul skiers, this is not necessarily an issue because their center of mass rides higher in the moguls, because they tend to ski on the elusive Glass Plate. Now if there is an opportunity on the other hand, such as a fairly steep backside that you can land on, you can plane out (rise to the glass plate) in as few as two turns. Sometimes, the obstacle is really flat icy moguls. All you need to do is lean really far forward on, until you're past them. Not only is it the best position for this kind of problem area, but doing so should remind you that you need to stay slow, and stay off your tail edges, which will slip on the ice.

Many schools of thought on mogul skiing teach mogul groups of six, but I like seven because it makes the entrance and exit of a difficult mogul symmetrical. Additionally, it makes the starting and ending turns leading into and out of "problem zone" the same turn (either a right, or left-handed turn). That way, you know instinctively when you have passed the problem area. This makes it far less confusing if you want to visualize your problem areas by saying: "Ok, the first 'problem area' (group of seven moguls) after the air starts with a left, and therefore is a 'lefty' problem area, then the next one starts with a right, and is, therefore, a 'righty' problem area, etc." If they all start and end on opposite turns, and you try to stack them, it gets complicated, and it has never worked for me.

Expounding on the above category locations, when trying to determine a plan of action, I choose to think of every small group of moguls as having a collective personality, and I break down the top section (before the top air) into two larger personality types. The moguls starting from the top of the course half way to the top air is the first group, and the other half of the moguls leading into the top air is the second group. Similarly, in the middle section, I like to break it down into three equal groups and the bottom section into two equal groups. If all this is too much for you, then don't stress about it. All in all, from my experience, a mogul course usually boils down to about two obstacles and one opportunity. Failure to realize any one of these can lose you the race.

You may want to ask the judges how well they can see the top section of the course. If you are shy and like to be discrete (like me), you can just hang out by the bottom of the judges stand, if there is one, and you will to be able to overhear their conversations. Many times, you will gain great insight on what the judges are particularly looking for if you just eavesdrop on their conversations. I used to like to keep my backpack closest to the judges' stand, or anywhere the judges might congregate, for the sole purpose of the possibility of overhearing anything that might give me even the slightest advantage. I highly suggest you do the same.

OPPORTUNITIES

> *"When we change the way we look at things,*
> *the things we look at change."*
> *-Wayne Dyer*

Opportunities come in three main categories: Line, Love, and Landings. The three "L's of Opportunity." Opportunities, simply put, are the parts of the mogul course and competition that can be exploited to your advantage. You must try to maximize every opportunity to the best of your ability on every course. Let me start with the oldest and most basic advantage any mogul skier is trained to find.

LINE

The "line" which you choose to take down the mogul course is the single most important aspect of any mogul skier's run. But to truly understand the importance and proper application of the "line" as an advantage, we must first look back to the history of the sport. The "line" can be defined as the average path a skier takes to get down the mountain. This generally refers to your center of mass and by how much you do, or don't, deviate from a straight line from where you started to where you finished the moguls—the he goal being to have the smallest amount of deviation from your line as possible.

Forty or 50 years ago, when mogul skiing was still in its infancy, all the way up to the point where we started to create man-made courses, the "line" that a mogul skier skied was as much of a virtue of his skill level as were his turns, airs, or speed. This was because, in natural moguls, the moguls were rarely in the perfect left-right-left-right continuum that they are today, and the mogul skiers of old had to do a great deal of work blending together broken sections of left-right turns into a seamless "line" that allowed him to not only continue his own left-right rhythm, regardless of the actual course conditions at any given spot, but to keep his balance, speed, and form all in check. It wasn't always easy, and the greatest of the natural-mogul skiers tied together even very large deviations in their lines in subtle ways and made it look easy. This took a great deal of talent.

However, all they used to do was to tie together sections of moguls that had good left-right continuums, by adding in a few extra turns as they gradually switched lines, where one line ended, or filled in some "razzle-dazzle" turns to tie to congruent lines (one just above the other) that didn't have good left-right moguls connecting them to each other. Good "lines" in natural moguls are inconsistent at best. And they are surprisingly quite short. It is truly rare to find a natural mogul line that rivals anything as long as a professional mogul skiing course is today. The best natural lines usually only have roughly ten left-right turns in continuum before they start to disappear. This is because most mogul skiers can't ski more than ten mogul turns consecutively. They usually get going too fast and blow out, get too tired, or fall. Mountains with better-than-average mogul skiers will have better, longer, natural mogul lines than those without.

Nowadays, "line" has been largely marginalized in mogul skiing competition by the advent of the man-made mogul course, which has a perfect left-right continuum of turns, in every line, from the start of the course all the way down to the finish. Therefore, short of any "razzle-dazzle," all the mogul skier has to do to have a good "line" is simply not blow out of his line, or change lines or drift on one of his landings—which the vast majority of mogul skiers have no problem doing nowadays.

However, going back to the roots of "line" in mogul skiing, we can tend to find it's true advantage, and thus our opportunity for an edge over our competition. The "line" as it existed in the "olden days" of mogul skiing—namely, short sections of 7-10 turns that are better and more consistent and rhythmic than those around it, before it, or after it—still exists in modern-day mogul courses. If you stop to look at a line more as a whole, you will start to notice large sections of perfect runs of moguls interrupted by an occasional smaller or larger mogul, or perhaps by an "obstacle" (see section above "Obstacles"). These sections of "line" or perfectly rhythmic short sections of moguls are opportunities. This is because you won't have to think about how to turn on them at all—they are, in essence, the easiest sections of moguls that a course will ever offer you.

Instead, focus a couple of extra seconds of your attention on more important things like obstacles. Always choose the "line" with the most continuous uninterrupted moguls in it. If you realize that you see the break in the lines, this will buy you a few moments to redirect your attention to obstacles or more pressing matters. Since a break in the line is, by definition, an obstacle, noticing it before you get to it buys you several precious moments to figure out how best to deal with it. It is one of the best lessons in focus that you can have while on a mogul course. This lesson from the natural mogul skiers of old still whispers in the ears of present-day mogul skiers who are open-minded enough to hear it.

LOVE

The second of the three "L's of Opportunity" is Love. Love can come from either outside of the course or from it. Generally speaking, "love" is any opportunity that can be exploited for your benefit while on the course. Anything that works to decrease the amount of effort or pain that you give, or get, from the mogul course is an opportunity. For example, nice soft freshly slipped moguls fall into the category of "love" from the mogul course to you. A big soft mogul to dissipate excess speed right where you need it, or fresh pine boughs on the course, that increase visibility and depth perception, are also opportunities for you. I like to think of these sort of things as "course love."

Off of the course, opportunities also exist that can be used to increase your chances of winning. These opportunities come from your teammates, coaches, judges, and the crowd. If your teammates believe in you—or talk about amazing things that you have done while skiing, on the water ramps, throwing new tricks, etc.—this can go a long way to intimidate your potential rivals before you even show up to the competition. Many times the very fact that you are intimidating to others can produce a self-fulfilling prophecy in their minds, which lets you win more easily and consistently.

Respect goes a long way too. Your coaches pick up on it, and tend to give it back to you. Usually, however, respect that your coaches will give to you comes largely from your progress and limitations as a whole. Sort of a "big picture" type of respect.

Also, coaches give proportionally more respect to athletes who have earned the respect of their teammates. To get maximum respect from your coaches, therefore, you must be progressing in all aspects of your life, as well as earning the respect of others through a combination of hard work, pushing the envelope, accomplishments, good deeds, and giving respect back. Judges, similar to coaches, can tend to get caught up in your life story, and sometimes give you that extra decimal point when you need it the most. Judges are people too. Make sure you treat them well, and if you have a good life story, share it with them. Be open and honest with them, let them get to know you on a personal level, and your scores will go up, way up. I promise.

The crowd can be one of the biggest influencers of them all, because no one likes to go against the crowd, not even judges. Although it is part of their job not to be swayed by the crowd, many times, judges can't help themselves. If the crowd loves you, no one wants to face the wrath of the crowd. To get the crowd to love you, you must have a good personal story, something that they can relate to. Additionally, you need to be an expert showman, have impeccable timing, and give back to them. Let them really know that any love they express to you, you express right back to them. If you do this consistently, you can "grow" the amount of love that the crowd gives you, just like watering a fledgling tree. "Crowd Love" is also an integral part in the "Leap of Faith" that some athletes make in their career to overcome overwhelming adversity. We will learn about that in Chapter 17.

LANDING

The "landing" advantage has two distinct and different meanings. The first meaning is the landing after both the top and bottom airs. The second meaning is the backside of every mogul. Landings of the airs are a key aspect in the proper choice of a mogul line. They are doubly important in the moguls because the terrain is so unforgiving. A true opportunity it is to find a landing that you are 100% confident with. The best landings have a good flat landing that you know has the least likelihood to change during the weathering process that a competition can bring. Learn to pick a landing where the majority of skiers don't check all of their speed on the first bump coming out of the air. This has the ominous result of creating a monster mogul that is difficult to deal with, right out of the air. Choose the landing that has moguls, or space where you know you can land, that is least likely to be disturbed as possible.

Speed is the benefit of the second meaning of "landing." This meaning dates back to the time before man-made moguls, and is basically intended to mean that the backside of any mogul is potentially an opportunity to generate speed, because it can be "landed on." When we land, we tend to generate more speed. When we combine that with pre-absorbing, which reduces the impact on the face of the next mogul, we can manually generate a good amount of speed quickly. The act of combining pressing (or "landing" on the backside of a mogul) with the pre-absorption of the next mogul (in order to generate speed) is known as "pumping." This skill is most advantageous when we can spot extra places (opportunities) to press hard down on (the back side of the mogul), followed by pulling up one's feet just before an impact with the next mogul to generate speed. The goal of pumping is to gain as much speed as fast as possible when it otherwise does not come of its own accord. One will usually use pumping most frequently in the first few moguls of the mogul course, to generate speed as soon as possible, or at after the bottom air, to make up as much time as possible. However, it can be used anywhere on the course you need to generate speed.

Other than that, pumping can be used after a great reduction in speed has occurred, such as after hitting a large abrupt mogul too deep in its rut (the most uphill part of the mogul). Pumping is an effective generator of speed, which allows you to gain it anywhere you need to, just as the great mogul skiers of old used to do. However, it is a very manual, mechanical, labor-intensive process.

The Glass Plate offers us an automatic generation of speed, which is both an obstacle and an opportunity—no doubt also the reason most people are afraid of it. Allow me to explain how it works. The first thing to know is that it works in reverse to the manual process of speed generation. So the "landing" on the Glass Plate refers to the contact one has with the face of the mogul, not the backside of the mogul like in "pumping." Since we rarely, if ever, come in contact with the back side of the mogul when we are on the Glass Plate, we have to generate our speed somehow on the front side. This is a highly advanced skill meant for contemplation by advanced mogul skiers. With that being said, this is how it works: As you contour over the previous mogul and head into the next, you pull your feet up slightly, and wait a little bit longer than usual to place your feet high on the crest of the mogul. The top crest of the mogul has the least amount of resistance to your speed because it is least perpendicular to you.

You want to "take the top" of the mogul—or even just past the crest of the mogul, so that you can make your turn, but don't miss! Then assume the hollow position and wait for the next mogul to come to you (remember Step 4, be patient!), and repeat the process. You will find that the generation of speed is so fast that your efforts will quickly turn into the mitigation of it, simply because you will feel the need to slow yourself down. To do this, you simply want to gradually increase the amount of the top of the mogul you want to take off, which will slow you down, but not too much! Remember, making contact too far down on the face of the mogul will cause you to break through the Glass Plate, and that can spell disaster. If that is still not enough, start to go higher and wider with your turns and the placement of your feet. (Refer to my interview with former US Team Head Coach Garth Hager for more insight into this technique.)

"Lucky means those who get the opportunity.
Brilliant means those who create the opportunity.
Winner means those who use the opportunity."
-H. C. Lodha

"Be a winner always.
If you miss an opportunity, don't fill your eyes with tears,
It may hide yet another opportunity lying in front of you."
-J. Cricket

CHAPTER 8
COMPET1T1ON

"Monotony is the awful reward for the careful."
-A.G. Buckham

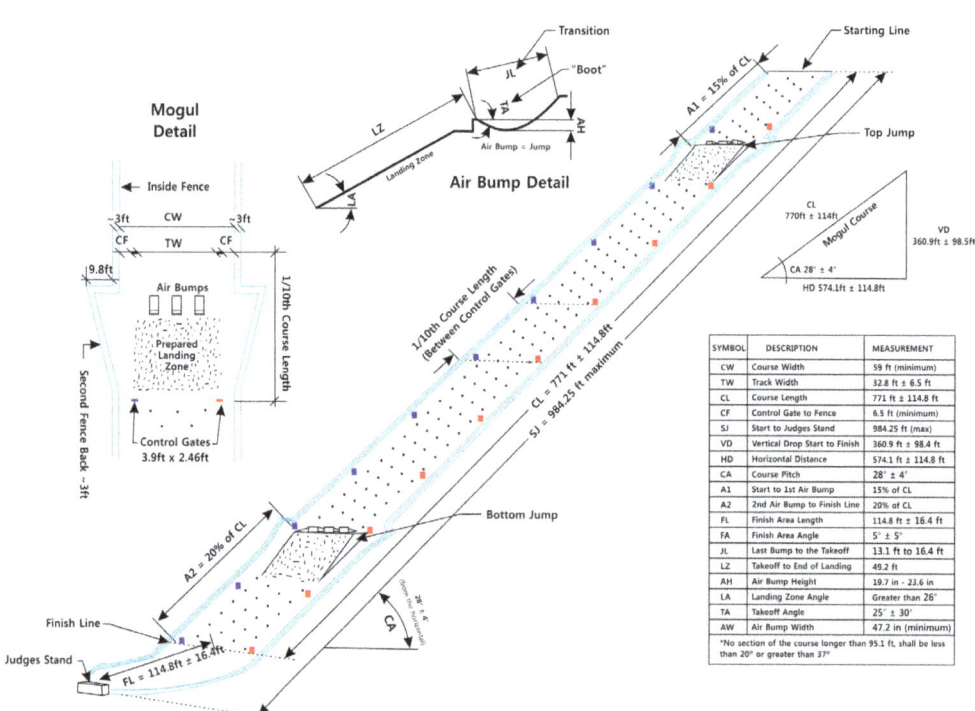

COMPETITION

Martynova Anna / Shutterstock.com

INTRODUCTION

*"Freestyle skiing combines speed, showmanship,
and the ability to perform aerial maneuvers whilst skiing. It debuted as a
demonstration sport at the 1988 Calgary Games."*
-Wikipedia, 2015

Everyone on the same team in mogul skiing is generally happy for their teammates when they execute their run well (of course, there are always exceptions to the rule). This is because it is so hard to do so. Mogul skiing is a difficult and complex sport that is very hard to do well. Therefore, whenever anyone makes a good run, everyone is happy for them because it is a beautiful thing. Of course, there are very competitive natures innate in competitive athletes and rivalries can spur up, especially in a sport that pits teammates against teammates, like mogul skiing does. However, this is a sport where no matter how well you ski, it can always be skied a little bit better. Every mogul skier instinctively knows this, and as a result, mogul skiing itself creates a unique dynamic that few other sport offers. It creates one collective community of mogul skiers vs. the course itself in addition to the singularity of competitors in the competition. The goal of the collective community of mogul skiers is to produce one athlete who is capable of dominating the course on competition day. It doesn't always happen, either. Sometimes the course dominates the competitors, and a lucky person wins. Therefore, domination of the competition course by a mogul skier community is always a sight to behold. If nothing else, truly dominating a competition mogul course demands respect, inspires awe, and sometimes boggles the mind. For all of these reasons, mogul skiing is a beautiful sport that commands respect and admiration from all who witness it.

"I mean, you never see like, others like… football teams… or anything training on the same field. But you can see people trying out their first mogul skis, and the top skiers in the world training the same course on the same day. And I don't think you can find that anywhere else…and that really shows how mogul skiing is a family all over the world…and it doesn't matter if you don't know each other before, just because you are mogul skiers, you have that connection, and that's really beautiful."

-Ludvig Fjallstrom, Swedish Olympic Mogul Team
(Bumps: A Mogul Skiing Documentary, Hoffman 2015)

THE ATHLETE'S ADVANTAGE

"Man is made or unmade by himself; in the armory of thought he forges the weapons by which he destroys himself."
-James Allen

The athlete's advantage is a very simple, age-old method that has been infinitely time-tested and remains rock solid. It is, has been, and will be the basis of every great athlete's mental toughness since the beginning of time, 'till the end of time.' It is so profound, yet so simple, that I will not gaudy it up with too many insights, or distract from its significance by rambling on with too many words. Here it is, in plain English. Learn it well. Own it. Become it.

When the going gets tough:

TALK TO YOURSELF, DON'T LISTEN TO YOURSELF.

Of course this means to be positive and talk to yourself in reassuring ways. Things you know you need to hear. We do that to block out all the automatic negative thoughts that pop into our heads. Don't listen to those automatic negative thoughts—create positive ones instead.

> *"Don't believe everything you think."*
> *-Thomas E. Kida*

TRAINING

> *"We don't rise to the level of our expectations,*
> *we fall to the level of our training."*
> *-Archilochos*

Training is paramount. Nothing prepares us for mogul skiing better than simple hard work and training. Most of the mogul skiing season is actually training days. The more training days you can get on a competition course before the actual competition begins, the better chance you will have to ski the course well during the actual competition. However, many courses actually limit the number of days that you can train on the course before a competition, so be sure to check in advance with the Chief of Course to find out when training officially opens, so that you don't end up wasting a training day that is better spent at your home course. Also, you most likely won't appreciate wasting the extra money associated with spending extra nights in costly ski town lodging, either. With that being said, there are a few important takeaways from training on competition runs day(s) before the actual competition begins.

WHEN TRAINING DOESN'T GO WELL

There are many reasons why training might not go the way you want it to. More often than not, it is because the airs are the wrong size or shape, the transition into or out of the airs are undesirable, and/or snow conditions are poor. The last reason that causes poor training runs is that the course is steeper than the course you usually practice on. Below, I go into depth on how to deal with each type of problem.

AIRS ARE TOO BIG

I usually find that if an athlete does not like one or both of the airs in their line, it is because they are too big. Usually, this is not the actual problem. The actual problem is that the course after the jumps is too steep for their taste, and the jumps are usually the regulation size or smaller. The solution to this type of problem is to realize that the steepness is the actual cause of the problem, and that the solution is to correct for the increased pitch while you are in the air. Landing on the balls of your feet and upright may not be enough to keep you from slamming deep into the back seat immediately after entering the moguls after the landing pad. The trick is to land very much in the front of your boots as possible. By having your center of mass in front of your feet, you will create a physical block that prevents you from throwing your feet out at the first mogul which will inevitably get you into the back seat. Since your center of mass is actually in front of your feet, it is mechanically very difficult to get your feet out ahead of you upon reentry to the moguls. It is a stomach-turning skill to learn, but when done correctly, it is amazing how easy it makes landing out of steep airs (usually only perceived as "easy" in hindsight, because of how nerve-wracking it can be at first).

Many of my students have pointed out that this method makes them feel like they are going to go over the front and tumble down the course. I have to agree that fear makes a lot of sense and compounds the problems many mogul skiers have after coming out of the top air. It is one of those things in mogul skiing that is counter-intuitive, and also one of those things that you have to rewire your reflexes not to act on. You need to actually reprogram the natural reflex of throwing your feet out at the first mogul when it is steep, to having your body feel like it is falling and your legs and feet trailing behind, because mechanically, it works better, maintains your balance better, and allows for you to use proper timing on reentry.

Sometimes, as Murphy's Law will have it, as you land far forward on a steep course, your feet will get bucked up, resulting in a "falling-down-the-course" feeling that should not be feared as unrecoverable, but can be corrected fairly easily. If you find yourself in this predicament, all you need to do is to make sure you keep your upper body square down the fall line by not tucking your shoulder (i.e., giving up), relaxing (which provides the means to create new movement that is not currently taking place), and gradually pull your feet up underneath you, so that you are almost in a tuck position. This allows you to gradually and lightly skim over the tops of several moguls as need be until you are finally in a position where you can once again get stacked, and then start putting your feet down on the moguls, as you gradually mitigate your body position back into the stacked position.

I've done this move many times after coming out of the top air. I have always called it a "getting-shot-out-of-a-cannon" feeling because of how fast it feels, and how much it feels like you are free falling, but it was always a relief for me because I never had to over-think coming out of the top air. It just sort of happened by survival type reflexes. It also had the added bonus of getting me several moguls ahead of my competition if I was dueling, and it was generally where the majority of my speed margin came from. When I use this method, my entry into the line is always cleaner, more dynamic, faster, and it scores better. The only time I ever got into trouble was when I had too much time to think coming out of a steep air. I would try too hard to over-control it, get stiff, get my feet out in front of me, and inevitably end up in the back seat. So try this tried and proven exercise instead.

AIRS ARE THE WRONG SHAPE

If the airs seem like they are the wrong shape to you, this means that they have too much "boot" to them, or not enough "boot." One of these is a timing issue, but both of them are strategy issues. First of all, it is important that you choose your line correctly. Because of the relative volatility in the moguls themselves compared to the jumps in size, shape, and texture, I recommend that you choose the line that has the jumps that you like the best, as opposed to choosing the line that you like the best. This is because, over the course of the competition, the jumps aren't as likely to change as much as the moguls will. The reason for this is because of the large amount of salt that is used on the jumps to help keep their shape, as well as the constant maintenance the jumps receive from jump scrappers during the competition. Each and every mogul, however, as well as the collective mogul "lines" are subject to vary wildly, so it is not wise to bank on them or try to predict the condition they will be in during your run. It is always good to bet on things that are less likely to change and more predictable of how they will be in the future (during your actual competition run). Also, it will pay dividends in the start gate knowing that you chose the line that has the jumps you like the best, because this fact will help you relax, as jumping usually tends to be the source of most athletes worry, stress, and focus. Make it easy on yourself; choose the jumps you like the best. Generally, even if you follow the obstacle rating scale from the previous chapter, airs tend to carry more weight because they show up in the obstacle rating chart more than any other obstacle. Airs have more occurrences in the obstacle rating scale because there are so many parts to an air that can be problematic, including the in-run, transition, jump shape, landing, and exit.

With that said, perhaps that still doesn't alleviate the whole problem, because "all" the jumps have too much "boot" or not enough "boot." As I said before, one of these is a timing issue, and both of them are strategy issues. If a jump has too much "boot" on it, it is a timing issue. The time to hit your pop can be much sooner than you are used to, and you need to be ready for it. As an aid, you need to come into the air a bit slower than usual, but not so slow that it hinders you from easily launching off the top of the jump. This will give you more time to hit that abrupt jump pop timing. I recommend slowing down three moguls before the jump and cutting down your speed by 25% to accomplish this. Jumps that have too little boot are often referred to as "loading docks" because of the flat trajectories and high speeds that they promote when hitting them. These kinds of jumps as well as jumps with too much "boot" require, at the very least, consideration of a strategy change. Jumps with not enough boot are bad for back inverts, and back off-axis tricks. Since these types of tricks tend to make up the majority of most people's "bread and butter" tricks at higher level competitions, they can be somewhat perplexing, because they make backwards style tricks much more dangerous than usual. However, these jumps are great for old-school upright tricks (quad twister, mute-twister-Kosak, etc.) as well as upright spinning tricks such as 360s, 720s, 1080s, and what have you. Additionally, they are really good for forward off-axis tricks like misty flips, rodeos, loops, etc.

Conversely, jumps with too much "boot" may actually make upright spins extremely difficult to pull off, as well as making forward-type off-axis maneuvers nearly impossible. Jumps with a lot of boot on them usually lend themselves best to back inverts, so stick with your straight backs, like back lay, back tuck, or back position, if they are really bad. However, most jumps with a lot of boot (but not too much) can be good for back inverts with rotation(s), such as back full, back double full, back off-axis tricks such as D-Spins, corks and what have you. Interestingly, when jumps have too much boot, even for backflips, they can lend themselves as great front flip kickers because they tend to put so much kick to your feet in the backward direction (back up the hill) that sometimes the best thing to do is go with it. I loved using jumps with a lot of boot on them as front flip kickers, because I found the extra energy I needed in those jumps that I needed to ensure I brought my front flips all the way around to my feet. On regular jumps, I usually struggled with landing front flips in the back seat. They came so much easier to me on jumps that had too much boot.

As always, it is up to you and your coach to help you choose which tricks that you feel most comfortable doing off of which jump, because only you know which jumps you have in your arsenal, and only you will be able to see the jumps that you have to work with. However, do not be a slave to doing the same jump off of the top air and the bottom air every single competition, no matter what. Don't ever limit yourself to just two types of jumps either. Your jumping arsenal should be under constant expansion. The more breadth your jumping arsenal has, the more secrets you will acquire for jumping that can be used to improve even the tricks that you thought you perfected, so never stop learning and never stop improving. Do your best to adjust your jumping strategy according to the above guidelines when the jumps are less than adequate in your eyes.

THE TRANSITIONS INTO THE AIRS ARE UNDESIRABLE

Many times, if the jumps don't get you, the transitions will. Meaning that if the jumps in and of themselves are not all that bad, sometimes the transitions coming into or out of the jump are poor. There are two main reasons for this: either the transitions are too short, or too long. If the former is the problem, then generally, the best course of action is to choose a different line. Transitions are the most important part of the jump. You can try to see if the Chief of Course will allow you or someone else to dig out the transition to your liking, but this is highly unlikely. Sometimes, however, athletes competing on their home course will be able to persuade the Chief of Course into allowing them to reshape the jumps. In World Cup skiing, this will be highly unlikely. Thankfully, most World Cup courses will have jump transitions that are the correct size. However, in mogul skiing, anything can happen.

The first course of action should be to pick a line which has the best transitions—after that, a strategic change of your aerial tricks choices may be wise. See the section above, "Airs Are the Wrong Shape," for guidance in choosing which type of trick to throw on which type of jump. Jumps with too short of a transition fall into the same category as jumps with too much "boot," so keep that in mind if you didn't already know. As you become more familiar with your aerial arsenal, you will instinctively know which trick you will feel most comfortable throwing off which type of jumps. However, more often than not, athletes don't pair their tricks wisely with the type of jump that they are confronted with, and too often try to force it to happen when they shouldn't.

The other problem is when jump transitions are too long. If the jump transitions are too long for you, my first suggestion would be to simply work in at least one extra turn in the transition before the air. There is no rule saying you can only turn on moguls, so turn as many times as you see fit. However, another solution would be to just ski faster. Fast mogul skiers rarely, if ever, think about any transition coming into an air as too long. It's almost like there is no such thing. So keep that in mind and work toward that type of mentality.

On rare occasions, however, some courses will have long jump transitions leading up to jumps with too much boot. This is the most difficult type of jump, and I suggest moving to another line. If changing lines is not an option for you, I would suggest a front flip, or a front-fly away. It may be counter-intuitive, but I feel it is one of very few tricks that will work for you on this type of jump. If you can't throw a front fly-away and don't want to learn it, I suggest you come up with some sort of attack plan that is best suited for you, in case you ever encounter a jump of this nature. If all else fails, just take the jump really slow and throw in a few extra turns coming into it to make sure your speed is in check before hitting it. Ski smart, and don't fight the mountain. The mountain is much bigger than you, and it will win. Ski wisely—you are already participating in one of the most difficult sports known to man, so don't make it any harder on yourself than you absolutely have to. In fact, you should constantly be looking for all the advantages that you can, and use them—no matter how insignificant you may think they are at the time!

THE SNOW CONDITIONS ARE POOR

There are many types of snow conditions that you will rarely, if ever, see—like a course with perfect snow conditions. There are many things that can go wrong with snow conditions, but it is important to realize that it is a part of the sport and as such, snow conditions will be completely out of your control (aside from what you can do during your course slipping). With that being said, a mogul course is more often than not a hodgepodge of different snow conditions, all occurring simultaneously—and not only that, the course conditions are constantly in flux (changing) due to weather, exposure to sun, time of day, temperature, wind, etc. It is a big part of what makes mogul skiing so challenging and rewarding. Few other sports have such interminably metamorphosing obstacles as mogul skiing. Yet for argument's sake, let's at least discuss the different types of snow conditions that are less than perfect. Namely, these problems are punchy snow, grabby snow, wet snow, icy snow, death cookies, and bare spots. Generally speaking, any type of snow that is tricky to set an edge on is considered poor snow conditions.

"Punchy snow," also known as "crusty snow," is typically a snow condition that refers to snow that has been hard-packed by high winds and cold temperatures from the night before, usually following a fresh snowfall. It can also be formed at times when the top layer of a fresh snow layer begins to melt, and then freezes again, creating a low density, "crusty" firm layer of snow on top of an otherwise soft, pliable layer of snow underneath. Crusty snow can be difficult to navigate anywhere on the mountain because of its layered nature. In mogul skiing, we are generally only going to see "punchy snow" like conditions in two places: in the landings and on the tops of the moguls. Thankfully, the landings are usually chopped, and punchy conditions in the landing pads are rare, but they do exist. This is because the soft bottom layer is usually trampled by the feet of the choppers, and the low-density crusty top layer is chopped up and left on top, creating a very deep, low density, somewhat solid landing pad. The danger of this is that when you land on the punchy snow, your feet punch through it much deeper than usual due to its low density, and a lot of snow surrounds your legs, sometimes all the way up to the knee. A mogul skier usually has a great deal of forward momentum when coming in for a landing, and he will want to keep moving forward while the punchy snow has nearly immobilized his feet, creating an often inescapable forward tumble. If you fear that your landing pads may be punchy, the best advice is to aim for a high spot or land where other people have already been landing. These are the least likely spots to contain punchy snow.

Punchy snow can also be a problem on the tops of moguls. This usually only happens on an active mogul course because the tops are the least skied part of the moguls. The danger with punchy snow on the tops of the moguls is that the it may grab your pole basket in the same way that it can grab your feet during a landing. It will penetrate deeper than expected into the top of the mogul, and it is difficult to pull out. This usually results in knocking the mogul skier off balance by turning his shoulders across the hill by force. It is best to avoid this problem, and keep your pole plants close to your feet, where the snow is firmer and more consistent.

"Grabby snow" is snow that has a higher coefficient of friction than normal. Most grabby snow comes from snowmaking machines, known as snow guns. Grabby snow can be difficult in much the same way as punchy snow, but the danger with grabby snow is that it is usually not as localized a problem as punchy snow is. It can be found anywhere, but especially on courses that have man-made snowmakers on them. There is a wide range where you can find grabby snow, from localized pockets all the way up to the entire course. Occasionally small, densely packed veins of grabby snow will get mixed into the natural snow, creating differences in texture in the snow, varying its consistency. These buried little "grabby veins" are known as "snow snakes," and they have been known to take down even the best skiers because of their unpredictable nature. The best course of action with grabby snow is to focus on being relaxed. Grabby snow will constantly be grabbing at you from this way and that. When it does, you need to correct your body position, and you can only do that if you are relaxed. The more tense you are, and the more you fight against and resist the grabby snow, the more it will harm your skiing.

"Wet snow" is a type of snow that retains more water than regular snow. Wet snow can actually be good for a course at times and is preferable to a lot of the undesirable snow conditions in this section, but it can still be challenging in its own right. This is because there is any number of different types of wet snow, varying from "heavy snow," to "damp snow," to "really heavy snow," all the way to "slop," which is little more than slushy water, or anywhere in between. They all vary in consistency and coefficients of friction. The main takeaway is that it is "heavy." Wet snow is heavier than regular snow, therefore it will slow you down more. You need to battle wet snow conditions by increasing your speed in the moguls. The moguls will try to steal speed from you, so you must generate more. Wet snow conditions can actually be a godsend to mogul skiers that like to ski on the Glass Plate, because it makes controlling one's speed easier. Be careful though, because wet snow is usually accompanied by its close friend, "icy snow."

"Icy snow" is the bane of most mogul skiers existence. It is the hardest type of snow condition to ski, and it is also the most common—often formed by the very way moguls are shaped. At best, icy spots are just right before the bottom of the rut, dragging your feet down into the rut and away from your center of mass. At worst, the entire course is bulletproof. If you are a competitive skier and you can spare it, you should consider not skiing that icy course. Pick your battles and save your body. If, for whatever reason, you decide you need to ski an icy course, the most important thing to do is to be patient and let the moguls come to you. Often times on bulletproof courses, I will set my edge before the rut or after it, whichever is more appropriate, because the rut will want to throw my skis in the wrong direction and it will be very hard to control. Also, before and after, the ruts are less steep than entering the rut itself, and are much less likely to trap your skis as you try to prepare for your next turn. Be very light on your feet, stay extremely relaxed, and be ever patient. Also, I highly suggest buying some skis with serrated edges, because they hold an edge on ice the best.

"Death cookies" are chunks of ice that have been kicked up or chopped up from an icy course, usually from the landing hill of the jumps and roll down the course, and they tend to come to rest at inconvenient locations like the bottom of a rut. "Death cookies" are dangerous because they can easily knock you off balance, or you can get your ski(s) stuck under them. They also hurt to fall on. It is best to avoid death cookies. Slip them off the course, or stomp on them during course inspection to break them up as much as possible. Death cookies are great for filling in ruts, so use them where you can. For the death cookies that escape course slip, just ski around them or simply avoid them by taking evasive actions. Usually, judges won't dock you very hard if you dodge them in a subtle way. It is best to plan a strategy for the possibility of death cookies in advance. However, usually just pulling up one's skis for a second is enough to coast over them, or just carefully choose where you place your feet to avoid all of them. Don't hit death cookies head on. Bad things happen. That's why they're called "death cookies!"

"Bare spots" are spots in a mogul course where there is no snow cover. Bare spots consist of natural grass, dirt, rocks, and sometimes roots. Bare spots are surprisingly common in mogul skiing, even at the World Cup level, due to the nature of skiing up moguls which actually "digs" the snow constantly from one location, and "places" it in another. It is good course etiquette to try to cover up bare spots as best as possible, but the chances of it re-emerging before your run are substantial. Therefore, it is best to know how to deal with them. You only need to do two things: First, look at the bare spot closely and remove any objects that might actually dig into the bottom of your ski. Sharp rocks can have immense "grabbing" potential as they can carve huge chunks out of the bottom of your ski. In many ways, rocks and other sharp objects are the ultimate "grabby snow" or "snow snake" condition, so you want to get rid of them if you can. Other than that, the only thing you need to do is to treat the bare spot like any other patch of ice. Realize that ultimately it is just frozen ground, and its consistency will be closest to that of ice. I have personally tested many different ways to ski over bare spots, looking for the best way. Treating them like average icy spots at the bottom of the mogul is the best. Remember this is done by being patient, and light on our feet. Therefore, it is best not to give them special treatment. However, you may want to wear you rock skis if you are worried about ruining your competition skis.

THE HILL IS TOO STEEP

This is a more common problem than probably anyone would like to acknowledge, but alas, it exists, so I will cover it here. In the United States, it is usually more of a problem for East Coast and Central Region skiers than Western Region skiers, because Western mountain mogul courses are generally steeper than Eastern ones. The best solution I can offer any athlete looking to improve her steep skiing skills, however, is to train on the steepest hill that you can find. If that involves moving to a different mountain or city, I highly recommend it. I know my skiing improved greatly when I moved to Killington from Holiday Valley, and to Steamboat from Killington, because of the increased steepness of not just the mogul courses, but because of the average steepness of the mountains themselves. Both were very beneficial aspects that helped my skiing technique immensely.

> *"Excellence is an art won by training and habituation:*
> *We do not act rightly because we have virtue or excellence,*
> *but we rather have these because we have acted rightly;*
> *These virtues are formed in man by his doing the actions;*
> *We are what we repeatedly do.*
> *Excellence, then, is not an act but a habit."*
> *-Will Durant, "The Story of Philosophy"*

> *"What we do on some great occasion will depend on what we are;*
> *and what we are will be the result of previous years of self-discipline."*
> *-H.P. Liddon*

SINGLES

*"And now that you don't have to be perfect,
you can be good."*
-John Steinbeck

Mikael Kingsbury, Deer Valley, UT

You never want to do a competition run that is more advanced than you have done in training. True, it might work out on some occasions, but in mogul skiing, it is too dangerous. Consciously setting out and competing at a higher level than you did in training is a gamble at best, and foolish by most standards. Competition itself might force out of you some faster speeds or some bigger airs than you planned on in the start gate—that is natural, and it is okay. But to intentionally set out to ski faster, jump bigger, or throw a more difficult trick than you ever have on that course, then you are just asking for trouble. Better to plan early on in the week what your strategy will be. Take a look at who is scheduled to appear at the event and try your best to pick the most suitable tricks for that particular competition. If you feel there is a chance that you might need to "pull out the big guns," then make sure that you at least practice that trick on the competition course. Think of it like bringing your best player to a football game—he might be stubborn, cocky, difficult to control, and doesn't like to listen. But he is the best player you got. When the game is on the line, he may be your best shot to win the game. But you have to dress him to have him on the sidelines; otherwise, he can't play. Practicing your "next level" airs is just like that: if you practice them during your training days on the course, then you can consider it "dressed." If it's not "dressed," don't use it. Mogul skiing is already a risky business, and there is no need to tempt fate. Compete just like you do in practice. This means do whatever you usually do in practice, wear whatever you usually wear in practice, anything; do all that the same way in the competition.

During the competition days, even in training before the game, the judges will be watching you. Always remember to keep a smile on your face, be courteous to others, and treat everyone with respect. It is best to start acting like a champion long before you ever win anything because your ascension to greatness will be quicker, your duration of greatness will be longer, and your fall from grace will be softer. So always remember, and be doubly sure to remember on competition day when you are being watched closely, that if you want to be a winner at the end of the competition, it's best to start acting like one at the beginning of it.

"If everything seems under control,
you're not going fast enough."
-Mario Andretti

DUALS

"You must be fast,
'cause you were hauling ass when I passed you!"
-"No Fear" T-shirt

To win at duals, you want to beat the other person to the top air, and cross the finish line first. Mogul skiing is a subjective sport, yet there are objective aspects to it. Objective aspects of mogul skiing are things that are black and white. The two most noticeable objective categories in mogul skiing are amplitude and speed. If you are higher in the air than the person next to you, that is a fact, not an opinion. That is what makes it objective. Likewise, if you have a faster time than the other person, that is a

Dmitry Kolesnikov and Andrey Uglovski compete in dual moguls

fact no one can argue with. Objective aspects are non-disputable, they just are what they are. Subjective aspects of mogul skiing require a trained eye to differentiate which athlete performed them better, hence the judgment aspects of the sport. Subjective aspects of mogul skiing are like points given for trick performance or turn scores. Subjectivity is nothing more than an opinion, so you want to win as many of the objective categories as possible. That way no one can argue, and you have more influence over winning more of the subjective points if you already won the objective categories.

Dualing brings the objective aspects of the sport to the forefront, more so than singles events. It's terribly hard to convince enough judges that you won a dual against someone who beat you to the bottom of the course, and had bigger airs than you did, when you skied side-by-side. In duals, win the objective categories first, then make your bid on the subjective categories. If you do those two things, you will be a great dualer. There is a strong natural tendency to want the person that crosses the finish line first to win, so there is a great advantage in getting to the finish line first. If you do, your opponent will have to have skied one heck of an argument to get judged the winner. Do bigger airs too. They don't need to be very high DD (degree of difficulty) tricks, just big. Meaning very high up in the air, and covering a lot of ground. People love to see huge simple tricks, compared to low and complicated ones. Especially on duals day. Therefore, winning duals is simple: Jump bigger and ski faster than everyone else (just make sure you stay in control). If you do, losing will be a rare trinket to you.

> *"Never write a check with your mouth,*
> *that you can't cash with your ass."*
> *-Scott Glenn in the movie "Sucker Punch"*

CONSISTENCY

> *"The hallmark of excellence,*
> *the test of greatness, is consistency."*
> *-Jim Tressel*

Consistency is probably the most elusive and coveted virtue a mogul skier can have. This is because mogul skiing is at its very essence a dance with obstacles—ever-changing obstacles at that. Consistency is largely a product of training, but the true secret to consistency has little to do with your skill level. It has everything to do with what you don't think about. I remember the day I realized the effectiveness of this strategy during a mogul competition in Telluride, CO, where I was coaching. I was the starting gate coach for all my athletes. During that event, all 12 athletes had the run of their lives after an in-the-gate conversation with me. It wasn't what I said to them, but it was what I took away from them that proved to be the elixir. Consistency is as elusive as love; it laughs at locksmiths. You must not overthink consistency. It can only be cajoled by the simplicity of your actions.

That is why the primary focus of the New Mogul Method is simplicity. If you think too much of too many things, you can't be focused on what you need to be focused on, and that is what makes you inconsistent. So in the start gate, with my athletes, I simply boiled down the entire run into as simple a means of my Mogul Method as possible, customized to that particular run. It was like a short little story, all about how the run would play out. The story reminded them that fear was a good thing. It comforted them when I told them exactly where they would need to get stacked, when they would need to be patient, and reminded them of the power that relaxation had when the moguls fought dirty. It isn't important to try to quell someone's fears. It is far more powerful to qualify it, put it into proper perspective, and use it to your advantage. Therefore, I didn't take away their fears, per se. I simply put them into the proper perspective. All my athletes already knew how to ski moguls, that wasn't the true test of their skill. It was the unknown they feared. What happens when... who knows? That is a mind trap of fear. It will lead you down a path of overthinking and over-preparation. Simplify, reduce your thoughts to all but what you absolutely must have to get to the bottom. In other words, do not add a multitude of exit strategies or "Plan B's" to your mind. That will make you inconsistent. Reduce, eliminate, and only focus on the bare minimum of what you need to do. You don't have to take my word for it, though:

> *"One does not accumulate, but eliminate.*
> *It is not daily increase, but daily decrease.*
> *The height of cultivation always runs on simplicity."*
> *-Bruce Lee*

What Bruce Lee is stating here is closely related to not only this section on Consistency, but also my section on Relaxation in Chapter 11, as well as Step Three to the New Mogul Method: Relax. It forces us not to react, but to allow. We do not DO a strategic maneuver—that would take too much time. We allow, then recover. The master martial artist knew all of the secrets of relaxing, and had so much speed because he removed all the clutter in his form of martial arts. What I have put together in the New Mogul Method attempts to parallel this same principle.

> *"It is vain to do with more*
> *What can be done with less."*
> *-William of Occam, Originator of "Occam's Razor"*

CHAPTER 9
VISUAL1ZATION

"People are never able to outperform their self-image."
-John C. Maxwell

One of the things that I learned from my conversation with Olympic medalist Bryon Wilson about visualization is that he actually visualizes waiting at the top of the course in every visualization that he does. Most mogul skiers forget this crucial step in their visualization of their runs. Planning out and visualizing your lead time before sliding into the gate can be a great way to alleviate yourself from those pesky last-minute jitters, especially when there are multiple course holds. Visualizing waiting at the top of the course and visualizing unexpected course holds should be a part of every mogul skier's visualization exercises, to help account for the unexpected. When doing team visualization exercises, it is beneficial to get your coach to interject random course holds as you are in the hole, on deck, and in the gate.

The process of visualization at the top of the course varies from team to team, coach to coach, and athlete to athlete. But in my 20+ years in the sport, the best method for visualization that I have come across for my athletes is as follows.

VISUALIZATION PROCESS OF AN ENTIRE MOGUL RUN

Close your eyes and imagine you are in the starting gate. Visualize a different length and number of course holds before your run. Then, as you actually take the course, imagine how your body should feel as you take the first mogul, what the perfect body position will be for that mogul. This is important, because it can set the standard for the rest of your run. If you hit it abruptly and it surprises you with how hard it hits you, it can make you tense, nervous and stiff. Whereas if you hit it tall and relaxed and with good form, you can coast right over it, setting a good first example.

Then, visualize yourself skiing fast into the top air and then picture yourself slowing down and controlling your speed three moguls before the top air. See yourself taking the transition to the jump with skis pointed straight and not snow plowing or turning on the jump.

Next, pretend that you are resisting the increased G-forces as you hit the jump with good hip position, and then lift off the jump with your arms and chest. Conceptualize how it will feel as you hit the weightless apex of your jump, and imagine as much information in your actual trick as you can. Think about where you will spot with your eyes, and when and where you will look for your landing. Then think about how you will land in a "four-point landing" with your feet together and both of your poles plants on either side of your skis.

See yourself taking the first turn out of the top air. Generally speaking, you don't want it to be right on the first mogul because it will be too big to take head-on. It is preferable to take the first mogul out of the top air in a mitigated manner, such as throwing a check turn in before you get to it. Or if you jump too far down the landing pad off the top air, make a check turn before you get to the mogul, visualize your landing a little further to the downhill side of the mogul, and take just the smallest part of the big mogul as your check turn on the very end of it, using the next few moguls afterwards to regain your control.

Upon landing and skiing out of the top air, the New Mogul Method Steps begin anew. The first step, "Scare Yourself," should happen naturally coming out of the top air if you jumped big enough, but you have to be committed to skiing your line. Right away, you want to get into a good stacked position (i.e., Step 2). Picture yourself in a good stacked position with your hips in the "Mogul Skier Hips Up" position. This is most important coming out of the top air because these moguls are usually the biggest on the entire course, and this position gives us an additional six inches of range of motion when we need it most.

Immediately after getting into a good stacked position, it is important to note that unless you have a major bobble, you will only have one chance to get into a good stacked position in the middle section. As you come out of the top air, the rest of the middle section's turns will be a derivative of how good that initial stacked position was, so it is extra important to envision a perfect stacked position as you come out of the top air. Then bring to mind the impacts of the big moguls right after the top air. Predict how you will relax your body and let the excess energy travel up, through and out of your body, while retaining only what you need to make the next turn happen.

Then perform Step 4: Be Patient. The first four steps should occur within the first three moguls out of the top air. As effective as they are, you must constantly repeat steps 3 & 4 in your head for the remainder of the middle of the course, all the way down till you get to the bottom air. We do this because, in mogul skiing, the unexpected must be expected. And these two parts of the New Mogul Method are both preventative and a cure for most of the mistakes we make on the course. Therefore, it is a good mantra to repeat to yourself: "Relax, be patient, relax, be patient, relax, be patient..." as you ski the entire middle section. By doing so, you should naturally be able to handle any bucks, bobbles, snow snakes, crossed skis, etc., as smoothly as possible. It should also prevent most of them from happening in the first place. Not to mention, it will improve your turn scores.

See yourself coming into the bottom air too fast, as likely will be the case, so it is important to prepare for it ahead of time. Disperse your speed over six moguls before the bottom air by widening your turn, using the flexion of the ski to absorb as much energy as possible, and hitting the mogul with more of your foot if possible. In short, you must create a plan of how you will slow yourself down as you come into the bottom air, and program that into your visualization routine.

Again, imagine yourself taking the transition to the bottom jump with skis pointed straight and not snow plowing or turning on the jump. Picture yourself resisting the increase of G-forces as you hit the jump with good hip position, and then lift off the jump with your arms and chest (again). Same as the top air, think about how it will feel as you hit the weightless apex of your jump and feel and see in your mind's eye as much information in your actual trick as you can. View yourself doing your trick, including to remember where you will spot with your eyes, and when and where you will look for your landing. Then think about how you will land in a "four-point landing" with your feet together.

As you land, the first four steps of the New Mogul Method should be repeated again. If you jumped big enough, you should be scared (at least enough so that your mind doesn't wander and lose focus), so imagine this in your visualization as well. Then once again repeat Step 2 for the last time by getting stacked all over again. Pretend to feel what it will be like to get the hips in the "Mogul Skier Hips Up" position. Then remember to relax and be patient through the bottom of the course. Remember to visualize yourself using the knee pocked to assist you in rolling your knees from side to side, so that you don't get deducted for straight running.

Then finally, picture yourself smiling as you cross the finish line because that will embed a good experience into your mind about the course, as well as remind you that you need to do it at the bottom of the course during the actual event.

VISUALIZATION CULMINATION

The entire process of visualizing an entire mogul run (above) should be done in its entirety without any visualized mistakes from start to finish, a minimum of three full times before your run. As you slide into the gate just before your run, close your eyes and visualize just the in-run, take off, trick, spot, and landing of both the top air and the bottom air. Then call to mind the image of you crossing the finish line with a big smile on your face and being genuinely happy. You will know that you have timed your visualization routine properly if you open your eyes (with a smile on your face) just as the starting official says, "Judges ready, racer ready..."

"As a man thinketh in his heart, so is he"
-James Allen

"Follow effective action with quiet reflection.
From the quiet reflection will come even more effective action."
-Peter F. Drucker

CHAPTER 10
PRACTICING GOOD MOGUL SKIING POSTURE

"The only way you can stay on top is to remember to touch bottom and get back to basics."
-Shane Black

THE PROGRESSION
A LESSON IN GOOD MOGUL SKIING FORM, FROM THE GROUND UP

In this lesson, we will begin the discussion of good lower body mechanics by a method I teach to all of my athletes, called "The Progression." This method introduces one drill after another in a specific sequence that is designed to stack together good lower body mechanics applicable to mogul skiing. These drills fit together like the pieces of a puzzle which are used to create a bigger picture. These conglomerated drills are flat drills, meaning they are intended to be practiced only on the flats. It is an intermediate step to improve your mechanics while skiing the flats so that you have an easier time applying the lessons in Chapter 5. Therefore, these drills are simple enough to do, and even moderate skill level skiers can practice them on the flats. The progression starts with a lead change because only after we lead change can we initiate and feel what a "knee pocket" is. So let's have a look at what all is in The Progression, and then I will go into more detail on how to practice each step later in the chapter. The Progression should be used as a tool to prepare your good mogul skiing posture at least once a week.

THE PROGRESSION

1. **LEAD CHANGE** - Puts your legs into the right position for the **knee pocket**.

2. **THE KNEE POCKET** - Puts your legs into the right position to have your legs remain tight together while skiing the moguls. Practice this while doing **short swing turns.**

3. **SHORT SWING TURNS** - The best way to practice keeping your feet tight together without discomfort, and still being able to carve your turns.

4. **THE JAVELIN DRILL** - This is a good flat training drill to feel and practice, and really accentuate the deep knee pocket position. Provides a lead way for a similar but much more advanced **Short Swing Javelin Drill.**

5. **SHORT SWING JAVELIN** - This is the best drill for practicing good mogul form and mechanics while skiing the flats. Great training for improving one's **knee angle**. Knee angle is important in the moguls, since it has a positive effect on turn scores.

   - **Knee Angle (in the moguls)** - Once you have good knee angulation on the flats, try it out in the moguls. If you find yourself getting off balance, this means your timing is off or you are washing out your tails. Start training your uphill hip drive to initiate sooner.

6. **THE Z-DRILL** - This is the best drill for strengthening and improving your uphill hip drive.

7. **UP HILL HIP DRIVE (IN THE MOGULS)** - Counteracts the "over-finishing" of the turn that a good **knee angle** can sometimes cause in the moguls.

LEAD CHANGE

When we are making a turn in a good upright position, our uphill ski and knee will naturally lead the downhill ski and knee by a little bit. A lead change is nothing more and nothing less than the changing of which ski/knee is in front. It happens at the inflection point between your turns as you link them. Chuck Martin's Mogul Logic website defines lead change as:

"When the body is stacked properly over the downhill foot, the uphill knee naturally advances forward. The leading knee changes as the weight shifts onto the new downhill ski."

The lead change initiates a new turn, but the hidden secret is its capacity for creating the knee pocket. The knee pocket's benefits are numerous. It is not only the best way for keeping one's feet together, without discomfort, but enables us to augment our knee angle, range of motion, and carve lightning quick short radius turns.

KEY #1: **"Lead Change"** *naturally gives birth to* **"The Knee Pocket"**

THE KNEE POCKET

The knee pocket is a very important concept to understand for any mogul skier. Have you ever seen those guys that throw out as many short radii turns as they can, and every one of them looks horrible and washed out as they are flailing about trying to throw their feet from one side to the other? Then too, perhaps, you have been lucky enough to catch a glimpse of a mogul skier who carves out the cleanest, shortest radius turns that you have ever seen, while their upper body remains perfectly still. So what's the difference? The knee pocket. The knee pocket is one of the most fundamental mechanics in mogul skiing. On the flats, we start our turns from the sweet spot of the ski. When we do this, the ski flexes and stores potential energy in the ski, just as pulling back on a bow string stores energy in the bow. Pressing into the knee pocket is what transfers this potential energy into kinetic energy directed across the body. It also prevents the over-finishing of a turn. Over-finishing a turn is the same thing as "washing out one's tails," and that is considered bad skiing. Since the knee angle created by pressing into one's knee pocket allows the ski to unload its coiled tension like a spring (in the direction of our knee angle), it affords us an easy transfer of the feet via this energy to the other side of the body for the next turn. Due to the fact that we transform the potential energy in the coiled ski into kinetic energy used to snap our feet from one side of the body to the other, it happens much faster and more effortlessly than we could ever do manually. In other words, we are using the knee pocket like a tool to transfer and transform potential energy into kinetic energy, just like a hunter does while using a bow and arrow.

PRACTICING GOOD MOGUL SKIING

While your skis pass from one side of the turn to the other, all you need to do is quickly switch your knee pocket from one side to the other. (This is the inflection point of the turn, at which the lead change occurs that I talked about above.) When you do this, "magically" your skis will be in another perfect lead change position, ready for another knee pocket, and ready to carve the next turn. Since all of the forces of the knee pocket are small and symmetrical, this allows us the ability to string together many tiny turns with little or no upper body movement. Okay, so now that we know what it does, HOW exactly do we do this, and WHAT even is this "knee pocket"?

Try this:

Find a nice straight flat bench or chair with a straight back to sit in that is not too high or too low to the ground for you to sustain good posture. (This works best in an office type swivel chair.) Place both your feet directly in front of you, knees bent at 90 degrees (your heels should be almost underneath your chair) and your feet placed hip distance apart.

Now, pick up your left foot and place the heel on your right foot, just where the toes meet the foot. Good. Now flex your left shin muscles and lift up your toes on your left foot as much as you can, without picking your left heel up off of your right toes. It should look like this (Right).

> Good! You are half way there! Now, take your right knee and without moving the placement of either of your feet, tip it towards your left knee until it connects with your left leg, and squeeze your thighs firmly together, like this (Right).

> Now, without moving the position of your knees and leaving your thighs pressed firmly together, take your left heel off of your right foot and place it next to your right foot with your left heel fitted tightly into the instep of your right foot, and place all your toes flat on the ground. It should look like this (Right).

Knee pocket

Now, squeeze both your legs tightly together. Feel how your legs just sort of mesh perfectly together? Notice how the heel of your left foot fits nicely into the instep of your right foot? Notice how the location of your calf muscle of your left leg is unobstructed and not "squished" because there is space for it in front of your right shin? Good, now take care to feel how your right knee fits perfectly just behind your left knee. Can you feel how there is no bone-on-bone contact going on in this position, and you can squeeze your legs together as tightly as you want without any pain whatsoever? This is what is known as the **knee pocket.**

PRACTICING GOOD MOGUL SKIING

It is called the knee pocket because it feels like your one knee has a nice comfortable "pocket" for your other knee that allows your legs to work together in unison. It is a strong position to be in, not only for keeping your legs together, but also the perfect position for carving a short radius turn. Which, in case you didn't know, is pretty much all we do in mogul skiing. Similarly, it is also the perfect position for accentuating your "knee angulation" in the moguls, which is good for turn scores. Now you know what a knee pocket is and how to do it.

Now, let us discover its benefits on the snow:

Why we need the knee pocket

While standing perpendicular to the fall-line, place your boots directly side by side, and then quickly touch your knees together. Ouch! Right?

Yeah, bone-on-bone action is bad, because it can cause a lot of discomfort. Can you see why we might want to avoid this in the moguls? Notice the uncomfortable feeling of the ball of the knee against the other?

Now, from the same position, shift your uphill ski half a boot length in front of your downhill ski, squeeze your legs tightly together, and then tip both knees in unison towards the uphill direction, while keeping your upper body and hips square.

Feel how well your legs fit together once the knee is in its pocket, even with ski boots on? It should feel much better than putting the balls of their knees together. That's the feeling of the knee pocket on the ski hill. Congratulations! That's another benefit to using the knee pocket. Not only is it mechanically the best position for your knees to be in while in the moguls, it's simply more comfortable.

Finding the knee pocket

It's important to point out that as a mogul skier passes through the moguls, his knees should only be "together," meaning "side-by-side" as they pass each other from one knee pocket to the other as he makes his turns. Furthermore, a mogul skier who puts his knees "together" but does not place them in the pocket will inevitably be drawn into the back seat purely by the uncomfortableness of the bone-on-bone pain. This is because the back seat—as bad as a body position as you can get while mogul skiing—does offer some relief to the pain of knee-on-knee action (since the weight is transferred through the tails of the skis and thereby reduces the collision intensity of the knee-on-knee action). An indicator of this would be when a skier enters each mogul turn at the top of the rut while sliding their tails out and ultimately over-finish their turns, which places them firmly in the back seat. Additionally, they are unable to drive their uphill hip effectively from this position.

MORE SPECIFICS:

- The knee pocket is felt by pressing one's legs together while holding the thighs tightly together, then tucking one knee in behind the other, in the cavity ("pocket") created between the bottom of the hamstring and the top of the calf of the uphill leg. That is the knee pocket. (See Figure: Finding the knee pocket.)

- The right knee gets tucked behind the left knee on a right-hand mogul. Likewise, the left knee gets tucked while turning on a left-hand mogul. Therefore, on a right hand mogul, the left leg is the uphill leg, and also the inside leg. On a left-hand mogul, the right leg is the uphill leg, and also the inside leg. Incidentally on a right-hand mogul, since your left leg is the inside leg, it is also called the uphill leg. Therefore, your left hip is the uphill hip on right-hand mogul. And your right hip is your uphill hip on a left-hand mogul. This is an important concept repeatedly used throughout this entire book.

- Once the knee pocket is tucked, it initiates knee angle. Knee angle is what allows us to place our skis on edge without doing so with our hips. (See Figure: Finding the knee pocket.) When we do this, the carve of the turn happens automatically when one is carrying the proper amount of momentum. Placing the skis on edge with the hips may be acceptable on the flats, in 2D skiing, but in the world of 3D mogul skiing, it is considered poor form.

KEY #2: *"The Knee Pocket" is practiced in the "The Short Swing Turn"*

THE SHORT SWING TURN

The first downhill drill in "The Progression" is the **Short Swing Turn**. The short swing turn is a staple of mogul skiers when they ski on the flats. It is the most simple method of skiing in which one can practice good mogul skiing form. The knee pocket naturally gives birth to the Short Swing Turn, because it puts our knees in such a position that all we have to do is rock them from one knee pocket to the other, and much of the rest of the short swing turn happens automatically if we are in a good stacked position.

To do good short swing turns, you want to first make sure you are in a good stacked position. This means having your shoulders and hips aligned over your downhill ski, while your hips are in a **Mogul Skiers Hips Up** position. Standing nice and tall with your knees slightly bent (to provide a range of motion and create space for the knee pocket) while at the same time having your hands out in front reaching for your next pole pant. It is also important to keep your chin and eyes up and looking down the hill, rather than down at your feet.

Good short swing turns happen when you initiate each turn with the sweet spot of the ski. This enables the ski to flex and absorb some potential energy in the process. One can then use that energy by redirecting it to help carry the skis and feet from one side of the body to the other side with minimal effort. It is important to initiate each new turn before the current turn is "over-finished." This happens when we "wash out" the tails of our skis. "Washing out" simply means that we have broken the carving edge of the ski, and the potential energy loaded into the ski has been dissipated without using it to our advantage. To prevent that from happening, we initiate an uphill hip drive before we get to the point where we risk "washing out" our skis. When we do this, we open up an avenue for the efficient transfer of our lower body to pendulate from one side of our body to the other. It also allows us to actually utilize the stored energy in the ski for this process. This is because the uphill hip drive forces the next turn to happen before the stored energy in the flexed ski is lost when the ski straightens out in the "washing out" process.

Washing out our turns is a bad sign because it indicates that we are pushing our feet at our turns, rather than pulling them back underneath us like we are supposed to. Pushing our feet at our turns is one of the biggest contributors to getting us into the back seat, not only on the flats but in the moguls. In the moguls, we combat the instinct to push our feet with Step 4: Be Patient, where we wait for the mogul to come to us before we try to turn on it. On the flats, however, we don't have the luxury of simply waiting for the next mogul to come to us. Hence, it is a much more manual process. To combat the instinct to push the feet at our turns while doing short swing turns on the flats, we use the method of **pulling the feet back underneath us**. When we pull the feet back underneath us, we are doing it when the ski is still flexed, and we are thereby allowing our hips a chance to catch up with our feet, thereby making the stored potential energy in our ski be released from the side of our body, which is what allows the efficient transfer of the feet to the other side of the body, directly underneath the hips. It also helps our feet remain directly underneath our hips, in a good stacked position as we initiate our lead change.

The short swing turn is one of the most similar forms of skiing to mogul skiing that one can do while on the flats. It is best to practice all your good habits on the flats so that you can use them in the moguls. Practice good stacked body position, square shoulders, quiet hands, mogul skiers hips up, eyes up, and a quiet upper body. Also, keep your legs together, utilizing the knee pocket, initiating the uphill hip drive, angling the knees, and learning how to harvest the potential energy from the flexed ski. All of these skills that we can practice in short swing turns are roughly equivalent to how we use them in the moguls. The only exception is how we have to manually pull our feet underneath us while doing short swing turns; this step is often replaced in the New Mogul Method with Step 4: Be Patient, only when actually skiing the moguls. But it can be a useful tool when our feet start to run away from us and we want to reel them back in.

For more information on how to harvest stored potential energy from your flexed ski while you are turning, please see below:

- ENERGY FROM NOTHING - A properly carved turn carries with it a packet of potential energy stored in the ski as it flexes into the turn. Here, at the pinnacle of the turn, the ski is acting like a coiled spring. A well-trained and efficient mogul skier can use that pent-up energy to his advantage. His goal is to release that energy to help transfer his weight to the other ski on his next turn. This happens during the lead change. He will release the energy before it is too late (before he washes out his tails) to augment the efficiency of his lead change and transition to the next turn. In other words, he will use it to help him initiate the next turn quicker and easier. Therefore, any work that can be done by redirected forces, harvested from outside one's body (such as coiled ski tension), reduces the forces that he will need to generate from within his body, thereby making him more efficient.

- "FORCING IT" FORCES BAD TURN SCORES - Furthermore, any forces generated from within the body needs an equal and opposite reaction, making them hard to hide. This reduces the smoothness of one's turns and, therefore, reduces turn scores as well. So it is best to limit forces generated from within the body to a minimum. In other words, to keep a stoic upper body, one must constantly use the forces created between the interaction of one's momentum with the mogul course to her advantage. We need to harvest, store, redirect, deflect, and absorb that energy in the most efficient and beneficial way possible. Redirecting those external forces properly is what allows a mogul skier to move his feet faster than he can on dry land, while maintaining a relatively stationary upper body. It is simply a very specialized, very intense form of jiu-jitsu. A good mogul skier is a magician of harvesting external forces to his advantage. The more efficient he is at this, the smoother and more effortless his mogul skiing will be, and the higher his turn scores also.

- GET OUT OF YOUR OWN WAY (LET THE ENERGY FLOW) —Now, combine the "Energy from Nothing" energy packet as described previously with an uphill hip drive. This should happen directly after the tension in the downhill ski is released. This is because it initiates symmetrical energy transfer to the other side of the turn by giving our lower body an axis that is square to the fall line on which to swing it underneath our body (from the energy of the downhill ski uncoiling, which was redirected by the knee pocket/knee angle). At the peak of the energy transfer, when the energy is directly underneath you, you should feel a weightless "hollow position" between the turns. Because in fact, you ARE weightless if you did the energy transfer correctly. In fact, you are "energy positive" at this point in the turn, meaning you have more energy in your body being directed by your will than you created yourself. Therefore, you can, with little to no energy on your part, place your feet directly into the knee pocket on the other turn after your lead change. An efficiently executed lead change can land the feet and knees in the proper knee pocket position on the other turn.

KEY #3: *"The Short Swing Turn" progresses to "The Javelin Drill"*

THE JAVELIN DRILL

The next drill in "The Progression" is the **Javelin**. The javelin drill is a turning drill in which the uphill foot is placed on top of the downhill foot, and therefore, the top ski is pointed down the fall line. This is a large radius turn drill. Therefore, when you are doing this drill, you will be taking up most of the width of the hill. Not only that, but you will be moving rather slowly, so be sure to be aware of your surroundings, especially of uphill skiers that you might be cutting off. It is a good idea to have your teammates or other coaches look out for you while doing this drill. With that being said, you want to start this drill by being able to locate and feel your "deep knee pocket." To do this, stand on one foot pointed across the hill so that you don't start moving downhill. Then, square your shoulders and hips to the fall line, while lifting one ski up and over the one that is perpendicular to the fall line, and point it as close to down the fall line as possible (see picture at right).

In this position, your skis should be in the shape of a large "X" since they will be perpendicular to each other. Be sure to bend your knees a little when doing this. As you place your uphill ski up, over, and perpendicular to your downhill ski (which is pointed across the hill), you will notice a similar feeling to the knee pocket. There will be no bone-on-bone action, and it will be a comfortable position similar to the knee pocket—except due to the semi-perpendicular nature of your skis in this stance, your knees will also be semi-perpendicular to each other. Now, if you raised your uphill leg up high enough when crossing it over the downhill ski, your knee pocket should come to a rest almost on top of your downhill knee. This creates a much deeper knee pocket (the knee fits just above the inside part of the calf muscle), which should feel deeper and tighter. This is what is known as the **deep knee pocket**. The deep knee pocket is good for accentuating the knee pocket skill, by stretching and strengthening the appropriate muscles. This is a major benefit of the Javelin Drill. Not only that, but it is also directly used to make the biggest "X's" possible in aerial tricks.

Standing Javelin Position

Once you have found the deep knee pocket by standing still, begin to slide across the hill in the direction of the ski that is perpendicular to the fall line, while maintaining that position. As you come to the end of your traverse across the hill, take your lifted (perpendicular) ski off the downhill knee and place it back down on the snow, yet somewhat perpendicular to the ski that is already in the snow. Doing so will create a big wedge as you go around the turn. As you come to a good point to start traversing back across the hill the other way, set your new downhill edge sharply as you lift your new uphill leg into the air, and placing it on top of the other knee in the **deep knee pocket** again. Then follow your sharply driven edge directly across the hill to the completion of your next turn, and then repeat the process back the other way.

BONUS KEY: *"The Javelin Drill" allows us to feel and practice the "The Deep Knee Pocket" Position*

PERFECTING THE JAVELIN DRILL

Make sure you keep driving the inside hip down the hill to initiate the lead change at the inflection point of the turn. This happens as the top foot is placed back on the snow in order to start the next turn. The uphill hip should be driven, which initiates the lead change. After the lead change takes place, the new uphill foot should be lifted and placed on top of the downhill foot concurrently finding the deep knee pocket again. If done properly, the motion of tightly tucking the downhill knee into the deep knee pocket will naturally help you carve the turn for you. If you find yourself trying this drill and your tails (on the top ski) keep touching the snow for balance, then you are in the back seat, and therefore, your hips are too far back. To correct this, make sure you keep your hips up and stay focused on your **Uphill Hip Drive.** If your tips touch the snow for balance, then you are too far in the front seat, and you need to find a more athletic stance. Although, it should be noted that this mistake is far more favorable than being in the back seat, because it takes considerably more effort to get out of the back seat. If an athlete makes this mistake, it is a sign that they are on the right track and are applying the skills well. A likely cause for being too far forward is having their eyes and/or chest down. Coach's discretion should be utilized, but remember to keep your chest up and your eyes as far down the hill as possible. Constantly practice improving how square your upper body is to the fall line. This drill works best with poles.

This drill is good for practicing correct pole planting, posture, and timing, as well as stretching and strengthening the same muscles used in the knee pocket. The correct pole posture is: The downhill arm and pole should be extended downhill and poised until the turn is made, then plant at the same time, just like in the moguls. The grip on the pole should be firm but not tight, gripping the pole with only the index finger and the thumb. The pole should be supported with the bottom two fingers and the pole strap. The hand should be placed on top of the pole strap. The pole strap should extend around the wrist, from the bottom of the hand.

The grip should be firm, but not tight. The index finger should grip the pole, the middle finger should be relaxed, and the other two fingers should

PRACTICING GOOD MOGUL SKIING

support the pole, as the top of it rests in the crest of the thumb. See picture to the right for more information.

The downhill pole should be planted just as you place the lifted leg back on the ground in the wedge position. In order to plant, one should simply just relax their two supporting fingers, which creates a swinging-like motion in the pole. As it swings, allow the tip of the pole to plant lightly on the snow, and then re-grip the pole firmly and pull with the all of your fingers as the pole swings past the two lower ones from which it was being supported. Use the motion of the swinging action to help you tuck it up and away underneath the armpit after the turn is made. (The lighter one makes their

Javelin Drill as Seen from Above

pole plants, the more swinging motion they conserve, and therefore, the easier it is to "tuck away" the pole underneath the armpit.) As one is planting the inside pole, the "tucked away" pole (outside pole) should be swung down and extended. This is achieved by simply relaxing the two supporting fingers and thumb, allowing the pole to swing down and through, as it does, grip firmly with the index finger and thumb, and prop the pole up onto the two supporting fingers. If done properly, very little effort is used to extend and tuck away the poles.

The position of one's poles in this drill is exaggerated when compared to skiing in the moguls. However, this drill is very good for strengthening your "pole-flicking" muscles. One needs to make good, light, and quick pole swings in the moguls. Thus, correct positioning of the poles is important throughout the entire drill. Always remember, pole swings and the switch of the pole positions should be light and quick.

KEY #4: *"The Javelin Drill" progresses to "Short Swing Javelin Drill"*

SHORT SWING JAVELIN DRILL

After practicing the Javelin Drill, the next drill is to take it one step further and move onto the Short Swing Javelin Drill. However, it is important that an athlete should have a good working knowledge and skill level of the javelin turn before proceeding to this exercise because this is an advanced drill. The Short Swing Javelin is similar to regular Javelin Drill, except it uses only short swing turns. It is a very difficult drill that world champions such as Patrick Deneen practice on a daily basis. But the idea is simple.

To do a **Short Swing Javelin** turn, you want to make a short radius turn while picking up your uphill ski and placing it in the air above the downhill ski, so that it points across the hill much like a regular Javelin Drill. However, it has to happen much quicker, and in rapid succession. Also, the downhill ski never comes as far across the hill either, which means you have to be an expert at controlling your speed with the flexion of the downhill ski itself while still keeping the uphill ski above your downhill ski, all without losing your balance. First, let's take a look at what this looks like from above:

PRACTICING GOOD MOGUL SKIING

Short Swing Javelin Drill as Seen from Above

Notice how square I keep my uphill hip and shoulder to the fall line. If you are having trouble with this, make sure you are standing up tall. If you hunch over or hinge at the waist at all, you will block your own ability to drive your uphill hip. If you block it, squaring your uphill shoulder to the fall line will be very difficult. The two go hand-in-hand. If you remain nice and tall and everything is in alignment, the knee pocket can be felt for a split second just as you finish each turn. The uphill hip is usually already in a good position by doing this drill, because it needs to be driven in order to get one's uphill ski over the top of the downhill ski. If you are dragging the tail of your raised ski on the snow, it is a good indication that you are not successfully driving your uphill hip down the hill enough. Therefore, this is a good drill to practice, as it both requires a lot of uphill hip and shoulder drive down the fall line (also known as "counter-rotation") and gives you very obvious indicators if you are doing it right or wrong. Meaning, if you can feel the knee pocket during your turn, you are doing it correctly; if you are dragging your tails, then you are not. When you are doing it the right way, you should notice that as you press your knee into the knee pocket, there is a very quick move to knee angulation. Here, you can feel the deep knee pocket for a split second before you need to switch lead change again. The Short Swing Javelin Drill has a lot more in common with the reality of mogul skiing than the regular Javelin Drill, because of how much you have to force your knee pocket and the knee angulation and how quickly the turns have to happen, which is good for strengthening the muscles required to do those things. However, regardless of how good it is at training important muscle memory, the deep knee pocket is rarely used in actual mogul skiing. It is mostly restricted to air tricks involving "X's."

BONUS KEY: *"Short Swing Javelin Drill"* gives birth to good *"Knee Angulation"*

PERFECTING THE SHORT SWING JAVELIN DRILL

While you are turning, drive your downhill knee up into your uphill knee from behind to feel the knee pocket. Just as you feel the knee pocket, if you drive the uphill hip hard and tip your downhill knee downward, you are then initiating knee angle. You may even force an even deeper knee pocket to the point where you begin to feel it stall out. This is the deep knee pocket. Then, immediately switch to the other side by placing your uphill ski on the ground and lifting the other, immediately crossing over the downhill ski. Repeat in quick succession. Remember to remain very tall so that you do not block your uphill hip drive. The requirement here is to use the uphill hip drive to prevent you from over-finishing your turn because it acts as a counter force to the skis washing out. This is the best drill we have for practicing knee angle and uphill hip drive on the flats.

PRACTICING GOOD MOGUL SKIING

Knee angle is of most use to us in the moguls, and not really an actual drill in "The Progression." Knee angle is simply an advanced skill that we are working to improve while doing the drills in The Progression. It is mainly improved on the flats by practicing the Short Swing Javelin Drill as shown above. By definition, knee angle in the moguls is the absorption of a mogul, so that one's knees come across one's body to the opposite shoulder during the absorption. Therefore, it can only be truly accomplished in the 3D world of mogul skiing itself. For the most part, "good" knee angulation is a conscious effort, and not natural in most cases. But it is required to know how to do so properly, so that one can make their turns look as dynamic as possible. That is why we first practice it on the flats. We carve our turns from our edges. Knee angle is what allows us to tip our skis on their edges in the moguls. It is incorrect to try to put our skis on edge with the hip angle, or anything else. We want our hips to remain as square to the fall line and parallel to the plane of the hill as possible. Setting our edges with our knee angle and not with our hip angle is what allows us to have an unimpeded range of motion in the moguls. This is because tipping our skis from our hip angle actually blocks our uphill hip drive, where doing it with the knee angle does not. In other words, if we initiate our edging with our hips, we are severely limiting our range of motion.

At this point, while you are in the moguls, one applies the techniques of applying the knee pocket, with the same skills learned during the Short Swing Javelin Drill. Good knee angle will happen automatically as one absorbs. However, as long as you can maintain good speed and balance, there is no such thing as too much knee angle. Too much knee angle can block your forward momentum and cause you to become un-square to the fall line. This problem is corrected by more "Uphill Hip Drive."

PERFECTING KNEE ANGLE

While making a right turn (the left foot is downhill), the knees should absorb up and across to the right shoulder. Make sure that you bring your knees up to your opposite shoulder, but be careful not to hinge your upper body over your knees by bringing your opposite shoulder down to your knees. Your knees should go up and across the hill as far as possible, but don't overcompensate by meeting them halfway with your opposite shoulder. Stand tall. Always stand tall. See picture above for a demonstration.

KEY #5: *"Short Swing Javelin Drill"* begs for more strength, which we gain by doing the *"Z Drill"*

THE "Z" DRILL

The last step in The Progression is the "Z" Drill. The "Z" Drill is similar to the Javelin Drill, except you keep both skis on the ground at all times. Start the drill by starting in a large wedge with your skis and your upper body straight down the fall line. Keeping your arms up, your pole should be extended downhill and poised the entire time; unlike the Javelin Drill, you will not be planting your poles in this drill. The grip on the pole should be firm, but not tight, gripping the pole with only the index finger and the thumb. The pole should be supported with the bottom two fingers, the crest of the thumb, and then supported by the pole strap. The hand should be placed on top of the pole strap. The pole strap should extend around the wrist, from the bottom of the hand, just like in the Javelin Drill—except in the Z-Drill, we don't make any pole plants.

Once you get into a good wedge, make sure you keep your eyes as far down the hill and keep your chest up. The object of the "Z" Drill is to follow the direction of your skis, exactly as they are in your large wedge when you are standing still. First, follow one ski, then planting the other, and following that one—so that if you were to look up the hill at your tracks, it should be a series of perfect zigzags, or "Z's" (hence the name "Z" Drill).

To do this, start on a fairly steep hill with your large wedge pointed directly down the fall line. Choose a hill that is best for you, but remember you will be losing a lot of momentum in this drill, so you are going to want a noticeable pitch to the hill. Then simply lift one edge, slightly releasing its grip on the snow. You will notice you will start to follow the trajectory of the ski's edge that you did not release. Now the whole point here is to leave the ski that you released the edge of, plowing through as much of the snow as possible without bringing you to a complete stop. Keep plowing the snow as you move, and try to keep your speed as constant and consistent as possible, regardless of the differences in the snow. To combat this plowing force on your body, you will want to be flexing your uphill obliques (your side abs muscles) while rolling and keeping your hips tucked into the Mogul Skier Hips Up position. Also, you will notice great strain on your uphill hip flexor as well. That is the last muscle that we use in our Uphill Hip Drive movement.

PERFECTING THE "Z" DRILL

Always keep your plowing ski as perpendicular to your downhill ski as you are capable of. This plowing of the snow while following the direct (slicing) edge of the downhill ski takes a very specialized set of muscles located in the butt and groin areas that are required to be extra strong for skiing moguls. These muscles, once strong, will only add to the strength and control you have in your obliques. Once you are ready to make your next turn, try to make as abrupt of a change as possible, by dropping your plowing edge firmly, while simultaneously lifting the edge of the downhill ski. If done properly, you will now be heading in the opposite direction on a new downhill leg, plowing with your other leg without ever have "washed out."

This is the sign of a good "Z" Drill because the tracks in the snow will be crisply shaped like a continuous "Z," rather than the natural "S" shape of normal turns. Making sure one has a very abrupt change in turn direction is important because it adds to the strength training purpose of this drill. The simultaneous planting of the uphill foot and the change in direction, all the while taking the weight off the downhill ski, can only be accomplished by a strong, conscious drive of the uphill hip, flexing the uphill obliques, and wrenching on the hip flexor. All of these muscles are what strengthens and improve our uphill hip drive. Other muscles that get strengthened by this drill are the upper groin area, lower front abdomen, and butt areas. The "Z" Drill is one of the best strength training drills for mogul skiing. Practice it as often as possible, and make sure to have good form when you do it, so you don't learn bad habits. Enlist the help of a good mogul coach if you can. Always take a look up the hill at your tracks when you are finished with the "Z" Drill to make sure you made good, clean, sharp "Z" shaped tracks in the snow, and that you didn't wash out in any of your turns (see photo below).

KEY #6: *"The Z Drill" gives birth to powerful **"Uphill Hip Drive"***

UPHILL HIP DRIVE

Uphill hip drive is one of the most crucial parts of the mogul skier turn. It is the reason that we push ourselves to strengthen up so many specialized muscles on the flats by doing the "Z" Drill. It is an important skill to have because it is what puts a stop to the previous turn and initiates the new turn, while simultaneously preventing the over-finishing or "washing out" of one's turns. The stronger the uphill hip drive, the more consistent they will be, because they will not be as "pushed around" by the moguls as someone who does not have good uphill hip drive.

It is important to initiate your uphill hip drive during the neutral part of the turn (i.e., the inflection point of the turn). This will drive the uphill hip forward to initiate a lead change and make way for the transfer of the feet underneath the hips from one side to the other. It is important to set it in place early because good knee angle could potentially throw you off from being square down the fall line. As such, it acts as a buffer for too much knee angulation or over-finishing a turn, which could be dangerous. In other words, drive the left hip forward in order to finish a left turn (mogul would be on the right-hand side in a left-hand turn). This helps get you out of the previous rut and up onto the Glass Plate as well, if that is your goal. It is important to keep the upper body square to the fall-line because it becomes too difficult to drive the uphill hip if the hips get too far across the hill. It is highly beneficial to practice uphill hip drive with no poles because it forces you to remain square to the fall line. Be sure to keep your eyes way down the hill and stand tall; you can't drive your uphill hip if you are hunched over, because it blocks your uphill hip drive trajectory.

KEY #7: *"Uphill Hip Drive"* initiates *"Lead Change"*

WAYS YOU BLOCK THE UPHILL HIP DRIVE

1. WITH THE DOWNHILL HIP

Make sure that you are not blocking your uphill hip drive with your downhill hip. There is a time limit on how long one can wait before it's too late to drive the uphill hip. This happens when the hips get to 45° from the fall line or more. This is because as one stays in the turn too long (ex. riding the entire rut from where it starts to where it ends), the hips continually counter-rotate until they are twisted so far across the hill, that the uphill hip is completely behind (uphill) of the downhill hip. When this happens, the uphill hip loses its "line of sight" down the fall line, and therefore, you lose the ability to drive the uphill hip effectively. When this happens, your uphill hip is considered "blocked" by your downhill hip, and the only way to get your uphill hip to become your new downhill hip is by "swinging" or rotating your hips, which is both bad form and function.

To correct this, initiate the uphill hip drive sooner before the neutral part of the turn, in order to square off the hips during the neutral part of the turn. When you do this, you hit the new mogul with your uphill hip already in place, preventing you from over finishing your turn. For an illustration of this, see "Photo Experience 2: When to Initiate Uphill Hip Drive" in the Appendix.

2. WITH THE UPPER BODY

You can block your uphill hip drive by skiing hunched over or by hinging. Skiing hunched over is a static style of skiing, where the body never actually gets tall, and severely limits one's ability to absorb large moguls. Hinging is a usually constant cycle of hinging the upper body down over the knees while absorbing the moguls as if one is bringing his chest to his thighs rather than absorbing

Drive uphill hip from the hollow position.

his legs to his chest, like he should be. Skiing hunched over is typically found in skiers who were never trained how to ski moguls. Hinging usually occurs in athletes that have at least had some training. Hinging at the waist can be fixed by consciously standing taller while also consciously driving the uphill hip. But you will not be able to drive the uphill hip at all if you are hinging. So stand tall first, and get out of your own way.

A hinging mogul skier is typically one that is most likely overcompensating his absorption for fear of too much speed. This problem is more difficult to correct, and requires a two-pronged approach. First of all, if this type of skier gets told to "Just try to stand up taller" or "Get your hips up!" like many coaches hurl at their athletes, they will continually find themselves struggling with the backseat, and to compensate, they continually throw their upper body down the hill again in an attempt to correct the back seat feeling. This just perpetuates the problem. Hence the birth of the "Battle for the Front Seat." The real solution lies in how you use your feet, not your upper body. It's kind of misleading, and it is true that the upper body can cause blockage of the uphill hip. However, the upper body is not the root of the problem—the feet are. Simply put, all one needs to do to correct hinging is to be patient and wait for the mogul to come to them. Wait for the mogul to come to your feet, do not throw your feet out at the mogul. That's it! Careful alignment of your posture over the properly timed placement of your feet on the right part of the mogul will allow you the CAPACITY to ski in a taller position. Once you get out of your own way in this manner, you will find it relatively easy to rise to, and maintain, a taller and stronger skiing position. Once properly stacked in this manner, the uphill hip is free to be driven powerfully and unhindered.

THE CALL FOR MORE STRENGTH

As you begin to practice uphill hip drive, and realize its fantastic ability to mitigate many of the problems a mogul skier will have, you may also be equally disappointed in how weak those muscles that initiate a good uphill hip drive actually are. They are a highly specialized group of muscles that most people never use much. What's more is that as little as they are actually used, they are used that much less in concert with other muscles that we need to use in the moguls. Once I show my athletes how powerful and useful the uphill hip drive can be, the first thing they want to know is how to make those muscles stronger. That's easy: Repetition! The best way to strengthen highly specialized muscles in concert with one another is to use them in that exact context over and over again, until they are strong. Also, as we talked about above, the "Z" Drill is great for strengthening many of those muscles. However, there are a few ways one can strengthen these drills in the off-season as well. The uphill hip drive is mostly powered by the obliques and hip flexors. These muscles can be strengthened by exercises such as TV Watchers, Sideways Planks, Hanging Cherry Pickers, Twisting Hip Drive Sit Ups, Backwards Lunges (straight back or 45° back), and Leg Throws (with a partner). They should be a large focus of your off-season training.

With the **TV watcher**, make sure your head is up, the line of your back is flat and your butt is down, like in the picture below. Work with a coach to ensure that you have the correct posture. This exercise should be held for at least 1-minute intervals. Try to work up to 2-minute intervals.

"TV WATCHER"

The **Sideways Plank** is a great exercise to strengthen our lats and stabilizer muscles. These muscles help prevent us from crushing side to side, like in a "C" Turn. They are very important muscles to keep strong for mogul skiers. Try to work these into a "Super-Set" with the TV watchers. Do 1-2 minutes intervals in each position, with no rest in between. Be sure to do both sides!

"SIDEWAYS PLANK"

Kettle Bell Planks are the next step in building your core strength in regards to your planks. They also have the additional bonus of adding free weight movement to the stationary nature of planks. To do these you must start with the kettle bell in front of you as you post up into a sideways plank. Then you want to pick up the weight, and extend it straight

PRACTICING GOOD MOGUL SKIING

David Colturi demonstrates a "Kettle Bell Plank"

out in front of you. Next slowly raise it in a large extended-arm sweep until it is directly above you. For additional difficulty, raise your top leg at the same time. Once the peak is raised, hold it still for a 5 count and then return to neutral in the same sweeping motion, taking care to move slowly. This drill is especially good at strengthening our stabilizer muscles that are so precious to mogul skiers. It is also a very good exercise because it combines strengthening our core to keep your body stable and well balanced while performing unstabilizing movements, which is essentially what mogul skiing is.

Hanging Cherry Pickers are great for strengthening your obliques (next page). To do these, they require special boots that allow you to hang inverted from a pull-up bar, as seen here. However, you can do the same exercise without the boots by lying on your back and raising your feet up at a 90° angle similar to above, and reaching across with each hand to the opposite toe (see next page). I prefer the inverted or "Hanging" Cherry Pickers because they require more stabilizing muscles while you are performing them. Plus, they allow for more range of motion. You tend to swing back and forth while doing these types of sit-ups, and it requires considerable stabilization to prevent the naturally induced swinging motion. If you need more of an explanation than that, simply try them out for yourself, and you will see what I mean. Any exercises that you can do that activate any stabilizer muscles are the best types of exercises.

"HANGING CHERRY PICKERS"

Twisting Hip Drive Sit-Ups (HD Sit-ups) are one of the best exercises that exist for strengthening your uphill hip drive, hence their name. To do these, lay on a declined bench, and do a twisting sit up like normal, but instead of breaking at the waist half way up, drive your hip on the same side as the elbow that you are twisting across your body. Take a look at the picture below. This prevents you from hinging at the waist, and drives your hips completely off of the bench!

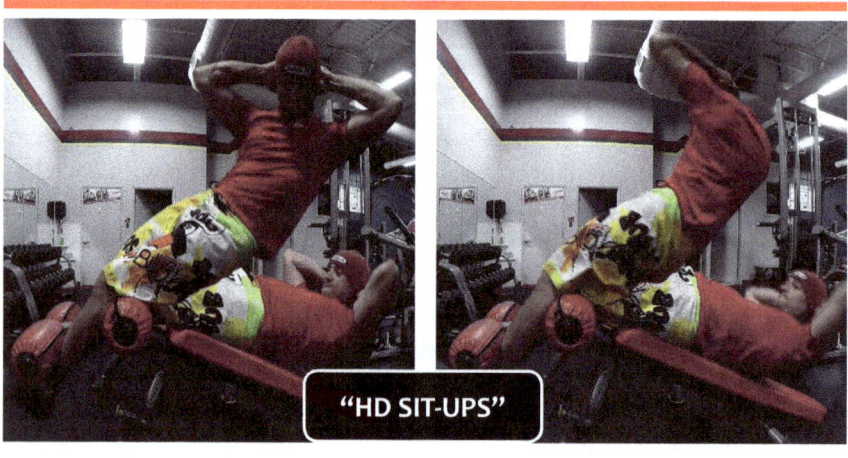

"HD SIT-UPS"

Backward Lunges are the other best exercise for strengthening your uphill hip drive. To do these, start off by standing straight, making sure there is nothing in your way behind you. Like so:

Next, take a big step backwards, but do not overextend yourself, as shown on the next page.

Then you want to slowly drop down to the knee that you just stepped back with:

Left Back Lunge

Right Back Lunge

The next step is the most important one. Here, you will be standing upwards and backwards into the standing position, using your back foot as a placement for where you are going to stand to. In this movement, you don't want to push off very hard with your front foot. Instead, you want to push off just enough so that you can actually engage your back leg's quad strength and hip drive. You want to drive the back hip (which represents your uphill hip, in this case) so strongly that it pushes your center of mass up and backwards until you are standing again. It is quite difficult at first, but practice it often, and it will get easier. Try not to rely on your front leg doing much of the work, as it is contrary to the beneficial aspects of this exercise. See how much I drive the back hip below.

Left Back Lunge

Right Back Lunge

Then simply stand back up from the momentum you gained by driving your back hip (which represents your uphill hip, hence why it is a good strength training for your uphill hip drive). If done properly, you should feel soreness in your buttocks the next day.

Left Back Lunge   Right Back Lunge

After you master doing straight back lunges like this, the next step is to do them at 45° backward angle. This is the absolute closest training you can get for uphill hip drive without actually being on snow. It is also the best exercise there is for strengthening your uphill hip drive, because of how similar a movement it is to actually being in the moguls. The first step is to again start in a straight standing position (1).

Then, step backwards just like the previous exercise, except this time step back at a 45° angle like below (2).

Next, drop slowly down until your back knee just barely touches the floor. Just like the previous exercise (3):

Good, now the important step. Carefully raise your center of mass up using your front foot, just enough so that you can powerfully engage your back hip drive, which will ultimately provide you the momentum you need to stand up the rest of the way:

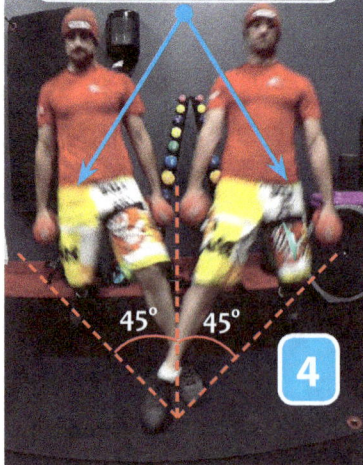

PRACTICING GOOD MOGUL SKIING

This backwards, upwards driving force with the back hip with a 45° twist to it represents the most accurate training we have on dry land to strengthening the uphill hip drive. Notice in the picture above how I am fighting to drive the hip, not only forward, but across my turned body (4). This is exactly the same way it will feel in the moguls. Pushing down the hill, but also across the body. This 45° angle also represents the maximum angle from which you can successfully do an uphill hip drive. Any more of an angle than this, and you would be considered "blocked" by your downhill hip. Pull yourself back up to the standing position like so (5):

A **"Ladder"** is a basically just two parallel strips of fabric joined together by multiple flat plastic "rungs." Its purpose is basically just to mark spots where you are supposed to place your feet as you do different drills on it. There is a multitude of **ladder drills** out there and all of them are good for mogul training. Ladder drills are especially helpful in building foot coordination and speed. They are also great for endurance training and strength building. In the above picture, David shows us how to do a "scissor" drill

David Colturi shows us how to do the "Scissor Drill"

in which he runs through the ladder by crisscrossing his legs forward and backward as he traverses the ladder. This drill is great at building strength required for lateral movements that we mogul skiers deal with constantly. It is one of the most important strength building ladder drills. Talk to a coach for more information and types of ladder drills, since there are simply too many to cover here.

Leg Throws are a great abdominal and oblique strength-training exercise. They are also a great speed training exercise, since the faster you can do them, the more you strengthen your quick twitch abdominal muscles, which are important in the moguls. To do these, stand with your head between your partner's feet and grab onto their legs for support, as seen below. It is important to grab onto the back of their legs because you can use it to increase the leverage with which you will be snapping your feet back up into their hands.

Leg Throws

Instruct your partner to throw your legs down at the ground as hard as he can, in random directions (angles). Your job is to resist the force of his throw and prevent your feet from slamming into the ground. If you can stop your feet more than 6 inches above the ground, find a stronger partner who will throw your legs harder. You want to just barely be able to reverse the direction of the leg throw a few inches before your feet hit the ground. After you have stopped your feet before hitting the ground, immediately "snap" them or bring them back up into your partner's hands as fast as you can. Then repeat the process. You should be able to do at least 60 of these per minute. Work 3 sets of 60 to start with, and work your way up from there.

SUMMARY

Uphill Hip Drive initiates lead change. Lead change initiates the knee pocket. The knee pocket initiates knee angle. Knee angle initiates carving a turn with the sweet spot of the ski. Edging on a turn is ended by uphill hip drive. Uphill hip drive makes way for the next lead change, and then the cycle repeats itself.

KEYS TO REMEMBER RELATING TO
CHAPTER 10
PRACTICING GOOD MOGUL SKIING POSTURE:

KEY #1: **"Lead Change"** naturally gives birth to **"The Knee Pocket"**

KEY #2: **"The Knee Pocket"** is practiced in the **"The Short Swing Turn"**

KEY #3: **"The Short Swing Turn"** progresses to **"The Javelin Drill"**

> **BONUS KEY:** **"The Javelin Drill"** allows us to feel and practice the **"The Deep Knee Pocket"**
>
> > ****Hint:** "The Deep Knee Pocket" naturally gives
> >
> > birth to large X's in all aerial tricks!

KEY #4: **"The Javelin Drill"** progresses to **"Short Swing Javelin Drill"**

> **BONUS KEY:** **"Short Swing Javelin Drill,"** gives birth to good **"Knee Angulation"**
>
> > ****Hint:** Good knee angulation gets you higher turn scores because it makes you look like a more dynamic mogul skier.

KEY #5: **"Short Swing Javelin Drill"** begs for more strength which we gain by doing the **"Z Drill"**

KEY #6: **"The Z Drill"** gives birth to powerful **"Uphill Hip Drive"**

KEY #7: **"Uphill Hip Drive"** initiates **"Lead Change"**

*"Before you can work smart,
you must work hard."*
-Pardo

*"Small disciplines repeated with
consistency every day lead to great
achievements gained slowly over time."*
-John C. Maxwell

"Deeds, not words."
-Dropkick Murphys

"Don't complain, just work harder."
-Grosser

CHAPTER 11
IMPACT, INJURIES, AND HOW BEST TO DEAL WITH THEM

"How wild it was to let it be."
-Cheryl Strayed

BACKGROUND

Mogul skiing can be a dangerous sport. Even though safety measures have improved immensely in recent years, injuries can still occur. It seems that the majority of injuries are reoccurrence of previous injuries, issues related to poor rehab dedication, or too little time spent in recovery. However, due to the nature of the sport, I feel it best to explain the best way to deal with impacts and injuries. This is because mogul skiers constantly push the physical limit of their bodies with speed and forces that the human body was never designed to withstand. Plus, they do it in the coldest, unforgivable, and unpredictable athletic platform imaginable. Remember that any given mogul course can change drastically in as little as an hour due to temperature swings in either direction, high volume of traffic, new snow, etc. In my experience as a mogul skier as well as a stuntman, I have seen my fair share of major injuries. However, I also learned in that two decade-long stretch of punishing my body how best to deal with those injuries. More importantly, I will disclose the single best strategy for avoiding major injury.

As I said, I have dealt with my fair share of injuries, both on and off of the mogul course. I have had seven surgeries in all to put me back together again, including four knee surgeries, two ankle surgeries, and a face surgery. Some of the highlights include driving a motorcycle into the side of a house (because the gas got stuck) so fast that I not only tore the siding off the house, but I ricocheted off the house and into the pool deck. Upon blowing through the pool deck and the pool's plumbing system, I stopped only after bouncing off the side of the above-ground pool. On a separate occasion, I was hit by a car while I was on my bicycle; the impact was so hard that my bicycle had to be pried out from underneath the guy's car with a crowbar. Meanwhile I was catapulted over the hood, bounced off the windshield, and spun into a flat spin. Eventually I landed all the way back on the sidewalk from where I started. One time I was skiing in A-basin and attempted to come to a stop above a 30-foot cliff, but as I stopped, my skis slipped backward by a mere inch or so, and the tail of my ski got stuck on the tip of a freshly snow-covered root or rock. This unexpected stop to my ski was just enough to knock me off balance, and since I had nowhere to catch my balance, I fell backwards, and head first, off the 30-foot cliff. Another time I got out of control in a mogul course, and hit the bottom air at a mind-boggling speed—which resulted in the most spectacular 30-foot moon drop (straight fall, flat on one's back) you have ever seen. My moon drop landed me onto the crest of a particularly unforgiving mogul. This particularly painful accident had me coughing up blood for a half hour after the event and resulted in two fractured ribs and a spine that has been out of alignment ever since. That one hurt, but it gets worse.

My most painful impact happened at Lake Granby, about 45 minutes north of Winter Park, CO, where I worked at the marina. One day, we needed to move the large docks out to deeper water because the water level had dropped so much that some of the slips were on dry land. To move the dock out to the deeper water required us to loosen all of the metal cables that anchored the dock to the bottom. Then we would use the winch-barge to lift up the huge cinder block anchors and move them out to deeper water, one by one. During the relocation of the dock, I was in charge of letting out one of the metal anchor wires which attached the dock to the enormous concrete cinder blocks on the bottom of the lake. As the barge latched on to the anchor and began to move it, the winch arm that I was using completely malfunctioned. Instantly, the cable snapped taught, and all of that force went into the large metal winch that I was holding onto. The which arm was instantly snatched from my grip, and on the next revolution, the large metal winch arm hit me in the face. I was struck with enough force that it knocked me completely off of my feet, and knocked all of my front teeth into the back of my throat. I landed flat on my back

IMPACT, INJURIES, AND HOW BEST TO DEAL WITH THEM

with a pulverized face, alone on a dock that was floating out to sea. Luckily for me, by that time, I had learned a great deal about the most important skill to exercise when disaster strikes. It easily could have turned out a lot worse, and I am very grateful for that it did not.

I have another story from when I worked as a stuntman that involves me flipping out of control after jumping off the top deck of a Russian aircraft carrier from a dizzying height. By that time, however, I had been fully versed in how to deal with dangerous encounters, and was well-practiced to boot. So instead of plummeting to my death, which seemed to be the only likely outcome, I escaped completely unharmed. In fact, it was this very skill that was solely responsible for saving my life.

Likewise, this skill is the sole purpose I am here today, writing this book. In my opinion, the importance of this skill cannot be overestimated. Since I owe my very life to it, I went through great pains to give you the best explanation, in the greatest detail available, to help you learn it. Not only that, but I break down how the skill is used in three different intervals.

The reason that I am telling you all of these stories is not to impress you or derive some sort of sympathy from you, but to try to explain to you that my way of dealing with disaster when it strikes was forged on the anvil of disaster itself. It is not an unproven theoretical methodology. It is distilled from experience. Distilled from survival. A two-decade-long concert of accidents, injuries, and pain itself is what birthed this skill in me. It took a lifetime of learning the hard way for me to finally learn it, but it thankfully doesn't have to take that long for you. All you need to do is take this lesson to heart. If you are at all interested in preventing as much pain and injury as possible, you will have to apply this skill in opposition to what your natural reflexes will tell you to do. That's the only catch, and you have to have enough control over yourself to monitor, mitigate, and mirror your reflexes.

Happily, most mogul skiers have a decent amount of control over their reflexes, since the sport itself demands it. Additionally, if you use my Mogul Method, overriding your reflexes is built right into the method. In that way, the method itself is a good teacher of the fundamental skills that you will need to practice this skill and is very congruent to dealing with injuries and disasters properly.

THE SKILL

So it has come now to the skill. The skill that I reveal below, you might recognize from the New Mogul Method. It is no accident. This skill is not only the single most universally applicable athletic skill in the world, but also the most poorly taught. It is what separates the best from the rest, the masters from the technicians, and the survivors from the dead. Well, here it is (again): RELAX! Is it really that simple? Well, it's complicated, but essentially, yes. You see, relaxing one's body allows the transfer of energy through your body unimpeded. When we get hit with a large instantaneous amount of energy, such as when we fall off a jump or into a mogul, that force goes into our bodies. Now the best thing to do is, of course, always do what you can to avoid major impacts like these, but that is not always possible. Therefore, we desperately need a way to minimize the damage to our bodies when these major impacts occur. It is a natural reflex to try to resist the impact by tensing up. We do this because we are attempting to ricochet, or "bounce," the energy generated by impact, from the outermost surface of our bodies in an attempt to prevent the force from entering our bodies and causing injury. However, if the force is too big, such that it will not be ricocheted anywhere, the force will get transferred into your body, whether you tense up or not. There lies the problem that most athletes face. Since moguls are generally immovable objects, they will not be deflected by your tense muscles, so your natural reflexes can actually work against you. If you are tense, then the energy then has nowhere to go and is localized; it may result in broken bones, torn ligaments, sprains, dislocated collar bones, even death.

When one is relaxed, however, a large percentage of the force from the impact can be transferred right through our bodies. Since this is not natural for us, it needs to be developed and practiced as a skill. Relaxing upon impact is counter-intuitive to our natural instincts. Naturally, when we are confronted with a fall or an impact, our instinct is to tense up. This is because tensing up does prevent injury up to a certain extent, but after that, stuff breaks. *You* break. Have you ever wondered why a drunk driver is often the only one that survives a fatal car accident? It is because, in his inebriated state, he is relaxed. He does not recognize or see the car accident as a sober person does; his instincts to tense up on impact are overridden by the chemicals in his system, preventing him from tensing up, thereby saving his life. The artificial state of relaxation that alcohol gives to a drunk person overrides his instinct to tense up when faced with major impacts, or threats.

Believe it or not, this is essentially the same thing that we want to do when we are confronted with a major impact. Except we need to be able to do it on command. We need a way to manually override our instincts of tensing up when danger is flying at our face, in a split second. Therein lies both the difficulty and the beauty. It is difficult because it is nearly impossible to reprogram millions of years' worth of evolution that gave you your reflexes in the first place. But the beautiful thing is that you don't have to do anything to do it. Just relax. That's it. That's all you have time for. Just resist the temptation to tense up. Just relax. Don't do anything. You are actually doing less by just relaxing than doing something by tensing up. Since relaxing, or remaining in a relaxed state, can actually have a quicker response time than tensing up, it is virtually the only signal you can send to your muscles to override your reflexes. This is why it is the most universally applicable athletic skill: because it allows all people to reprogram their instincts, and reflexes to however they see fit. This makes them faster, less likely to get injured, and more efficient in their movements.

People from all walks of life who have lived a hard-knock life generally learn this skill, either consciously or subconsciously, the hard way. But they were never taught how to use it and harvest it properly. That's what I am hoping to do in the next section. I will break down this skill for you in hopes that it speeds up your learning process, resulting in your ability to apply its beneficial aspects sooner, and save you from any more pain, injuries, and broken bones. It may even save your life one day, as it did for me.

HOW TO RELAX

How to relax may sound self-explanatory. However, I am not talking about how to relax while you're sitting there, comfortably in your chair, reading this book. I am talking about how to relax when you are about to get hit by a car, or a mogul at 40 mph. It is even the same skill that you need to use to prevent the scared sensation when your older brother tries to scare you by popping out from around the corner. It's all the same thing. So for brevity's sake, for the rest of this book, when I say "relax," what I really mean is, "Relaxing in the face of danger." So that when I say "relax," you know what I really mean.

The problem is, though, how do we go about rewiring our brain to relax when we are scared? First is to understand the problem. The problem of being tense has three main sources: surprise, reflexes, and blame. The solution to being tense is to relax. Relaxing has three main steps that you will need to practice. They are: **Monitor, Mitigate**, and **Mirror**.

MONITOR

Monitor means to constantly watch what is going on in our environment. To sum up: all we can see, and also what we can't see to predict the likelihood of all things that may trigger our reflexes into action. If we can predict to some extent the probability that something bad is going to happen, then we are not surprised when it does. This allows us to remove surprise from the equation and the natural tension that it brings along with it. Being able to remove surprise from the equation greatly increases our chances of properly mitigating our reflexes. For example, if your brother is not in the room when you go to leave, and you are aware of your surroundings, you can predict some percentage that he is likely hiding and going to try to scare you when you go to walk around the corner. If he does try to scare you, and you still get tense, even though you knew he was going to do that, then that is your reflexes trying to prevent you from impact or injury. But at least you weren't surprised.

The main takeaway is that the undesirable action of tensing up comes from two sources: surprise and reflexes. Surprise happens when something unexpected happens. Reflexes usually occur in an attempt to prevent you from injury. You need to handle both to be able to successfully control tensing up your body. If you can separate surprise from your reflexes, it is a great advantage that you will have over others, because most people can't do that. **Monitor** removes surprise from the equation. I like to think of it as a type of "Spidey-Sense." It's one of Spider-Man's superpowers, and it allows him to know when danger is approaching, regardless of whether he can see it or not. If you know danger is coming, it is much easier to remain relaxed. Prediction is the attribute that **monitor** affords you. Then all you have to worry about is how to mitigate your reflexes when they happen.

MITIGATE

Mitigate - To moderate (a quality or condition) in force or intensity; alleviate. To become milder.

-From the American Heritage® Dictionary of the English Language,

4th Edition (wordnik.com)

First of all, allow me to point out that our reflexes developed over millions of years for a reason, so there are times when we should allow them to occur naturally, and unencumbered. But since they did not evolve for the type of environment and circumstances that a mogul skier has to deal with on a daily basis, there comes a time when we need to **augment, mitigate,** or **nullify** those reflexes. Many times, however, you need to do all three of those things at the same time. For example, if you have come off your skis and are falling sideways into a large mogul, your reflexes will want you to do two things at once: avoid the mogul (flee), or fend off the mogul (fight). If you are not well-practiced at falling, your reflexes will inevitably force you to fend off (fight) the mogul, since you are incapable of fleeing from it while you are falling. To do that, your reflexes will likely tell you to stick out your hand or "stiff-arm" the icy monolith rushing towards your face, while also telling the rest of your body to tense up, in an attempt to have the mogul "bounce off" you. Well, I've been skiing moguls a long time, and I've never seen one "bounce off" a person. Usually, it is the person that does the bouncing, and/or breaking, as the case may be. Depending on how fast you were going when you fell, you are likely to break your collarbone, dislocate your shoulder, or both. Not to mention it will likely end your ski season, which makes this set of reflexes bad for your health, and your skiing career. Therefore, we need to override those reflexes, so that we can ski another day. So how do we do that exactly? As I said above, you need to do three things, **augment, mitigate,** and **nullify** those reflexes. Here is how I would do it:

If I found myself falling sideways down the mogul course heading straight into a mogul, I would first nullify the "fight" reflex of "stiff-arming" the mogul, because I know that the most injury-prone part of this particular type of fall is extended appendages. If I did nothing else to modify this fall, I would have less injuries, simply by not fighting (stiff-arming) the mogul. So that is the most important one. In other words, the first thing I would do is to **nullify** the "fight" (the mogul) reflex. Then, if I had time to do so, I would **augment** my other primary reflex of flight. In this case "flight" would mean to avoid the mogul. Since I can't simply "fly away" in mid-air like perhaps Superman would, to completely avoid the mogul, I need to **augment** my natural "flight" reflex. I would do this by simply tucking my downhill arm in close to my body and rolling my shoulder, pointing my back at the mogul. This protects my face, my ribs, and my arms. The impact will then take place on my back, which is better than taking the impact on my shoulder, and much better than taking it in the face. Also, tucking into the fetal position is good for preventing my extremities (and my skis and poles), from getting caught on something, twisted, broken, and/or torn. This ability to choose where I take an impact is a product of **augmenting,** or "improving" my "flight" reflex. In other words, if you can't escape, you can usually choose where you will take the impact, to some degree. It is usually best to take major impacts on the back and then roll out of it, if possible. So I make that my go-to "flight" reflex. If you have a go-to reflex or plan of action before the fall actually happens, you stand a much better chance of carrying out that augmented reflex when it matters most.

Upon impact, I would **mitigate** my "fight" reflex of tensing up. Now it should be noted here that tensing up is good pre-impact. Tensing up helps you control the fall, control your extremities, tuck your shoulder and get into the fetal position. Therefore, I **mitigate** or "moderate" my tensing up reflex by tensing up only when it is appropriate (during my fall) and relaxing when it is not, thereby **mitigating** it. So upon actual impact, I relax. I let the force dissipate through my entire body and "through" me, delocalizing the impact. I delocalize the impact because if I didn't, it would hurt more in the one spot that I took the impact. In other words, when I delocalize the impact force, I decrease the amount of damage given to any one part of my body. In explanation, if some of the force of impact goes into my arms and legs because my whole body is relaxed, then the overall energy of impact on my back is less. By these means, I stand the greatest chance of surviving that impact unharmed. As a mogul skier and stuntman, I was renowned for my ability to take a huge impact and then walk away unharmed. People called me "tough," which most people mistakenly assume is an innate (inborn) trait. It's not. "Tough" is a skill, and must be practiced like any other. All I was doing when people called me "tough" was exercising this simple skill—the very same skill that you just learned. Well, that and getting used to living with pain. I learned this skill the hard way from a hard-knock life, but now, hopefully, you don't have to do the same. Hopefully, now that you know the basics, you can limit the amount of pain and injury in your life.

A great way to practice these aspects of **mitigate** is to practice taking falls on a trampoline. If you don't have a trampoline, see if you can scrape together some old mattresses and or couch cushions and practice jumping from elevated positions and crashing (i.e., not landing on your feet). You will find really quickly that sticking out any of your appendages is bad and it can hurt. Hopefully, you learn the lessons above quickly and tuck your shoulder into the fall as you impact. As you become more comfortable with it, try landing in as many different "crash landing" positions that you can. It is almost preferable to land on a pile of old spring mattresses and couch cushions because they can offer inconsistencies and variable soft/hard spots much like falling in actual moguls. So it's a good practice. It's just a lot safer. Practice landing half on balance and half off balance too. Learn how to flex your muscles to force yourself to regain control, but also learn your limit and when you need to let go. My first knee injury was an ACL tear. I tore my own ACL because I fought too hard for my landing, and I literally pulled my own knee apart with my leg muscles while fighting the rut of the mogul. So knowing your limit and living to ski another day should be the ultimate goal. Remember, not every jump needs to be landed. Not every fall needs to be personal. But every jump and fall needs to be survived.

Another thing that you can do to practice the **mitigate** skill is to do regular or flying somersaults. A flying somersault is like a regular somersault, except you jump into it from a standing or running position (1). Run only for three or four steps, and then jump up and forward (2). Once in the air, fully extend your body and then dive towards the ground (3).

Upon impact, you will want to **mitigate** the impact of the ground with your hands. What is meant by this is that you are not going to stop your body from hitting the ground simply because you stick out your hands. However, what you can do is to control or mitigate the initial impact a little bit by slowing down and redirecting it (4). As you use your arm strength to slow down your impact, use it to redirect the impact to allow you to tuck your head between your arms by touching your chin to your chest (4). This elongates the back of your neck, which can be used as the initial fulcrum (point of rotation). As you make an impact, gradually lower yourself so that the back of your head touches the ground first. Before this point, you want to have the rest of your body tense so that you can retain control over it while you are initiating your flying somersault. Use a tense body to control your flight, fall, and rotation. That part should be easy because to be tense is natural. The majority of the impact with the ground happens on your upper shoulders and back (occurs between steps 4 and 5 above). This is the point at which you want to **augment** your natural reflexes to relax your body upon actual impact with the ground. It should be noted that at first, the impact will likely come all at once. But with practice, it is possible to dissipate the impact over your entire back by timing your rotation and "rolling through the impact." If you get a localized impact near the top of your back, that means you set your rotation too slow, or you didn't control your descent enough with your arms. If you get a solid blow to the middle of the back, but your rotation stops, that means you abandoned the fetal position and didn't tuck your legs and arms in enough. It also means that you didn't flex your abs throughout the entire maneuver. If you take the majority of the impact on your lower back or tailbone, then you didn't successfully lower yourself into the roll with your hands, or your initial rotation was way too fast, so you didn't initiate the roll with the top of your head and neck. It is important to keep your legs and arms in during the somersault because it helps with the rotation itself. If you stay tight enough, you may be able to actually just stand right up out of the somersault. This is great practice and similar to how we actually need to fall in the moguls as well. We must force ourselves (nullify the "fight" reflex) to keep all of our extremities close to our bodies when we fall in the moguls, no matter what our reflexes tell us to do. Especially if it is an uncontrollable fall.

Once you get good at standing up from out of the somersault or flying somersault position, you can take it one step further. In order to gain even further awareness and control during your falls, you can practice getting up out of the flying somersault to the left or right, instead of just straight ahead. Position 6 above shows me getting up out of the flying somersault to the right for a demonstration. This involves breaking away from the fetal position earlier than a standard flying somersault by scissoring the legs and putting the right leg down on the ground and then the left foot if you are going to get up to the right (5). Alternatively, you can place your left thigh down on the ground first followed by the right foot if you want to get up out of the somersault to the left. After you stand up, you are facing 90° away from the direction from which you started (6). This is a great way to learn body awareness and control while falling, since it teaches you how to move and what to do while "crashing" so that you can achieve the desired result at the end of it. Additionally, it is fundamentally a good way to fall in the moguls should you "go over the handlebars," because this method will bring you back to a standing position with your skis already across the hill so you can stop. This skill is helpful because even when we have an uncontrolled fall in the moguls, assuming the fetal position gives us a better chance of controlling our fall once we slow down. The better that you are able to control how you come out of a fall or a "tumble," the less likely that you will get hurt. Sometimes you will surprise yourself just how soon and smoothly you can come out of a nasty fall if you have well-practiced body awareness and control.

MIRROR

The last part of being able to relax properly is to exercise the **"mirror"** skill. **Mirroring** is the ability to depersonalize the danger and/or the pain. When you make the pain of the impact or the injuries personal, it hurts more. It also makes you tense when you make a personal association to the danger before the actual impact, thereby increasing the pain upon impact. I like to use the word **"Mirror"** because it helps me detach myself from the pain. I like to envision myself looking at myself as if through a mirror. I see me, but it's not me; it's a mirror copy of me, and therefore different. In explanation, when you look at yourself in the mirror, you do not see the same version of you that other people see when they look at you. You see your left ear as if it was your right ear, and your right ear as if it was your left ear, your entire body is likewise reversed. Therefore, it's you, but it's different. Looking at a **mirror** copy of myself as danger approaches is the best way I have found to become "detached" from any impending danger, impact, or pain. This is because, in my mind's eye, it's happening to "that" person instead of "me." This version of detaching from yourself by imagining you are looking at a **mirror** copy allows you to still have all of the proper survival factors in place to protect you in case you need them, but detaches you a little bit from the drama of the situation and also of the pain.

To **mirror** also removes responsibility from the action of falling, getting hit by a car, or even a metal winch arm. What I am trying to say is that when I got hit by that car, I did not say to myself, "You bas**rd!" or "Why me?" I put zero energy into trying to "will" him to stop or avoid me. I removed the blame. I dealt with the situation as unavoidable, and dealt with the action as any other happenstance in real time. That allowed me to walk away with a simple scratch on my thumb, rather than the normal injuries one might expect from being run over by a car. That is the power of the **mirror** skill. **Mirroring** is an important step to being able to relax. When you blame things, you get tense. If you just accept the fall or impact as unavoidable happenstance, you are free to deal with it properly by being able to relax.

"Shock" is a form of the **mirror** attribute in its most extreme form. When the body goes into shock after a traumatic event, one is truly detached from what is going on. Be it pain or injury or whatever. Shock is actually the body's built in override system to force you to relax in extreme situations. The problem with shock, however, is that you have zero control over it, and many times can actually put you into harm's way if you are not properly cared for by someone. **Mirror**, as the way I describe it, and use it, is like a milder form of shock. It gives you almost the same benefits that shock gives you, but in **mirror,** you still retain control over your faculties. It is one of the more difficult steps to learn when one is learning to relax, but should be practiced nonetheless. My advice is to practice it on little things first, like stubbing your toe, or when you get a paper cut. What I mean to say is when one of these things happens, imagine in your mind's eye that you are looking at yourself in the mirror, and the injury happened to the person in that mirror, not you. Also, to disassociate from the pain, it helps to relax that area of the body as much as possible, and then just stop caring that it hurts. Pretend, if you like, that it is simply empathy pain for the person in the mirror that it actually happened to. When the pain gets really bad, remove all personalization from the injury. Prevent yourself from using the words "my," "me," "I," etc. For example, don't say "MY knee hurts," "Why did this happen to ME," "I am not going to be able to compete with this." It is better to say, only that "It hurts, but it is too soon to know what the problem is, so I am not going to worry about it." Or, "Well this happened. But I'm still alive, and I need to be aware of other or more pressing dangers," and so on.

However, the best thing to do is to just stop thinking altogether. I find that even when I am trying to do positive self-talk when I am injured, negative thoughts still seem to invade my mind. But when I try to not think at all, I am more successful at keeping negative thoughts from entering my mind. If you can practice all of this stuff on a daily basis, you will get better at it, and you will experience what I am talking about. Then when you need the mirror skill the most in a dangerous situation, it will be increasingly available to you, depending on how much you practiced it.

AFTER THE STORM

A career in mogul skiing can leave a person with any number of lagging injuries that never seem to go away. I am certainly no exception. I have suffered the setbacks of seven surgeries and countless other sprains, strains, and broken bones—injuries that have left me with pain that I have always assumed would be lifelong sentences. Thankfully, I have discovered that many of these injuries don't have to stay with me forever, and I would like to share with you some new and fairly uncommon medical rehabilitation procedures that have worked absolute wonders on my badly banged-up body. I am sharing them with you in the hopes that you will be able to prevent, mitigate, or eliminate some of the common ailments that plague mogul skiers.

First off, I would like to explain the types of injuries that I have suffered from, so that you might be able to compare and contrast my ailments to your own. That way we can be on the same page with regards to the types of pain we are trying to heal—this will help you determine whether or not my described solution will work for your circumstances. Additionally, I will list all of the treatments I have tried for my injuries and list their relative effectiveness on a 0-10 scale, with 10 being the most effective and 0 being the least effective. Additionally, I will also use a 0-10 scale to convey recovery time for each procedure as well as the associated medical costs of each procedure. Here, a 10 represents the highest recovery length and the highest associated medical costs. Lastly, I will also add insight as to how I dealt with each particular injury that I endured, and whether or not I would deal with it the same way again, or do it differently the next time given my current perspective.

KNEE PAIN

- Torn ACL - Repaired by patellar tendon graft
- Torn MCL
- Torn Meniscus x 4

ACL - All in all, I am pretty happy with my repaired ACL. The knee feels pretty strong and I haven't had any problems with it since it was repaired. If I could do it again, I might do a cadaver graft, since that way my patellar tendon wouldn't have been cut into, but the choice is completely up to you. It's a really hard decision to make, since it's going to be a long and painful recovery no matter which road you take. I chose not to get the hamstring graft, because the hamstring always felt like it had such a paramount importance for mogul skiing, and I didn't want to risk diminishing its strength, feel, or flexibility, even the slightest bit. But again, it's your choice. Either way, if you're currently struggling with this injury, my heart goes out to you. It might seem like the end of the world when you tear your ACL, but remember, there are mogul skiers who've kept skiing moguls after they tore their ACLs and did quite well. Take Evan Dybvig for example. He skied in the Olympics with no ACLs!

SOLUTION RATINGS:

Knee surgery (ACL Reconstruction)
- Short term effectiveness = 0
- Long term effectiveness = 9
- Recovery Time = 10
- Medical costs = 10

No knee surgery
- Short term effectiveness = 3
- Long term effectiveness = 2
- Recovery Time = 0
- Medical costs = 0

MCL - The MCL tear I had probably could have healed on its own, but I chose to have surgery on it because I was told that was the best course of action. If I could do it again, though, I probably would've just let the stupid thing heal up by itself. Having the surgery cost me thousands of dollars that I didn't have and contributed to my skyrocketing personal debt. If nothing else, my wallet would've thanked me.

SOLUTION RATINGS:

Knee surgery (MCL Repair)
- Short term effectiveness = 1
- Long term effectiveness = 8
- Recovery Time = 7
- Medical costs = 9

No knee surgery
- Short term effectiveness = 3
- Long term effectiveness = 7
- Recovery Time = 5
- Medical costs = 0

Meniscus - I tore my meniscus multiple ways, multiple times. The story is so similar to my MCL that if the actual physical tracking of my knee joint was still working, chances are I probably wouldn't get them scoped again. I probably would have waited until several years down the road if at all possible. I've officially had four MRI-confirmed meniscus tears, but I recently had another one that I have not gotten confirmed via MRI—but I am convinced that it is indeed a meniscus tear. This time I opted for a different solution, and I have seen remarkable results. My knee was locking up very badly and walking was difficult. I had pain in the back of my knee, and I was also experiencing the popping and locking up of the knee that usually coincides with a torn meniscus. Instead of getting my knee scoped, however, I decided to try Rock Tape (stretchable athletic tape), and wow! I can walk again! It's not perfect, but the swelling went way down and the locking stopped. If I had a big competition coming up and I tore my meniscus, I would definitely go this route instead—especially since I never really saw much improvement even after my scopes. But that is just my opinion and you should choose based on your own experience.

SOLUTION RATINGS:

Knee surgery (scope)
- Short term effectiveness = 7
- Long term effectiveness = 8
- Recovery time = 3
- Medical costs = 8

Neoprene knee brace
- Short term effectiveness = 3
- Long term effectiveness = 0
- Recovery time = 0
- Medical costs = 1

Rock Tape Athletic Tape
- Short term effectiveness = 7
- Long term effectiveness = 1
- Recovery time = 0
- Medical Costs = 1

BACK PAIN

Conventional Western medical knowledge says that lower back pain is usually caused by weak abdominal muscles. A quick Google search will confirm this. However, that has never sat right with me. Mogul skiers with weak abs? Don't be ridiculous! One time, I was complaining about my chronic back pain to a doctor and he had the audacity to look me in the eye and say, "It's probably just weak abdominal muscles." Excuse me? Weak abdominal muscles? I could do 120 sit-ups a minute, and I did hundreds of crunches, six days a week! Planks, TV watchers, all of it! Doctors nowadays don't care about who you are as an athlete, and they don't really know how to treat you properly. If you search the web for "lower back pain," countless websites will tell you that they know the true cause of your pain, and that no matter what your ailment is, they will be able to cure it once and for all. Most of it is garbage, designed to keep you coming back week after week for tiny, insignificant, incremental improvements. I know from experience, because I tried many of those treatments. My chronic pain lasted for a very long 17-year period. During that time, countless web searches got me no closer to finding a cure for my back pain. See below for the list of treatments I've tried and their relative effectiveness.

First, though, let me be clear about what type of back pain I have. That way, you can judge for yourself whether or not your back pain is similar, and therefore if any of these treatments are relevant to your unique type of pain. I have had three distinct types of pain:

1. BULGED DISC - I once had a bulged disc in my back that was so painful that I could not walk without assistance. This was an acute pain and the solution was remarkably simple.

2. **UPPER BACK PAIN** - I had lingering upper back pain that resulted in constant knots underneath my shoulder blades, as well as along both sides of my spine. These were relatively benign compared to other parts of my body that lingered with pain—but make no mistake, these knots were big, and permanent.

3. **LOWER BACK PAIN** - "The Dragon's Mouth," I called it. A chronic knot in the lower left side of my back that never went away and was about the size of my fist. This muscle knot ailed me fiercely for nearly 20 years, constantly draining energy from me like some kind of energy vampire. It was as solid as a rock, and it grew to twice the size of the same muscle in my lower right back. To give you some perspective on how solid it was, I once had my cousin—a big strong man (6'-2" ~270lbs) who bends ¼" wire all day long with his big burly fingers for a living (he's an electrician)—try to work the knot out for me. He tried hard for nearly 10 minutes, but I couldn't even feel it. I've had countless deep tissue massages that had no effect on my lower back. I also tried blind massages, in which a blind masseuse looks for knots inside your body because they are supposed to be more "in touch" with what ails you and are able to find knots that nobody else could. Well, my back was blind to their touch. I've had people massage it hard with the tip of their elbow, and had tons of people walk on my back. One time, I even had a ballerina stand on just that part of my back on her tippy toes. Nothing, nothing, and still nothing. I mean, don't get me wrong, my back was constantly in a lot of pain—but after 15 years of non-stop discomfort, I was practically immune to any sort of touch or pressure in that area of my body. I had reached a point where I was no longer able to relieve some of the pain by self-massaging, and the only thing that kept me going all these years is stretching. I stretched every day, for as long as I could, whenever I could. That is, until I discovered the solution below. When I did, it practically brought me to tears. I feel like if any section of this book will change someone's life for the better, it will be this one. I can honestly say that there is probably no other chapter in this book that I am as proud and grateful to write for you as this one.

So now that you know what my lower back pain was like, let me see if I can help you out. If I know mogul skiers at all, and I like to think that I do, then I know their pain. Because I experienced it myself. I've lived with it for nearly two decades. Hopefully, my persistent testing of various treatments will mean that you will not have to suffer the same fate. It seems that almost all of the former mogul skiers that I talk to experience and complain about some sort of lower back pain which never goes away. Typically, mogul skier pain has four main characteristics:

1. It does not stem from a ligament damage.
2. It does not stem from spinal damage.
3. Constant knotting of the lower back muscles.
4. It is a deep, muscular pain that never goes away, not caused by weak abdominals.

Does this sound like you? If so, then the very next treatment you should try is Active Release Techniques (ART). Active release techniques involve working with a certified doctor who combines assisted stretching (usually in ways you cannot stretch yourself) with targeted deep pressure on the associated knots. The combination of these two seemingly mundane strategies is utterly amazing! The first time I had ART done on me, the doctor found a knot that was as large as a kiwi and as hard as a walnut on my upper hip flexor, about half way between my belt and my rib cage. I hadn't even known it was there! He then turned me to my side and dug in his strong hands as hard as he could. While that was happening, he made me move my top leg and top arm as far backward as I could, in order to stretch the muscle while he pressed on it. The pain was pretty intense, but let me tell you the relief that I felt from those few minutes changed my life. The relief was instantaneous. And my energy skyrocketed the very next day! All these years I thought the source of my pain was in my lower left back strap, but the vast majority of the energy vampire that has plagued me for so long was in this hard-to-reach area. Even though I could have technically reached this area myself, there is no way I would have been able to get the knot out like he did. To this day it still remains the worst knot that he's ever seen.

After that first day, I was immediately hooked. I still go to ART therapy twice a week because my injuries are so deeply imbedded. My doctor always says, "We have to peel back the layers one at a time." He has indeed healed me, one layer at a time, and every single time I get a little bit of my life back. Knots that he gets out using this technique stay gone! For days at a time! He also adds in quick chiropractic adjustments after releasing my knots, which gives me days of relief—as opposed to the usual 45 seconds or so of relief I would get from self-massaging or regular chiropractic.

IMPACT, INJURIES, AND HOW BEST TO DEAL WITH THEM

My knots usually come back in different places now, but I like to think of it as a game of "whack-a-mole," until finally none are left. I really couldn't be happier with this technique—nothing else that I have tried has even come close. I even tried the Chinese version of this technique when I lived in China, and the doctor there was very thorough and could relieve my pain in largely the same way. Although I didn't spend enough time with the Chinese doctor to heal me, it was actually him who led me to find this method here in the United States. Although in China, the doctor would follow up a session with cupping, which made it even better.

SOLUTION RATINGS:

Standard Massage
- Short term effectiveness = 2
- Long term effectiveness = 0
- Recovery time = 0
- Medical costs = 2

Blind Massage
- Short term effectiveness = 3
- Long term effectiveness = 0
- Recovery time = 0
- Medical costs = 2

Deep Tissue (Thai) Massage
- Short term effectiveness = 4
- Long term effectiveness = 0
- Recovery time = 0
- Medical costs = 2

Acupuncture
- Short term effectiveness = 1
- Long term effectiveness = 4
- Recovery time = 0
- Medical costs = 4

Dry Needling
- Short term effectiveness = 2
- Long term effectiveness = 4
- Recovery time = 0
- Medical costs = 4

Cupping
- Short term effectiveness = 7
- Long term effectiveness = 3
- Recovery time = 0
- Medical costs = 2

Hot Rocks
- Short term effectiveness = 1
- Long term effectiveness = 1
- Recovery time = 0
- Medical costs = 2

Chiropractic
- Short term effectiveness = 1
- Long term effectiveness = 1
- Recovery time = 0
- Medical costs = 1

Active Release Techniques (ART)
- Short term effectiveness = 7
- Long term effectiveness = 7
- Recovery time = 0
- Medical costs = 2

ART + Chiropractic
- Short term effectiveness = 8
- Long term effectiveness = 8
- Recovery time = 0
- Medical costs = 3

ART+Chiropractic+Cupping
- Short term effectiveness = 10
- Long term effectiveness = 10
- Recovery time = 0
- Medical costs = 4

As mentioned above, there was one time I managed to get a bulged disc in my back. Unfortunately, over the years and with the number of injuries I've had, I can't even remember how I got it. What I do know is that I was living and going to school in Boulder, CO, at the time, and that it was the absolute worst years of my life for back pain. Not only did I have the aforementioned chronic back pain I've always had, but I had a bulged disc on top of it. Being a poor college kid at the time, and already heavily in debt from paying for my skiing career, I begrudgingly sought out professional help. The decision didn't come lightly, however. It came after I collapsed on a staircase because I couldn't feel my legs, and a buddy of mine had to physically assist me as I walked back to my dorm room. I decided that if it was bad enough that I couldn't walk, it was probably time to go to the doctor.

At the time, I had no money, no room on any of my credit cards, no insurance, was WAY too far in debt to take out another personal loan, and in the middle of my semester at college. Getting a surgical procedure to fix my back was simply out of the question, regardless of whether I could walk or not. So with a little research and some helpful pointers from some strangers, I stumbled upon a tiny alternative medical office that employed a little-known medical technique that seemed viable to my engineering mind. The concept was simple enough. Physically my bulging disc was nothing more than a piece of cartilage and soft tissue that was spilling out of my spine from between my vertebrae. Therefore, if I was able to somehow separate the vertebrae for a long enough period of time, the resulting negative pressure would "suck" the bulging disc like a vacuum back into the spine where it belongs. It made sense to me, so I tried it.

The treatment is called Decompressive Traction System, or DTS for short. At $150 per treatment, it wasn't exactly cheap for a poor college kid, but I forked over what little money I had left on this unproven system. The doctor took me back to what could only be described as a torture table, fully equipped with arm, feet, waist, torso, and neck straps. The table might have given a normal person cause for concern, but I was in so much pain I simply shrugged and hoisted my hell-bent carcass upon the futuristic torture table and hoped for the best. Then he strapped my waist with something very similar to a weight-lifter's belt, and clipped a metal carabiner onto it, which was attached to end of the table with a metal cord. He strapped a similar device to my upper waist, just above where my bulged disc was, and attached that to the head of the table. Both of the harnesses began pulling my body in different directions, powered by automated winches on either end of the table.

At first, I must admit that I was not completely convinced that this doctor was not out to kill me, but it hurt so good, I didn't care! The process took about a half an hour or so, and the doctor came back in the room every 5 or 10 minutes to check on me and increase the pull a little bit more. When it was all over, he laid me down on a simple table and let me ice my back for another half hour. The procedure was fantastic for loosening up my rock-hard lower left back muscle, and it was worth it to me just for that. I did three treatments in all—and I even convinced him to do it on my neck for two of those times, and that was almost as good as the lower back part! I honestly don't think I could've ever come up with another $150 for a fourth visit no matter what I did, because I was already so far behind on my payments from the first three visits that I would've had bill collectors calling me. Lucky for me, three visits were all I needed. I honestly wanted more, but hey, I don't have a bulged disc anymore! The treatment was the best thing I ever found, other than ART therapy. It helped my specific pain so much that I even vowed to one day buy a table like that for myself, but ART therapy has helped so much, that I don't really need DTS anymore. It's still the best option for a bulged disc, though!

SOLUTION RATINGS:

Decompressive Traction System (DTS)
- Short term effectiveness = 8
- Long term effectiveness = 10
- Recovery time = 1
- Medical costs = 4

DTS + Icing
- Short term effectiveness = 9
- Long term effectiveness = 10
- Recovery time = 1
- Medical costs = 4

NECK PAIN

I have suffered from neck pain almost as long as I have suffered from back pain, except that my neck pain was on the opposite side of my lower back pain. The knots would occur and condense on the right side of my neck, so they were in a constant state of tug-a-war with the knots on the left side of my low back. The result was a spine that was constantly out of alignment, which meant that chiropractic work did no good because my muscles were pulling so hard on either side of my spine that it snapped out of alignment and hurt again before I even got back to my car. As a result, I experienced headaches, neck pain, and loss of energy. I found that DTS worked surprisingly well for my neck pain, but ART works much better because it is so adaptable to any and all muscle groups that might be hurting that particular day. But I don't mean to downplay DTS's effectiveness. If I still want to really wrench on my muscles to loosen them up, DTS is my preferred method of relief. The scores below are similar as above, but specifically in regard to my neck pain.

SOLUTION RATINGS:

Decompressive Traction System (DTS)
- Short term effectiveness = 7
- Long term effectiveness = 7
- Recovery time = 1
- Medical costs = 4

DTS + Icing
- Short term effectiveness = 8
- Long term effectiveness = 8
- Recovery time = 1
- Medical costs = 4

Cupping
- Short term effectiveness = 5
- Long term effectiveness = 3
- Recovery time = 0
- Medical costs = 2

Chiropractic
- Short term effectiveness = 1
- Long term effectiveness = 0
- Recovery time = 0
- Medical costs = 1

Active Release Techniques (ART)
- Short term effectiveness = 7
- Long term effectiveness = 7
- Recovery time = 0
- Medical costs = 2

ART + Chiropractic
- Short term effectiveness = 9
- Long term effectiveness = 9
- Recovery time = 0
- Medical costs = 3

ART + Chiropractic + Cupping
- Short term effectiveness = 10
- Long term effectiveness = 10
- Recovery time = 0
- Medical costs = 4

In summary, I would just like to remind you that I am not a doctor of any kind, nor do I assume to know what is best for your given ailments. I am merely stating and rating my own experiences to the treatments that I have undertaken in hopes that perhaps they will help you, too. Please consult a medical professional before trying any of these treatments. I wish you the best of luck and a speedy recovery for you. I hope that if nothing else, this was an enlightening section!

*"One who wins without troubles gets victory.
But the one who wins with lots of troubles gets Glory."
-S. U. Haniel*

*"Life is not the way it's supposed to be. It's the way it is. The way
you cope with it is what makes the difference."
-Virginia Satir*

*"Expecting the world to treat you fairly just because you're a
good person is a little like expecting the bull not to charge
you because you're a vegetarian."
-Dennis Wholey*

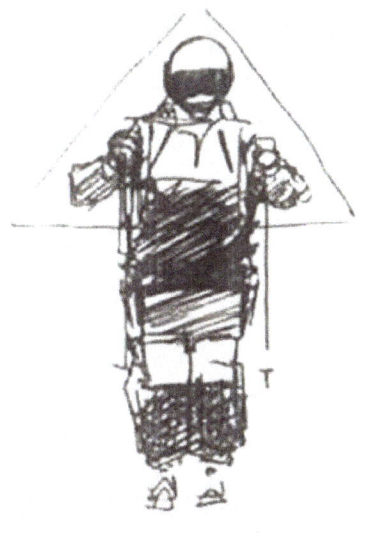

THE INVINCIBLE MOGUL SK1ER
PART 3
THE BOOK OF ICE

PSYCHOLOGY OF MOGUL SKIING
How Not To Get Burned By Your Own Mind

Artwork courtesy of John Dowling

CHAPTER 12
THE CAVE OF THE M1ND

*"Truth is often stranger than fiction,
but the strangeness comes from the clouds surrounding our minds,
not from the mystery itself."*
-Ronald A. Beck

Most coaches, in my opinion, don't do enough at the top of the course to ensure that you are in the best mental state of mind before heading off down the hill. Mogul skiing is one of the world's most dangerous sports, and we shouldn't leave as much to happenstance as we do. I've seen coaches send kids down mogul courses and off jumps that were terrified at the time, and shouldn't have been. Granted, there are times when you just need to overcome your fears by doing the thing you fear, but your coach should be there to make sure you are mentally prepared for that task. Each and every time. For as many times as it takes. Many coaches out there will try to force their athletes into difficult situations by guilt tactics, authoritarian demands, anger, and even complete withdrawal of their coaching services until you accomplish what they wish. All of these are more damaging than helpful.

The mind is like a cave under a lake. I see these coaches acting as if they were swinging pickaxes in your mind. If they swing a pickaxe haphazardly, like I often see happening, then it can all come caving in. As a result, that athlete feels belittled, demoralized, has a bad competition, or can even get hurt. Yet, I see coaches doing it all the time. They don't place enough emphasis on your state of mind as you are learning. They don't know how to settle your insecurities, mitigate your fears, all the while implanting in your brain everything that you need to remember to successfully accomplish your task at hand. You don't need a pickaxe in the cave of the mind; you need corks and plugs. In fact, you need to extradite all the pickaxe wielders out of the mind before the framework of good "frame control" can begin to be built up in the mind of the athlete.

Coaches are not the only ones who can be pickaxe wielders, though. Pickaxe wielders can be anyone wielding fears, guilt, or subjugation of any kind. "Frame control," as I use it here, means that intangible interaction that happens between one or more people who "get inside someone's head," who control what they focus on. It is the product of strongly conceived expectations. In other words, "frame control" means the person with the clearest expectations of a situation usually gets those results.

The goal of this chapter is to help you identify, in your own life, all the potential pickaxes that are swinging about in your delicate mind so that you can begin to regain your own frame control. After that, you should be more able to work with a coach who can help you "plug" all of the remaining fears that leak through. Once you remove all the pickaxe wielders from your mind, you should only have to deal with the actual fears that arise from the present situation, without all the extra baggage imposed on you by others.

TYPES OF PICKAXES: (TYPES OF FEARS)

> *"Named must your fear be, before banish it you can."*
> -Yoda (Star Wars: The Empire Strikes Back)

PARENTAL FEARS

Parental fears are especially devastating to an athlete's performance. But usually, the fears that are the most hazardous to the elite athletes are not native to the athletes themselves. They are usually injected into them by their parents. In my experience, the athletes that do the best are often the ones who have parents with little or no fears that they impose on their offspring. So, if you were not blessed with John Wayne and "The Bride" from Kill Bill as parents, you will need to eventually build up strong boundaries to prevent them from infusing their fears on you. If your parents' fears have already made it into your experience, don't fret. Simply start by identifying that this is, in fact, a problem for you, then start to question those fears that were never native to you in the first place.

More often than not, parental fears tend to keep "re-emerging" in conversations with their kids. This is how we acquire them in the first place. The first step to expelling their fears in you is to question it or deny it the next time it comes up. You will often catch you parents off guard. Usually, they will come up with a counter-argument that will be difficult for you to reject, because they are your parents and they know you so well. Don't let this bother you either. All you have to do is keep questioning or rejecting the fears in all the following conversations in which they re-emerge. Eventually, they will begin to realize that you don't share or partake in their fears, and they will stop using them on you.

The beautiful thing about this method is that you don't even need a good reason to reject a fear. You don't really need a good explanation, either. Simply by rejecting it multiple times (usually about 10 times is more than adequate), you can separate yourself from ownership of the fear. It is enough to reject a fear simply by saying to the person who is attempting to impose it on you that, "I don't believe in that fear," or "I don't accept that fear." This is a powerful indicator to the other person. You can say, "I see that you are afraid, but I choose not to be, despite your fears." It is a very freeing feeling, and very effective as well. They are unlikely to re-impose that fear on you in the future if you say that to them. Again, you don't even really need a good explanation or reason for doing so. Simply rejecting it verbally at the moment it is presented to you is often enough to set you on a path to recovery from that fear.

Probably the most common fear is that bad things like injuries will happen to you. However, fear of injury will be far more devastating to your learning curve, and overall career as an athlete, than any actual injuries will be. Learn to transform "fear of injury" into "risk management," and you will be much better off. You can reject this fear simply by saying, "I am not afraid of getting hurt, because I am learning to manage my risks well." You must do all you can to prevent the continual injection of fears from those that are close to you. Over time, fears become more entrenched as the years go on. Eventually, they will become so ingrained in your habits that they will be impossible to get rid of. Identify and oust parental fears as early on in life as you can.

It should be made clear here that I am strictly talking about mogul skiing, and not about the fears your parents have of you walking down a dark alley at night, for example. There are some instances where your parental fears are good for you—but as a mogul skier, you will quickly become more skilled in the art of mogul skiing than they are, therefore you should learn to value your own opinions more, and trade in their fears for your own risk management ability. Once you learn to value your own opinions and experience more than theirs, their fears and opinions will become irrelevant to you.

BYSTANDER AND FAN FEARS

Fears tend to seep in through crevices in our mind that we thought were sealed. They can come from the most innocent of places, like from bystanders. An innocent phrase or comment from a bystander, laden with their own fears, can be enough to let those very same fears seep into our own thought patterns. Fears, after all, are contagious. They can leak like water through the cracks of our mental fortitude and into the cave that is our mind. They make it weak and brittle. It also becomes fertile ground upon which additional fears can take root. An example of this would be if a bystander makes an innocent enough comment to you while they are on the side of the course, perhaps saying that they "Would never ski this course because it is much too steep." Or maybe they ask you, "Why did they have to put the course on such a difficult hill? Aren't you afraid you are going to get hurt?"

Sure, you might try to blow it off as a meaningless comment, but inevitably, somehow the seed of doubt begins to take root. You start to question if the bystander's comments weren't all that far off point. "The course is kind of steep," you say to yourself. "It is steeper than the last course," you continue. "Yes, if they put the course on the next run over, I believe I would do better over there." Then, you try to fight the negative self-talk: "But this is where the course is, and I will make the most of it!" But now steepness, difficulty, and the fear of injury have crept into your conscious thought. Fear has leaked past your mental defenses, and into the cave of your mind. It is all you can think about: "Well, I hope I don't get hurt. If I do, I won't be able to make the most of anything. What would happen if I got hurt? What kind of injury would it be? What if my season comes to a screeching halt? What would I do then?" Now fear grips you, just as it did the innocent bystander. You begin to get angry: "Why would they build the course like this? They are so stupid!" Now you are tense. And being tense is where the majority of all injuries and mistakes come from on the mogul course. Forget about posting good results. Never mind having a bad competition. Consider yourself lucky if you get out of there injury free!

I have found that it is best to find a way to "tune out" all bystanders. One good way that many mogul skiers use is to listen to music while they ski. There are many different types of earbuds and earpieces that fit underneath the helmet without discomfort. There are also helmets on the market with built-in speakers that offer a similar experience. Earbuds are the better option in my opinion, however, since they physically get lodged into the ear which provides an added layer of protection from unwanted background noise. Plus, the ear flaps of your helmet will prevent them from falling out. In the analogy of the cave of the mind, this would be likened to putting a cork in that particular leaky hole.

The most effective method that I have found has been to simply identify the creeping fear as a foreign entity. It is important to consciously identify that the fear belongs solely to the particular fan or bystander from which it came from, and not to you. By doing so, you separate your consciousness from the fear. Fears can only take root in your mind if you identify with them. Disidentifying with them helps prevent them from getting into your tough patterns. Once you realize that the fear is not of your own making, you can give yourself permission to dismiss it and let it go. It will take some degree of self-confidence to do it, but it's really not as hard as it sounds.

The next best way to get rid of a fear that has accidentally gotten through is to use the Athlete's Advantage from Chapter 8. It tells us that when the going gets tough, talk to yourself. Don't just listen to yourself. In other words, if you tell yourself reassuring statements like, "It is fine, I've skied this course a thousand times before and I was fine." Or, "My training and reflexes are very good, and I have the skills necessary to ski this course well." That is how you "talk to yourself" as indicated by the Athletes Advantage. When you are listening to yourself, you can start to pay attention to small little negative thoughts, like: "I can't ski a steep course today because my shins hurt." Or if you start asking yourself a lot of open-ended questions like: "What if I do get hurt?" "Why didn't they put the course on the other hill?" "What kind of injury will I sustain if I fall?"

I find that I am most easily able to identify that I am falling victim to negative self-talk when I notice that I am asking myself a bunch of questions. Likely, you will be able to do the same. Then, that is your cue, and your opportunity to convert your thoughts into more positive ones. If you become good at it, try to reserve the entire time you are at the top of the course where everything that you say to yourself (in your head) has to be a statement, not a question. Questions are more likely to be negative and fear-ridden than statements are. After you get good at that, then you can start weeding out all of the negative statements and replace them with positive, reassuring ones. It is fine if you have a negative thought or statement cross your mind. They tend to be automatic anyways. Just as soon as you notice it crossing your mind, replace it with a positive one of opposing kind. An example would be like, "Wow, my shins and toes really hurt right now." = Negative thought. A suitable replacement would be, "That may be true, but once I start skiing and the adrenaline and rush of competition sets in, I won't even notice!" = Positive thought. It is very powerful to talk positively to yourself, and that IS the Athlete's Advantage.

EX-ATHLETE FEARS

Sometimes, ex-athletes (mogul skiers) will like to converse with you about your competition or their "good old days." These former athletes like talking to athletes about mogul skiing because they have had shared similar athletic experiences in their own lives but, for whatever reason, decided to stop. These individuals like to recount their past golden days with elite athletes who are capable of understanding the difficulties, the jargon, and all the nuances of mogul skiing. More often than not, however, I find these conversations to be a Trojan horse of sorts. These conversations usually seem innocent enough on the surface, but they can be riddled with fears that may strike uncomfortably close to home for you. This is because their fears are usually of a much higher quality, or "potency," because they once shared the same path as you.

For example, they may say something like, "Oh it's an icy course today, those bumps will never build-up enough for you to be able to control your speed… So be careful out there!" Not that we wouldn't be aware of such a situation on comp day, but the smugness, combined with the accuracy of the observation, and the "relief" she has that she doesn't have to ski this course, will often times be more than enough to get to us. Ex-athletes can be brutal in the things they say to current athletes. The best thing to do is to be inaccessible to them. If you can't be inaccessible to them, then try to curve the conversation back at them. For example, using the example above, you could respond, "Oh, you can't ski icy moguls? That's too bad, but a simple change in strategy is all it takes to ski them well. Are you afraid to ski all types of moguls, or just icy ones?" Notice the emphasis I put on the word "you" in that statement. You are consciously branding the fear back onto him and choosing to not share in it. Any time you can turn the tables on them, and send the fear back in their direction will be an added confidence booster for you, and at the same time, eradicate their fears in you. A little bit of their own medicine used back at them can often be enough to get them to back down or carry on. This is because they want to see you stub your toe, so to speak, because it will validate their own reasons for retaining their fears and quitting mogul skiing. They want to see if you, the athlete, can handle their inner demons and fears. At best, they are merely seeking insight as to how to handle their own problems and fears, and are looking up to you to provide them insight. However, if you are not careful to set up strong boundaries, you can become a magnet for potent fears from ex-athletes. So you have to be on the lookout for that. Finally, it is important to remember that it is neither your responsibility nor your obligation to entertain the demons of others. Mitigating your own fears begins with focusing your attention squarely on managing your own inner demons, and protecting yourself from those of others.

INNATE FEARS

Parental fears are often confused with innate fears, because we may have had them for most of our lives, but if we really stop to think about the true origin of many of our fears, we can begin to outsource their origins to the people they really belong to. By doing so, we disassociate ourselves from many of our parental fears, and thereby alleviating the responsibility to entertain said fears in our own experience. True innate fears are primal fears. Fears that we evolved to be afraid of, in order to improve our chances of survival, both as individuals and as a species. Innate fears are those particular fears that you were born with, such as the fear of:

- Death
- Embarrassment
- Loss of love
- Rejection
- Falling/heights
- Darkness
- Sudden loud noises

Luckily for us, many innate human fears are not really of consequences on the mogul course, such as loss of love, rejection, or darkness. Additionally, fear of death is not really a real concern in mogul skiing either—for the most part anyways. However, there is quite a substantial reason for fear of injury. Other than that, all we really have to worry about in the moguls is the fear of embarrassment, falling/heights, and sudden loud noises. Most of the time, sudden loud noise only happen on the mogul course at large events in which there are many spectators. Occasionally, you will encounter some bystanders that will try to scare you with suddenly yelling when you aren't expecting it, or using an instrument such as an air horn. Since the fear of sudden loud noises is hard-wired into our bodies, this one can be hard to cope with at times. I already mentioned in the previous section to tune out all bystanders as best as possible. This is one of the reasons why. Having earbuds in and listening to music of your own choosing is always a good choice. Another method that I use, which has been exceptionally effective for me, is to constantly be expecting loud noises or interruptions. Then, when they happen, they don't surprise me. Try it—it is easier than it seems. This is the same as the "Monitor" skill that we learned about in Chapter 11.

Fear of falling/heights can be difficult to overcome in the moguls. It is best dealt with by repetition of big jumps, and the constant honing of your basic mogul skiing mechanics. The more confidence you have in your ability to control the falling or control the heights, the less you will be afraid of them. However, if you have a naturally high level of fear associated with heights and/or falling, mogul skiing might not be the best sport for you to pursue.

I see the fear of embarrassment holding a surprising number of athletes back from achieving their true potential. Granted, sometimes they are also afraid of getting hurt, but more often than not, they are afraid of looking stupid in front of their friends and peers. Mogul skiing is a difficult sport. It requires countless failures before it grants you much success. It is important to realize this, because the more you are willing to fail, the more you are able to achieve. In other words, the thicker skin you have, the more opportunities for success you can give to yourself. To aid you in overcoming the fear of embarrassment, try to find at least one other person on the team who puts the desire to learn and improve their mogul skiing ability above the fear of embarrassment, and make friends with them. Use each other to push and encourage one another. This type of friendship is most important when you are trying something that you may actually fail at doing. Combined with your small support group of friends, the more you can distance yourself from the fear of embarrassment by trading it in for the chance at success, the less fear you will have.

Many schools of thought teach that you need to face your innate fears head-on. Although, speaking as someone who has actually had to face most of his fears head-on, I want to tell you that I believe that there may be an easier way. What I have experienced is that over time, we are all confronted with many lesser fears in the same category as our greater ones. It is important to face those lesser fears and problems with good character and consciousness head-on and do what you can to face that particular fear. Think of it like a step ladder: work your way up to the bigger fears by conquering incrementally larger fears, but by first starting with the smallest ones. Once you have acquired confidence through the successful handling of your lesser fears in life, you can use that as momentum to conquer your greater personal fears.

FEAR MANAGEMENT

It's not fear; it's risk. My advice is to completely ignore the fears of others, and discard them without a thought. Repeatable victory is achieved through careful analysis of the lowest risk method in which winning is a realistic possibility. In other words, there is a risk vs. reward strategy. This not only exists in mogul skiing, but is prevalent amongst all the top competitors. The tougher the competition is, the more risk one will need to take on in order to win. Therefore, someone who thinks like this does not take on unnecessary risk when one does not need to. They only take on as much risk as they think they need to win, no more. This is how to manage fears as well, by managing risk, and by ignoring the fears of others, thereby extracting the pickaxe wielders in the cave of your mind. If the risk degree required to win is too high, and you do not need to compete, then don't. Why risk getting hurt when there might be a less risky way to acquire all the points you might need in the next competition? Mogul skiing is a brutal sport on the body, and you need to take as good of care of it as you can. Compete with a strategy in mind. Don't do every competition out there. Learn to compete in the ones that are most likely to give you the most points, with the least risk. Manage the unnecessary dangers you expose yourself to, as well as the necessary ones.

Winning is like a poker game. Fears and risks are your poker chips. Bet too little, and you could blow the hand; bet too much, and you could be out for the rest of the game. The better your fear and risk management, the better your chances are of winning and continuing to win. The tougher the competition, the higher the stakes. The higher the stakes, the more careful risk management strategy you will need. The better your risk management strategy is, the bigger the bets that you can make, and the tougher the competition that you can win. Many a poker game is lost by a person who starts with the most chips and throws them away by betting on every hand, or by betting in an undisciplined manner. A good poker player doesn't place a huge pile of chips on every bet either. It is the same for mogul skiing. Fear and risk management are the key to a long and successful career in mogul skiing.

> *"Indeed, no one can thwart the purposes of your mind --*
> *For they can't be touched by fire, steel, tyranny,*
> *slander, or anything."*
> *-Marcus Aurelius, Meditations, 8.41*

> *"When you are able to create a lonely place*
> *in the middle of your actions and concerns,*
> *your successes and failures slowly can lose*
> *some of their power over you."*
> *-Henri J.M. Nouwen*

CHAPTER 13
MEDITAT1ON

*"Your vision will become clear only when
you look into your heart.
Who looks outside, dreams.
Who looks inside, awakens"*
-Carl Jung

INTRODUCTION

This section is intended for those who want to understand the basics of meditation, and what it can do for their mogul skiing mentality. This is not intended to be an advanced training on the subject, however. It is intended to only introduce meditation and its calming principles to athletes, so that they may analyze it, use it, and then seek further instructions in the future. You might want to visit the "Further Learning" section at the end of this chapter if you would like a suggestion on where to start.

HOW TO MEDITATE

When left on their own, thoughts run like a frantic, sporadic monkey, whipping through the jungle. It is surprising just how little control we have over our thoughts when we stop to think about it. How many things have you thought about today that actually came from you consciously deciding to think about them? Conversely, how many different thought patterns came into your mind accidentally? For example, if someone cut you off on your way to work, did you make a conscious decision to evaluate how their driving affected everyone on the road, or just you? How quickly did your thoughts catapult straight into blame without a single thought of the bigger picture? In fact, most of our thoughts are like that. The people who can consciously control what they think about, with consistency, are the most level-headed. They do not let their productive thought patterns get distracted by happenstance. Most of us, however, are unable to control our own thought for even 45 seconds at a time! If you doubt this, just try to do a simple experiment. Put this book down and try to hold your mind still for just 45 seconds. Just be still, silent and don't think about anything at all for 45 seconds.

...

...

...

Welcome back! And congratulations on doing what very well may have been your very first meditation exercise! So, how did it go? What happened? Well, if you are like most people, chances are you weren't able to keep your mind free and clear of all thoughts for the entire 45 seconds. Our thoughts have a way of crawling in from the back door, even when we don't want them to. They pop-up in our minds, even when we are actively trying to keep them out. Fears and worry can be especially invasive thought patterns. Even though we consciously don't want them in our minds and try not to think about them, they always find a way to re-emerge in our thought patterns. This is why the Chapter 12: The Cave of the Mind gave so many examples of how to free yourself from all of the different types of fears that we are constantly surrounded by. The fewer fears we have, the more control we can have over our own minds.

Most likely, as you read this book, your thoughts are like a wild monkey jumping from thought to thought, and then back to what you are reading. You need to practice letting your unsolicited thoughts go without entertaining them as they pop up in your mind. The key to accomplishing this is to realize that the thoughts WILL come into your mind from ANYTHING other than what you want to be thinking about. Consciously, acknowledge to yourself what your intended thought parameters are, and then simply bat away any thoughts that come into your mind that don't meet those parameters. Bat them away and simply let them go. Don't think about them, don't even attempt to entertain them; just let them go. You may find it helpful to close your eyes...take a deep breath and exhale slowly and completely. At the same time, let all the "wild monkeys" (thoughts) go. Don't judge them or attach any feelings to them, just let them go, stay in the present moment, while freeing yourself of thoughts. With a blank mind, relax and stay without thoughts for as long as you can. Then, when you are ready, breathe them back in ("the monkeys" or "the thoughts"); the faster they are "whipping through the jungle," the deeper and harder you must breathe in. Breathe them back to you like the whole world/space/time is getting sucked in by your breath.

Then hold your mind still, wrap it up and hold it tight but gently, like a frantic puppy, transferring your calmness to him by being relaxed, being still, being present in the moment. Then breathe it out again. Letting it go, just a little less frantic, until you breathe it back in, and calm it down some more, repeating the process until your mind no longer feels the need to run rampant through the jungle, but stays by your side and obeys your command. This is how you gain control of your mind and your thoughts. It's not an immediate process; it takes some time, some focus, and some techniques. This is meditation. This is how you think intentional thoughts—by first controlling our thought patterns that are out of control. When your mind is relaxed and so are you.

Without the constant torment of your thoughts, listen to your heart, listen to your breath, and finally just "be" in the present moment. Be aware of all of your surroundings. Even with your eyes closed, be aware of what is to the left of you, and to the right of you. Try to imagine all that is beyond the walls of the space you are in. Now, with your left and right awareness expanded, try to imagine all that is in front of you. In the same breath as your left and right awareness, without losing their awareness. Then try to imagine all that is behind you in the same manner. Then do the same for what is below you, try to feel yourself "rooting" to the earth. Feel connected. Then try to increase all that expanded awareness, the perimeter, all of it, left, right, front, and back awareness to above you for as far as you can. Just "be aware" and "be present" in the moment. Try to expand the perimeter by which you expanded your awareness every time you meditate by a little bit each time. That is all meditation is.

You will realize a calming sensation by doing this exercise. Not to mention I find that after I meditate for at least seven minutes, it is like I just awoke from a good nap. It is very rejuvenating to relieve your mind of thoughts. I usually find that about 20 deep breaths are enough to calm me down even when I am really upset. The most difficult thing is not the calming down itself, but actually forcing yourself to take those deep breaths when your mind is racing and you are impatient. You might want to do as

I do, and count to three as you breathe in to start with, and match it as you breathe out, then breathe in to a four count, and match it on the way out. Do this all the way up to a 20 count and maintain that for as long as you want to meditate. Then, to come out of meditation, simply reverse the process. On your next breath, breathe into a 19 count, match it on the way out, and so on, until you get down to your normal breathing rate again (which for me is about a 3-4 count). One important thing to realize is that you don't have to follow each thought in your mind like a dog following every smell they encounter during their walk. Recognize the thought, realize it's there, and then let it go without attaching any emotion to it. One of the greatest spiritual men in history was Lao Tzu, the founder of Taoism; he put it this way:

> *"To manage your mind, know that there is nothing,*
> *and then relinquish all attachment*
> *to the nothingness."*
> *-Lao Tzu*

Another great hero likes to think of it this way:

> *"I have a system of ridding my mind of negative thoughts.*
> *I visualize myself writing them down on a piece of paper.*
> *Then I imagine myself crumpling up the paper,*
> *lighting it on fire, and burning it to a crisp."*
> *-Bruce Lee*

Meditation is merely detaching yourself from your thoughts. Simply be an observer. As you watch new thoughts come into your head, imagine putting a box around them and then closing up the box and simply put it aside and out of your perspective. As more and more thoughts come into your mind, simply capture them with boxes and stack them away. Don't entertain the thoughts. As you stack more and more thoughts away, just imagine that they are like all of your stuff going into storage before a big move. It is all still there, safe and sound if ever you should need them, but you are now detached from them. Then after you put a lot of thoughts into your boxes, as soon as they come into your mind, you will notice that they will begin to emerge less frequently. Notice in between thoughts; there is a little bit of nothingness. This is what Lao Tzu was referring to in his quote. With practice, you can increase the intensity and duration of the nothingness. Simultaneously, you will increase the amount of rest you experience during your meditation. Some people get so good at clearing all of the thoughts out of their heads that they find themselves forgetting to breathe. You know when you truly have nothing going on in your mind if you are forgetting to breathe!

Meditation in mogul skiing is no more than the ability to quiet the mind and hold it still while skiing. At best we can hold only the things we are working on in the mind while we ski. Most of the time, however, we settle for meditation in mogul skiing to keep negative thoughts out of our head, by using the methods described above to silence the voice in your head when it is negative and transmute it into a positive thought. It is important to strive to not only remember the things that we are working on, but to paint them in a positive light in our minds while we do it. If we can hold the negative thoughts out via meditation, and then paint the things we are working on in a way that is beneficial to us, that is the best way to not only ski in a competition, but to improve ourselves in general. To do this, it helps to think about the thing that you are working on as "I am doing it this way because it WORKS better," or "I am going to do it that way because it SCORES better."

Sometimes, especially when I am thinking about my mogul method while I am skiing, I think to myself, "I am doing it this way because it makes mogul skiing EASIER." That is what I mean by painting it in a positive light. Try to stay away from telling yourself things like, "I will do it this way to make HIM happy," or "I'll do it that way because SHE wants me to do it that way." Those thought patterns detach us from all benefits to ourselves, and make our efforts less effective. We want to keep our minds as positively reinforced as possible at all times, so do yourself a favor and paint all thoughts in a positive light if you can.

On the flip side of meditation, we can enter the "zone" while skiing. Most mogul skiers know that of their "best" runs happen when they "just sort of zone out" or "are in the zone." Many times, they can't even remember the details of their run exactly. It "just sort of happened." It is surprising, but also usually a good sign to just have the mind go "blank." Many mogul skiers report that they ski their best runs when their minds go blank. Sometimes they don't even have a recollection of a run they just did. As puzzling as this sounds, more often than not, it appears that these are some of their best scoring runs.

Eckhart Tolle, in his bestselling book, *The Power of Now*, states that one should "die to the past every moment." Meaning that one should stay completely and totally in the present moment. Certainly, if a mogul skier cannot remember his run that occurred just a few seconds prior, then it may be said that they sufficiently "died to the past"—each of those moments while they were on the course, at least. Obviously, when mogul skiers experience this phenomenon, they are utilizing the massively popular technique as described in *The Power of Now*. This may seem like a far out there stretch to claim that mogul skiers are meditating on course without even being aware of it, but in the book *The Rise of Superman*, author Steven Kotler claims that is exactly what is happening.

So how does one "turn off" his or her mind in the moguls, exactly? Well, there are several approaches but the one that I use and have the best results with is simply to scare yourself. It is no coincidence why this is the very first step in my mogul method. You must scare yourself to such a degree that is sufficient for real danger to be present. "Real danger" is relative to the risk tolerance of each individual mogul skier, but generally, the concept goes like this: In life-threatening emergency situations, the shift in consciousness from time—and the mind-bound noise-making activities (talking to oneself)—to the present (the power of now) happens naturally. The personality that has a past and a future momentarily recedes and is replaced by an intense conscious presence. Very still, but very alert at the same time. At this stage of consciousness, whatever reflex is needed will arise naturally and without thought. That is why we scare ourselves in the first step of the mogul method, and also why our best runs happen without thought. It is hard to believe, but it's as real as can be.

It is important to point out here, however, that sufficient training is required to lubricate this process. For example, if you are physically incapable of doing the required response, then it will not happen for you simply because you can still your mind. In other words, if you don't have a skill practiced into reflex yet, it will not be able to come to your rescue when you are scared. This is why it is important to train so much. You need to transform the Mogul Method into muscle memory. Muscle memory is the avenue to which our reflexes are restricted. This is important because although we cannot directly control our reflexes, we can train anything we want into muscle memory. If our muscle memory is programmed well enough (by lots and lots of training) and becomes sufficiently fast enough, it can replace our default reflexes; whatever those may be. As a guideline, it takes about 10,000 repetitions (or 10,000 hours according to Anders Ericsson, Professor of Psychology at University of Florida, and an expert in human expertise research), to train that particular movement to become muscle memory.

According to Eckhart Tolle, the reason why so many people engage in dangerous activities is that it forces them into the "now." The "now" is that intensely alive state that is free of time, free of problems, free of thinking, free of the burden of the personality, where slipping away from the present moment, even for a second, might mean death. If you have ever been in a life or death emergency situation, like I have, you will know that it wasn't a problem. The mind didn't have time to make it into a problem. In a true emergency, the mind... stops, and something infinitely more powerful takes over.

> *"In any true emergency, either you survive, or you don't. Either way, it isn't a problem."*
> *-Eckhart Tolle*

This is the same reason why people can become capable of seemingly impossible deeds in true emergencies. In mogul skiing, we are faced not only with enough potential pain (from crashing at full speed) that we don't want to consciously think about, but there is also so much information coming at us from the different sizes, shapes, textures of moguls, which is complicated by speed, line, momentum variance, balance, plus our airs (which is a whole world in itself). Sometimes, our mind just plain gets overloaded and shuts off. When our mind shuts off, it has access to something greater. That something greater is the ability to process all of that information in a split second, and it's what keeps us alive.

Again, this is the reason why my first step to my Mogul Method is to scare yourself, because if you are thinking about it, you are handicapping yourself. Eckhart Tolle and other spiritual leaders proclaim constantly that being able to quiet the mind is one of the most powerful things a human can achieve. It is known in Eastern religions as enlightenment. The concept is also pervasive in modern pop culture as well, though it goes largely unnoticed by the vast majority of the population. For example, in the recent movie, *Avengers: Age of Ultron*, there was a scene in which all of the Marvel characters tried to lift Thor's hammer, but couldn't. This was because Odin, the "All-father" (basically God in the Marvel universe) put a spell on the hammer that only the worthy shall be able to lift it. No one, not even the Incredible Hulk, was ever able to lift it from where it lay. Thor gave the secret in this film that, "One must be able to hold the mind still, in order to lift the hammer." It is quite interesting that the same secret that all of the great mogul skiers use to formulate good runs is the same exact secret used by the "gods" to be able to wield one of the most powerful weapons in the Marvel Universe. Of course, it was meant that one must be able to hold the mind still, at all times, as does Thor—but hey, we are working in the right direction, aren't we?

PRACTICAL MEDITATION

Recently I was talking with some colleagues of mine about this book, and I was asked to explain why I had incorporated meditation into it. During the conversation, I realized that not a lot of people understand the benefits of meditation, or why almost all super-successful people use it, or even that athletes use it in the first place. So I decided to add an extra section to this book to explain the benefits of practical meditation from my own personal experience. Meditation is something that never came to me naturally—because I learned it so late in life—but after you read about my experience, I hope you will be encouraged to give it a meaningful try.

As a competitive mogul skier for over twenty years, I spent many of those years focusing on strength training and power-training my legs. Therefore, for nearly all of my adult life I have had very strong legs. I used to do reps at 315 lbs., and once squatted 405 lbs. I am not saying this to brag or to compete with anyone, but the reason this is important to my story will soon become apparent. As part of my daily training, wall sits were a very important (and difficult!) exercise. As athletes we regularly did five minute wall sits. Perhaps some of you can relate to that. As I got stronger, I would work out in the gym and could usually "grit-it-out" to about 12 minutes and 30 seconds. But doing that was excruciating, and I constantly had to put my mind on other things to take my focus off the pain and my shaking muscles. I would casually look around the gym and make up stories in my head about people I saw, or I would day-dream, or even read the funny pages in the newspaper. Anything to get my mind off the pain. One day I was feeling particularly "froggy," and I did a 16-minute wall sit! I was 21 years old at the time, and I was in my physical prime.

Years later, I learned the benefits of practical meditation from a very unlikely source: a juggler. Brandon Birchak was a high diver on one of my stunt teams, and in his spare time he was also a circus-grade juggler. Many nights we would just sit around and watch him juggle. He could juggle anything! And there seemed to be no limit to the number of things he could juggle. In awe of his uncanny abilities, I asked him how he was able to focus on so many things all at the same time. At first, the answer he gave was perplexing.

"Simple," he said. "I don't."

"What?!" I exclaimed. "But obviously you do. You have to focus to keep all of those things in the air at the same time."

"Nope," he said simply. "I just sort of let mind go blank. It's actually quite relaxing to juggle."

We ended that conversation with me no closer to the truth than when I started. But finally one day, a good old competition between friends dislodged one of the most powerful "keys" I've ever discovered.

One day, bored after a day of shows, we were sitting around in our condo, and we got to bragging like friends do sometimes. It wasn't long before we decided to have a little wall sit competition. Brandon was sure he could beat me, and I was positive I could beat him. Even though I was out of practice, I was convinced that my mogul skier legs would decimate this skinny diver in a wall sit competition. So we began. As simple as that.

I was expecting him to drop out at the four-minute mark. Perhaps five or six minutes, tops. But four minutes came and went. Then six minutes was a distant memory. Around 11 minutes, my legs started to shake. But Brandon was still as solid as a rock. Then 14 minutes approached. I began to sweat. Then 15 minutes came and went. Holy crap! I thought to myself. This guy is ridiculous!

I collapsed to the floor just under 16 minutes. But Brandon was still going. Not shaking, not sweating, just sitting there, staring at me like he was on a sofa watching TV. I couldn't believe it. How could I be defeated so easily when I had such a clear advantage? Brandon sat in a perfect wall sit position for a solid 45 minutes, but he looked like he could've gone longer if he wanted to. He didn't just beat me—he CRUSHED me! It wasn't even close! I had to know his secret. I pestered him for a long time about it.

"The answer is simple," he said. "Clear your head." There it was again! Not thinking. I thought to myself, "How in the world could that be so powerful?"

"Is it like mediating?" I asked.

"Yes," he said. "Thoughts take effort. You can't afford to expend any extra effort in something like this."

I was floored. Could it really be so simple? Well, being a very competitive person by nature, I couldn't let him beat me with such a simple trick, so I decided to try it out for myself. And let me tell you, man did it work! In less than 10 attempts, the key of meditation (and my mogul skier legs) catapulted my personal best all the way up to a full hour! That's a 400% improvement over my personal best from back when I was working out my legs everyday!

Just to let you know that it is ever-effective, I recently went to the gym for the first time in years, much older and way out of shape from my desk job, and tried out my wall sit just to see how I would do... and... 20 minutes! Right out of the gate, weak, out of shape, and I beat my personal best from my mogul skiing days by 25% just by using this one simple technique. So how is that for practical meditation?

The meditation technique that I learned as a stunt man has stuck with me all these years, and I have used it to great success to increase my running speed, distance, endurance, focus, and just about everything else I do. Just to make sure that you don't feel left out, I intentionally built this power right into my mogul method that you just learned about. Step 1: Scare Yourself is the technique that I use when I ski to shut my brain off, and introduce meditation into my mogul skiing! It was done very intentionally. Now you too know the secret!

PRACTICING PRACTICAL MEDITATION

There are three different forms of the zone, or "flow states," if you will. The first flow state (Level 1) is derived via circumstances, or environment, and is mood dependent. As fickle as it is, most of us are familiar with this one. It is when everything just seems to be going our way and we can't help but win at whatever we are doing. It feels great at the time, but is difficult, if not impossible, to replicate on command. The second flow state (Level 2) is intentional. It is derived by blocking out all thought, except for positive thoughts when you really need them. It is far more difficult to hone and hold onto the Level 2 Flow state at first, but it is much more powerful once you learn to harness it.

You can practice this level of flow while doing your everyday training exercises. The more strenuous the better. It is especially useful and produces outstanding results when it comes to endurance exercises such as running, or wall sits like I mentioned earlier. To practice it, simply close your eyes, shut out all sense of time, and remove all thoughts from your brain. Don't let any thoughts enter your brain at all. If a thought pries its way into your consciousness, simply acknowledge that it is there and then let it go as soon as possible. And that's it. Remain in that state of mind for as long as you can. When the pain of your exercise pulls you out of the zone, or when negative thoughts occur—such as "this sucks" or "when is this going to be over?"—just refocus your mind and re-enter the zone. It is a muscle like any other in your body, and it needs to be worked out like one. You will inevitably have weak spots as well as moments of strength, so keep practicing until all the moments in your exercise are strong, controlled moments of focus in the zone.

    Meditating like this while doing strenuous exercise can actually recharge you, and that is the point. Thoughts take energy, and if you don't think, you have more energy to apply to your exercise. This is where my extra strength and will power came from when I took my wall sits from my personal best of 16 minutes to an hour. The third and final flow state, Level 3, is the just like the second level flow state, however, you do it with your eyes open. This is the pinnacle of intentional flow, because it most closely resembles the real world state of flow that you will need in competition. When you can sustain a Level 3 flow state on command, you are ready for high-level competition—mentally, at least. For feedback on how strong my current zone holding skills are, I like to write three extra columns in my workout logbook at the end of each exercise. I write L1, L2, and L3 at the top of each column. These designate the different types of the zone: Level 1, Level 2, and Level 3. Then after each workout, I write a percentage of the time that I honestly felt I spent in each respective zone. So for example, if I am running for ten minutes and I barely enter the zone (or do so via a Level 1 flow state), I may just put 5% or 10% in the L1 column and a 0% in the L2 and L3 columns. However, other times that I intentionally focus really well—like my hour-long wall sits—percentages were up around 80% or 85% but my eyes were closed, so I put these numbers in the L2 column, 0% in the L1 and L3 columns, and so on. Doing this allows me to track my progression of how long I am able to stay in which level of flow, and which types of exercises in which it is easy or difficult for me stay in flow. It has helped my ability to stay in the zone.

    So now the question you should be asking yourself is that if I could do an hour-long wall sit years after my strength training, with only 80% of time spent in a L2 flow state, what can you do in the peak of your training, with 95-100% of your time spent in a L3 flow state? Even more so, what will you accomplish if you bring that level of focus to your competition runs? One thing is for sure, greatness awaits! But either way, by applying this type of training to your workout routine, you acquire the ability to force the zone to your every beck and call!

> *"Peace comes from within.*
> *Do not seek it without."*
> *-Buddha*

> *"Sometimes just by sitting,*
> *the soul collects wisdom."*
> *-Zen proverb*

> *"Reflect on your present blessings of which every man has plenty;*
> *not on your past misfortunes of which all men have some."*
> *-Charles Dickens*

> *"When I started counting my blessings,*
> *my whole life turned around."*
> *-Willie Nelson*

FURTHER LEARNING

Meditation mechanics, purpose, results, and understanding:

https://www.youtube.com/watch?v=TcX-CBrF9m

CHAPTER 14
TAP YOUR 1NNER STRENGTH

"I took a deep breath and listened to the old brag of my heart;
"I am, I am, I am…"
-Silvia Plath

    In my 20 years as a mogul skier and coach, I've seen all types of athletes make it to the top. Some you expect to, some you do not. But they all have seemed to have a weird and powerful characteristic that goes largely unnoticed by most. It has been practiced by elite individuals for thousands of years. This weird but very powerful trait was coined by Todd Herman as "the Alter Ego Effect."

    Todd Herman is someone who has worked with over 10,000 high-performance athletes around the world, including 86 Olympians, pro athletes in the NHL and NFL, pro golfers, Broadway actors/actresses, high-performing CEOs, self-made billionaires, and even royalty. The world of entrepreneurs, high-performing athletes, and CEOs look up to Todd for his training and advice, which he learned by working with extremely high performing athletes like Olympians and professional athletes for more than 18 years. Todd says: "The very best athletes I was working with, the 'pros,' all left themselves on the sidelines." He goes on to say, "They all had a mask or alter ego they would step into, so the hard-earned skills they practiced and honed wouldn't be disrupted by the insecurities, worries, or negative self-talk they would carry around with their everyday ego. Instead, they would manufacture a 'new version' of themselves to ensure they had the greatest chance of performing at their peak levels." He developed a performance masking model of sorts that is useful to help us create and sustain our own, self-manufactured "Alter Ego Effect." For more information on the topic, I highly suggest you check it out for yourself, at: https://www.facebook.com/toddhermanconnect. It is good stuff, and I can tell you from my own experiences that he was on the right track.

Take for example Bo Jackson, one of the greatest athletes of all time. He played in both the NFL and major league baseball, and is the only person to be an All-Star in two professional sports. Todd got to speak with the living legend, and Bo said that "Bo Jackson" never played a down of football in his entire life. He said that if he took the Bo Jackson that his family knew, that his friends knew, and competed on the field, he would have never been successful. Because that Bo Jackson doesn't want to hurt anybody. He isn't violent, but the reality of it is, football is a violent collision sport. He said one day he was watching Friday the 13th and thought to himself, "What if I was Jason from the movie? A relentless, cold attacker… instead of ME?" Now he obviously didn't want to carry that type of personality off of the field, so in his mind, he created a space where only Jason lived. And he created a certain move to trigger "Jason" when he would walk out of the tunnel: he'd make a very deliberated heel to toe gesture with his foot, and when the ball of his foot would strike the turf, he imagined a blue shock entering his body, which was "Jason." Jason lived on the field. And if you've watched any highlights of Bo Jackson, there's no denying that he was absolutely relentless on the field. (Bo) went on to say that when he was on the field, his only mission was to destroy anything that got in his way. And as a running back, that is a core fundamental skill to have.

The way I like to call forth my inner strength is a little different from how Bo Jackson does it. There are several steps involved in my method, but they all happen more or less at the same time.

Firstly, I initiate the process at the top of the course or mogul line that I will be skiing. I stand with my skis pointed perpendicular to the hill and I look down my line. I try to internalize the entire run into a single thought or feeling. Then I close my eyes and lean heavily on my poles. Once the "general feeling" of the run is internalized, I jump up and down three times, stomping my feet heavily as I land. This gives me several benefits. The first one is that I feel the abrupt, sharp impacts of the stomps surging through my body, preparing my muscles and my joints for the series of similar sharp impacts to come. Secondly, I use it to gauge the snow conditions, trying to get as close to true high impact conditions as possible. Is it firm, icy, punchy, sticky, slow, or soft? Since I am not just "feeling" the snow, but jumping up and down on it, I can more accurately predict the current feel and give of the mogul course at full speed. This information is then used to calibrate and prime my muscles and reflexes for the type of impacts and rhythm (from my general feeling of the run) that they will most likely encounter.

Next, the increased movement and physical exertion warms up my muscles and increases my breathing. This process oxygenates my muscles in advance. As this happens, I feel my inner strength increase via a surge of energy through my entire body. When this happens, I can feel my breath get short and tight. My muscles begin to tense, itching for the fight to come. It is at this point that we must take considerable precautions. Calling forth your inner super-persona is no mere illusion or trick. It is an actual biophysical transformation that makes chemical changes in your brain. At this juncture, it's arrival is only partial. All of the power of your inner strength rising to the surface at once can be intoxicating, and like most intoxications it cuts off oxygen to the brain. So although the power is immense, it is unstable. Therefore, we need a way to stabilize it in for at least 30 seconds to get a good mogul run in. The best way I have found to harness this power is to measure my breaths, following a steady rhythm and counting each one to make sure they are equal to each other. This makes sure the brain and body gets the oxygen it needs for this advanced level of performance, thereby sustaining it throughout the run.

At this point I open my eyes and look down the course with my avatar seated squarely in my consciousness, but he is not fully in control yet. There is one more important ingredient required to kick my everyday consciousness into the back seat. Do you know what it is? If you guessed, "Scare yourself," from Step 1 of the Mogul Method, you would be correct. I push off out of the gate with both of my "consciousnesses" having one hand on the wheel. Then, as I am skating down the course, I exhale deeply, waiting until I scare myself, then immediately inhale deeply as I get stacked (Step 2), and right then is when my calibrated inner *Flash* puts both hands on the wheel, kicking my feeble everyday consciousness into the back seat. My inner avatar then skis the entire rest of the run for me.

Some of the pitfalls of acting in "super-persona mode" would be that you tend to be susceptible to being over-prepared for what is to come, or so focused on transgressions of the past, that you project into the future. It is important that we don't let ourselves slip into these thought patterns, because they are poisonous to "flow," or to being in the "zone." You see, by all accounts, the feeling of time slows or even stops when we are in the zone. The zone exists nowhere else other than our mind (which is where thoughts occur), and one of its main features is timelessness, so it is not much of a stretch of logic to deduce that thoughts of past and or future can dislodge you from the "flow" of the present moment. They cannot exist together. Try to stay focused on the present. Feel the breeze on your face or the clean, cold air in your lungs—do not entertain the thoughts in your head!

Conversely, some of the pitfalls that I have seen for someone acting in their "Superhero mode" is that they get too attached to everyone in their surroundings. Superheroes tend to have an easier time existing solely in the present moment than Juggernauts do, but it is easy for them to get too dispersed with their awareness, thereby drawing them out of the intense focus that being in the zone requires. They may disperse so much that they forget what they were working on, or where the difficult spots in the course actually are—or, sometimes, that they even exist at all. Fear of what others are thinking is a good example Superheroes being too dispersed in their focus. Whereas Juggernauts tend to get lost in the past or future. Wrapped up in dissecting their past or plotting the future instead of being present. You need to be able to let go of everything and everyone except the task at hand if you are to ski at your best. For more on Superheroes and Juggernauts, see Chapters 15 & 16.

It's great to be able to get in the zone, but in order to stay in that high-intensity space, you need to be aware of these common mistakes that can prevent you from being able to sustain it.

Bo Jackson invented a superhuman monster in his mind that he used to augment his strength, reflexes, focus and personality, in a much the same way I did. In fact it is similar to most professional athletes. The key is to find your own catalyst for bringing forth your inner strength that works for you. It is a bit of an iterative process, but once you find something that works. Keep it, and use it as a trigger every time you want to call it fourth. This consistency will help expedite the process. However, a word of caution; one of the most common mistakes that I see many people make is that they don't ever take their superhero "cape" off when they leave the mogul course. Being this alter ego, whoever your own enhanced version of yourself is, is simply supposed to exist for a very specific "all-in" purpose. Once that very specific purpose is accomplished, however, it's time to take off your cape. This is because, this inner superman or woman is simply not sustainable outside of the specified task(s), nor should it be. For example, just because your car can rev up to 8000 rpms doesn't mean you should leave it pegged at 8000 rpms all the time, does it? You need to survive, live, breathe, eat, and hang out with your friends and family. Just like the engine in your car, your alter ego needs a break from time to time as well.

It is also not good to overdo it with your Alter Ego, either. Similar to your car, it can wear out, and even break if you push it too hard, too fast, or too often. You dilute the power of your alter ego by taking him everywhere you go. The "Law of Familiarity" says that to which you become accustom, you do not value. Plus, you never want to train your super persona into thinking it is okay to do trivial or mundane things, like brushing your teeth or flossing. He/she exists for one purpose, and that is to accomplish that which your everyday persona cannot. They exist to channel your focus and energy to a very specific goal, all at once like a laser beam. Even Superman hangs up his cape at the end of the day. He doesn't return home after saving the world and do dishes in his Superman outfit, and neither should you.

We may see professional athletes interviews on TV in which they seem to be so nice or humble, when in reality, they may very well be some of the greatest athletes in history. This is because after the game, they hang up their cape, and they can be a real person again. The reason the niceness, genuineness, and humility of fantastically iconic individuals catches people off guard is because most normal people try to live in a constant state of enhanced character and expect the same from professional athletes, but that is simply not the case. What I am trying to say is that most people never learned to hang up their cape, so they automatically expect that no one else ever hangs up theirs either. The truly successful learn early on that it is silly to wear your cape around everywhere. They know that it is okay to relax when they are not in competition. It is simply not sustainable as a personality characteristic. Do not dilute its power by wearing your cape everywhere you go.

> *"If you don't design your own life plan,*
> *chances are that you'll fall into someone else's plan.*
> *And guess what they may have planned for you?*
> *Not much."*
> *-Jim Rohn*

CHAPTER 15
THE LEARN1NG PROCESS

*"There is no veil more opaque than ignorance.
It is the divine task laid upon each man to lift his own veil."
-Unknown*

COMPETENCY 101

First of all, let us understand how we learn to become competent. Competency is the basis for all our endeavors in life, and the core reason competition exists is to allow us to gauge competency in each other. Otherwise, our brain is programmed to gauge ourselves far more favorably than it does others by default. This is an illusion that is not beneficial to our species, which means that competition may be more important than it seems at first. This is because without competition to stratify us amongst each other, the wrong people may have an unwarranted influence over the next generation. In effect, this would weaken our species. Thus, as a pack animal, humans must compete with one another to separate the effective strategies and skills from the non-effective ones; for example, leaving the most effective athletes with the most reverence to pass on what they have learned to the next generation. The way we categorize competency is simple.

There are four main components of "competency" which make up the heart of the graph that I use later in the chapter to illustrate more advanced concepts. They are affectionately integrated from the "Four Stages for Learning Any New Skill" theory what was developed at Gordon Training International, by its employee, Noel Burch, in the 1970s. It has since been frequently attributed to Abraham Maslow (although the model does not appear in his major works). So as strange as this model may seem, it is based on science.

FOUR STAGES OF LEARNING:
1. UNCONSCIOUSLY INCOMPETENT
2. CONSCIOUSLY INCOMPETENT
3. CONSCIOUSLY COMPETENT
4. UNCONSCIOUSLY COMPETENT

As we practice more, we learn more. The more we train, the more skill we acquire, the more skill we acquire, the more competency we have. The more competency we have, the less we have to think about our cultivated activity. It is as simple as that. These four stages of competency listed above are merely a stratification of the major "quantum leaps" that we as humans can have in our learning process. As such they provide a good basis for the graphs below that show the similarities as well as the contrast between the two most successful psychological archetypes of competition. I am aware that there are many books out there that describe (usually four or five) psychological archetypes of humans, and most people are a blend of two or three of them. Or sometimes all of them. I am not talking about those archetypes. I am simply talking about the two most commonly successful archetypes there are amongst successful competitors. More specifically, we will learn how these personality types can be used as a powerful catalyst, which we already know from Bo Jackson, how powerful that can be.

Other than the quantum leaps in the for stages or categories of learning listed above, learning is largely a linear process. So in order to compare two very different psychological personalities (which have to follow a learning process that is more or less the same for both of them), I used a circle graph, split down the middle with each of the competency quadrants on either side. Later on in the chapter you will see how the different personality types deal with these learning stages. They both follow their own linear path around the circle. These different paths, or "a journey in competency," if you like, will be hence-forth be known as "Ways."

The previous chapter introduced us to the powerful methods that can help us improve our performance. They are meant to be for short-term goals; a presentation, competition, an event, etc. Your "Way" is intended to provide you a beacon, a lighthouse in the dark to provide you clarity and focus on the long term goals of your athletic, as well as professional careers. It is when we combine the two—the "who we are" and the "who we would like to be"—that gets us through the greatest tests of our lives. As a mogul skier, it gets us through our competition runs. Helps us brave new tricks, increase our speed, and enhance our reflexes and focus.

This powerful synergy is what we will be learning about in the next few chapters. It is so powerful in fact, that many people tend to believe that they can be even "superhuman" at times. This may sound a little silly, but practically all elite athletes do it. Therefore, it is worth talking about and exploring in greater detail.

As people grow from children to adulthood, they acquire skills and traits that they didn't have before. These new found skills and traits give us a sense of power and entitlement that we didn't have before, especially, when we make one of the "quantum leaps" in competency as previously discussed. As we begin to gain more and more skill, we begin to fancy ourselves as being vastly more powerful, qualified, or skilled than the "other guy(s)." In large part, this is merely ego and arrogance at work. But now I will teach you how to hone those negative and harmful attributes into beneficial ones.

First, let me explain why arrogance and ego are only natural. You see, our brains are programmed in such a way to value ourselves much higher than others. It's a survival instinct, and it has existed in us throughout time. The need to feel significant is, after all, one of the basic human needs, according to self-help guru, Tony Robbins. This means that, even if we don't feel we have significance in our lives, we will create it in our minds. Thus arrogance and ego emerge, even if they are hollow and unwarranted. The way we do this is by our own personal story. Our personal story is that nonstop inner dialog that we have with ourselves about who we really are, and why we are "always right" or "better." When our inner story pits us as a victim for some reason, we emphasize with ourselves more because we are better at focusing on the faults and wrongs of others, than our own. It is a self-narrated story which places us firmly as the protagonist, and everyone else in the world as lesser roles, friends, enemies, etc. Everything that happens in our personal story is narrated only as it pertains to "me." How does this or that affect "me?" We ask ourselves if it is significant to us, or not. It can be a "big deal" for someone else, or even a lot of people, but if it is not a "big deal" for us, we will pay it little mind. The opposite is true for things that are important to us. Even if no one else thinks that the happening is significant. In this chapter, we will learn about these traits that we all share, in an effort to both gain a better understanding of how we as humans work, but mostly to help us better understand our competition, and their weaknesses.

Happily, there are really only two main ways that competitors tend to cultivate their inner strength. The two most effective competitive personality archetypes are **Superheroes** and **Juggernauts**. The ones who associate most closely with the Superhero archetype are said to follow "The Way of the Superhero." Conversely, Juggernauts follow "The Way of the Juggernaut." While this may sound silly at first, I can assure you that most competitors adhere to one of these two life paths whether they talk about it or not. It's very common amongst athletes. After all, I derived this theory after being one, and hanging out with elite athletes for two decades.

Superheroes and Juggernauts have different core values and use different methods to achieve the same goal: to be significant, to be a success. What differs is what that means to different people. The ultimate success that any athlete can dream of is to be the best in the world. Olympic Champions and World Champions are commonly viewed with the highest prestige and significance in any sport. These titles are often fought over viciously from the highest ranks of a sport. Therefore it is only prudent to learn about the stratification of the ranks and how one ultimately can achieve this lofty goal. Additionally, since our athletic goals usually have a time limit on them before we get too old to achieve them, it is important to achieve them in the most efficient way possible. Therefore, the chart below can be seen as a "race" of sorts. The Superheroes vs The Juggernauts in a race against time as well as skill.

The "goal" here is to make it to the finish line first. The "finish line" represents the highest honors of the sport, the highest skill level, and the most renown. The "starting line" represents where we all start in life, with no skill or renown, ignorant of our own ignorance. Thus the section to represent those near and around the starting line is the Unconsciously Incompetent people, and the section near and around the finish line represents the Unconsciously Competent people. The rest of it breaks down as seen on the next page.

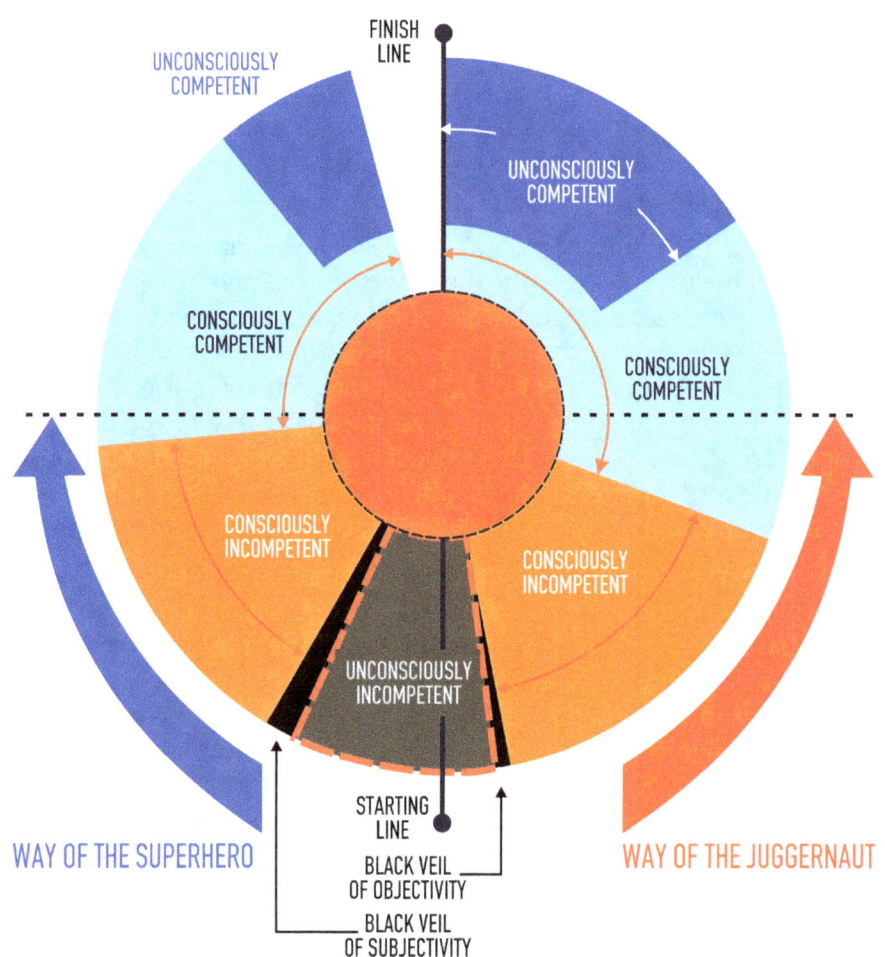

The Competency Wheel Chart

UNCONSCIOUSLY INCOMPETENT - The first stage is the default stage that everyone is born with or begins a new profession/career or skill as they start their training in any particular endeavor. This is the unconsciously incompetent zone. In this stage, you don't know what you don't know. Your ego may think you know, and it may also give you confidence. But ultimately, in this stage, you are just plain ignorant. It is very easy to be overly confident, because it is human nature to assume that everyone else is in the same boat you are, while you give yourself the benefit of the doubt. This, of course, is ridiculous, because there are people out there that know things that you don't know, and what you don't know can indeed hurt you.

This stage is the most difficult one to break out of because it is barricaded by the **Black Veil of Ignorance.** This is a psychological barrier that separates us from knowing that which we do not know. It can be a difficult psychological barrier to break through, because to do so, we must admit to ourselves that we are less significant than we are programmed to believe, even if it is only temporary. Only you can lift your black veil of ignorance, even though it can be painful to go from thinking you are slightly better than everyone around you (Unconsciously Incompetent) to Consciously Incompetent—meaning you finally realize just how few skills you actually have, compared to others. To admit that others are better than us can be the most painful step in the learning process, but a necessary one for us to go through in order to be able to find a mentor, coach, etc., and to reach our ultimate potential.

"Unconsciously Incompetent" is a natural stage of the learning process, and is a growth process for everyone. The most important thing to do when you are in this stage of learning is simply to graduate from this zone as quickly as possible. At this stage, even though you don't know what you don't know, you are 100% confident in your opinion. You are 100% confident that your opinion is the right one, because you have no evidence to the contrary. Hence why this is the source of your ignorance. This can be because you are in denial, or because you are simply that egotistical. However, as you begin to learn a little, and the more you are exposed to, the self-opinion evaluation abruptly drops to zero. This is a defining symptom that you have finally broken through the "black veil." Once the black veil has been lifted, you are no longer ignorant, and you therefore have graduated to the next stage in the learning process. In other words, the moment you realize that you have been unconsciously incompetent or unaware of all your incompetencies, this realization event marks the beginning of the next "quantum leap" in the learning process.

Once you are in the consciously incompetent phase, you become aware of just how bad your skills are, and what you don't know as compared to everyone else that you are competing against. It is a very scary time in our learning paths. Many people hate lifting the black veil so much that some people live their entire lives without lifting it. It is important to point out that many people, non-athletes especially, can live their whole lives without ever lifting their black veil of ignorance. Although it may seem tempting at times, it is ill-advised to point it out to them, or to try to lift it for them. The longer they have lived with it, the more likely they are to hate you for it, regardless of whether you are successful or not. Besides, they are the only ones that can effectively lift it for themselves. But not everyone wants to. Remember that.

Notice on the chart above how much sooner a Juggernaut will be confronted by his black veil than the Superhero typically would be. Additionally, look at how much thinner the Black Veil is on the Way of the Juggernaut than it is on the Way of the Superhero. There are two different types of Black Veils in actuality. One is the Black Veil of Objectivity, and the other is the Black Veil of Subjectivity. The Black Veil of Subjectivity is so much thicker because, as we discussed above, our brains are geared towards giving ourselves and our opinions the benefit of the doubt on all things subjective. If we believe that we are constantly right, it can be a vicious cycle to try to break free of in the learning process. More on this in Chapter 19: Your Opinion Betrays You.

For Juggernauts, on the other hand, who intrinsically value objectivity over subjectivity, it is a much quicker process for them to become aware of just how far behind they are. In other words, notice how much closer to the starting line the consciously incompetent stage of learning is for "The Way of the Juggernaut," than it is for "The Way of the Superhero." This is because it takes much less for a Juggernaut to be motivated into action than it does a Superhero. One who is acting in their "Juggernaut Mode" only cares if someone is better than they are, objectively. Since skills and talents are so much easier to stratify objectively than subjectively, this gives the Juggernaut an initial and powerful head start over the Superhero. What's more? Since it is one of the defining characteristics of a Juggernaut to want to dominate, they will be heavily motivated to improve their skills the moment they realize that anyone is objectively better than they are. This can actually be a deterrent for a Superhero. For Juggernauts, on the other hand, it may be all that is required for them to get motivated to brave lifting the veil of ignorance and the fortitude to stick it out through the consciously incompetent stage. One who is in their "Superhero Mode," however, takes more motivation because what people think of them and what they think of others is of much greater importance than it is for a Juggernaut. It requires more motivation to cut through the red tape of approval, and at times Superheroes must realize they may never get the approval they crave. When this happens, they must grant themselves their own approval.

It is important to know that anyone who has mastered any skill can often skip this stage entirely when attempting to learn a new one, because

THE LEARNING PROCESS

they have already experienced and been presented with a multitude of examples of things, they didn't know. They are open-minded enough to start at the next stage. In other words, they are consciously, ravenously searching for all of the things that they don't know. In other words, they consciously realize that they are incompetent before they start to even learn the new skill. Therefore, they are able to bypass the unconsciously incompetent zone completely, thereby speeding up their learning process. This is an important milestone when learning new skills like aerial mogul tricks.

Assuming they are willing to learn, they will humbly, yet manually, set their self-opinion level to zero as one of the defining characteristics of the consciously incompetent zone. You can spot someone like this because they tend to ask a multitude of questions, and they clarify rather than object to any new training. It is important to point out here that this might be the single greatest catalyst for developing mastery in any given skill—not talent, not even determination. One who consciously defers his opinions to someone who knows more than himself will learn faster and better than anyone who holds to their old opinions. Even times which may seem silly or obvious, it can be beneficial to hold your opinions in check. The fact that an individual can skip this phase entirely drastically decreases the amount of time required to learn any new skill because, after all, how can their opinion betray them if they consciously nullify it?

CONSCIOUSLY INCOMPETENT - In this stage, you begin to realize all the things that you don't know. You start to become aware of all the skills that others have that you don't. You also begin to piece together just how difficult it will be to learn some of those skills. In this stage, one begins to piece together a hierarchy in their mind of who is better than who, why, and by how much. At this stage, it is a good idea to choose role models, or other mogul skiers that have a style or skills that you want to emulate. It is a long road, but it's good to set your goals early.

This is a very difficult stage in the learning process. It is plagued by troubles, worries, and difficulties. In this stage, you are freed from the bliss of ignorance. It can be a rude awaking for most people, but it is a necessary step in the learning process to become aware of how bad you actually are, compared to the best. This is a necessary and important stage in the learning process because if you don't have an accurate assessment of your skills, none of your goals will be realistic. Without a realistic set of goals, you cannot plan out the road map to your success. Additionally, none of your achievements will feel adequate enough to you, which can be very discouraging.

An example of this would be a good skier who has had 10 years of skiing experience (but never learned how to ski moguls properly) joining a mogul team or a mogul coaching program. The skier's family all think of him as a great skier. He can ski all the black diamonds and rarely, if ever, falls. He is complimented often on his technique by friends, family, and ski instructors. He joins the mogul team with intentions of mastering moguls as well, because they are the "one last thing" he has to master. He knows he doesn't know everything, but with a few short lessons, he feels confident that he will be the best skier on the team.

However, upon his joining the mogul team, he slowly becomes aware of just how far behind his skiing skills actually are. He sees first hand just how mind-bendingly fast competitive mogul skiers ski through the moguls, and how big their jumps actually are. So he begins to train the moguls, feels good about himself, until a little 7-year-old girl blows by him effortlessly (I've seen it happen). He sees the mature athletes do huge jumps, spinning on three axes, landing in the moguls, and skiing as fast in the moguls as he can on the flats. In short, he begins to see things done on a daily basis that just a few days before he never even knew were possible. What's more, he begins to hear stories of athletes from far and abroad who can do mind-twistingly difficult tricks. Reality sets in quickly for certain skills, and slowly for others, as the months of hard work and training fall off the calendar. He has earned few of the skills that he sought on his first day, and more and more of his shortcomings become apparent to him, one by one. It is a very disparaging time. He may feel discouraged, fearful, weak, slow, and generally all-around inadequate. It is always a difficult time when one becomes aware of their shortcomings. The consciously incompetent stage of learning is the time when most people decide to give up. They feel if they aren't good at something when they first start, then they figure it is better to give it up altogether, before they embarrass themselves. The majority of people get to this stage and then stop, rather than choosing to put in the time and effort it takes to get to the next stage of learning.

It is important to know that every great athlete and great person has somehow managed to make it through this stage at one time or another in their life. Some people, like myself, go through this stage many times in life because they want to have many different skills. It is important to point out that if you complete this stage, or stick-it-out to the next stage, it will become easier the next time you go through it with your next set of skills. This stage becomes easier every time you go through it because we become less and less sensitive to the shattering of our ignorance. We tend to give little effort in order to protect our egos. We seek proper instructors faster, and are more coachable. Plus we are intimately familiar with how much work valuable skills take to learn. Therefore, we are not as easily discouraged. We are also more capable of planning out achievable goals and take pride in the smaller accomplishments as we achieve them. We also tend to be more determined to "make it work." This is because we know it will work if we just put in enough time, don't let our own opinions betray us, have the proper coaching, and think about the task at hand in the right way. Below is a quote based on this same concept from one of the rarest types of people in the world: An individual who possessed both worldly power and intellectual wisdom:

> *"If anyone can prove and show to me that I think and act in error,*
> *I will gladly change it.*
> *For I seek the truth,*
> *by which no one has ever been harmed.*
> *The one who is harmed*
> *is the one who abides in deceit and ignorance."*
> *-Marcus Aurelius, Meditations, 6.21)*

CONSCIOUSLY COMPETENT - This is the stage of learning, in which all your hard work and determination begins to pay off. It usually comes after you sacrificed and invested way more time than you originally planned on, but that is to be expected. It is also when you begin to appreciate and value those skills that were so hard to acquire. You can do things well at this stage of the learning process, so long as you set your mind to them. The major learning goal of this phase should be **focus**. Practice how long you can keep your focus on your body as you move it intentionally, precisely as a good mogul skier should. Focus on your jumps, on your take-offs, and on your landings. Stay focused and control every muscle intentionally as you take flight. Stay positive. Keep reassuring yourself that you know how to do things correctly, and listen to those thoughts. This is the stage that you know what to do, but you have to focus on it to do it. Just remember your training. Remember what you learned in this book, and hold it in your mind as you train. The longer and more often you can do that, the faster you will improve, and the faster those movements will be written into your muscle memory.

A consciously competent person, for example, would be someone who has practiced how to do a D-Spin many times on the water ramps, and has taken them to the snow. They may not have many on-snow D-Spins under their belt, but they have enough to have them qualified. They can do the trick consistently and always land on their feet. They may take a little longer before each jump to visualize the D-Spin before they go, but they can do it. They just need to remain focused and think about it in order to do it. In other words, they need to consciously implement each of the mechanics required to do the D-Spin, but when they do, they can do it competently. Hence, "consciously competent."

UNCONSCIOUSLY COMPETENT - In my opinion, there are two kinds of Unconscious Competence: physical and mental. Your muscle memory and augmented, mitigated, or nullified reflexes are your physical auto-competency assets. In the New Mogul Method, Step 2: **Get Stacked** is an example of a learned muscle memory skill. Whereas the choices you make in the moguls, along with your self-talk (see "Athletes Advantage"), as well as the ability to monitor, mitigate, and mirror our reflexes are all examples of mental auto-competency skills that we need to be able to rely on. Steps 1, 3, 4, and 5: **Scare Yourself, Relax, Be Patient,** and **Smile,** are all mental toughness traits built right into the New Mogul Method.

Your muscle memory is just a storage bank of information on how you move your body in any given situation. It is similar to your reflexes. When you have good mogul skiing technique programmed into your muscle memory, you don't have to think about a movement to make it happen. All you have to do is present yourself in a situation where those muscle memory moments were programmed to occur, and they will. This is exactly the environment Step 1: **Scare Yourself**, was designed for. It is also the reason Step 1 is at the beginning of the method. It serves as the catalyst that allows you to tap into your reflexes and muscle memory, which speeds up your reaction time, as well as stops you from overthinking. Additionally, it reassures us (when we get out of control in the middle of the course) that we can actually re-enter the New Mogul Method cycle. Simply by being scared, we begin the cycle anew from Step 1. Being scared, or out of control, therefore does not prevent us from getting back into good form.

Furthermore, for those of us who think too much on the mogul course, scaring ourselves serves as the "off switch" for all those burdensome extraneous thoughts.

Since mogul skiing is riddled with herculean difficulties, it is very hard to do consistently. Therefore, being able to ski moguls well in an unconsciously competent manner should be the ultimate goal for any mogul skier. Surprisingly, however, it is not necessarily the ones that are the most consistent at skiing moguls (in an unconsciously competent manner while maintaining perfect form) who are the best mogul skiers in any given competition. There are a lot more factors that come into play, and this is where it gets fun. In the following section, I attempt to explain in detail why the "best" skier doesn't always win—nor is he even perceived as the best by his peers or by the public. There is a skill that is far more elusive, fickle, and powerful than unconscious competency that we need to learn how to hone as well. There is also great power in learning how others perceive us, as well as the great power that comes from how we see ourselves.

"This is the very perfection of a man, to find out his own imperfection."
-Saint Augustine

CHAPTER 16
SUPERHEROES AND JUGGERNAUTS

"Superheroes don't often get their powers in one fell swoop.
It's like superhero puberty.
-G. Willow Wilson

Superheroes and Juggernauts are the two most successful competitive personality types, therefore it is important to not only understand how they learn, but how they value things and how they stratify themselves in the different stages of learning. As we've seen from the chart in the previous chapter, those who follow the Way of the Juggernaut would follow the chart from the starting line, counterclockwise around the wheel to the finish line. Conversely, those who follow the Way of the Superhero would start their journey of increasing competency as they travel around the wheel radially to the left (clockwise). The chart is broken down in the following pages into further detail. It is a representation of the paths or options one must take to become the best at almost any competitive endeavor. It is broken down into two main paths or "ways": The Way of the Superhero, and The Way of the Juggernaut.

This may all sound silly, but the number of people in competitive endeavors that follow one of these two paths is staggering. In general, *The Way of the Superhero is concerned with integrating and utilizing the strength of networking and social circles as an augmentation tool for their training and competitive successes. The Way of the Juggernaut is integrated with the desire or need to become completely dominant in a given skill or set of skills to have complete objective domination over their competition.* Fewer people tend to follow the path of the Juggernaut, but there is still more than you might think.

> **How to Use This Chart:**
> If you are new to the sport, imagine yourself starting at the bottom of the circle at the starting line, and then you would "walk" or work your way up the right side or the left side of the circle, progressing through the different stages of learning. So, the first thing you would do is choose which direction around the circle you would like to proceed.
> If you choose the Way of the Superhero, your journey would take place clockwise, otherwise, counterclockwise. Either path provides a different set of advantages and disadvantages. But, both paths share the ultimate goal of eventually leading one to becoming a legend at the finish line. However, their means, methods, and values are different.

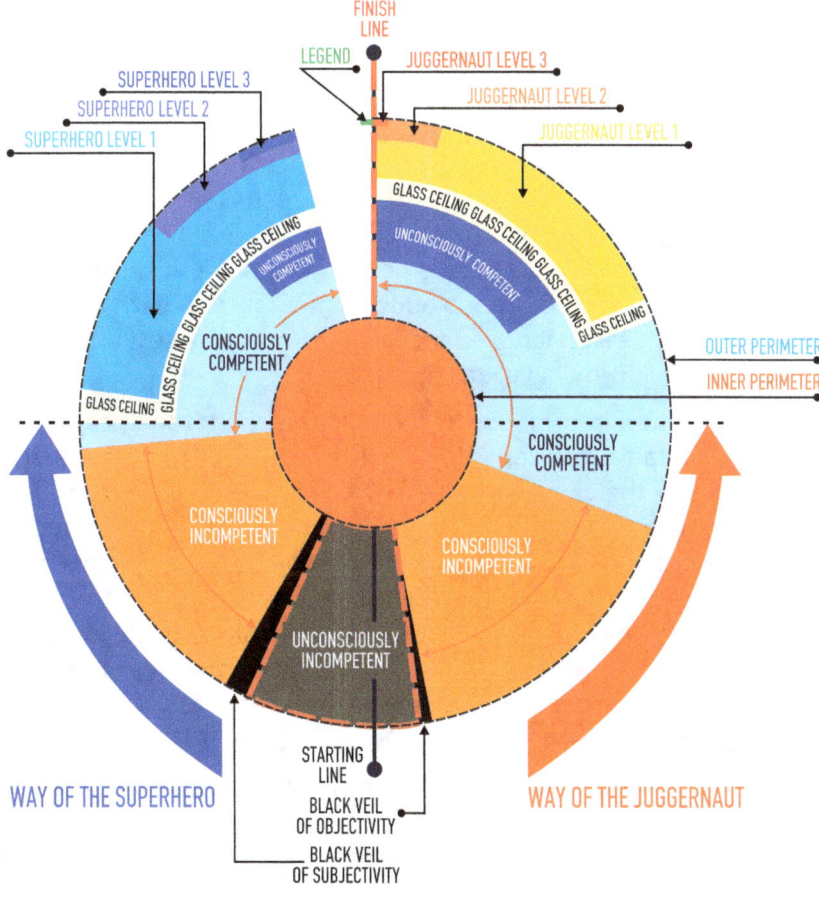

The Way of Superheroes and Juggernauts

If we are honest with ourselves, we have all felt the desire to be both of these types of individuals at times, and therefore, both traits live within us. In reality, we are all some combination of the two, to varying degrees dependent on any number of variables. We all have the desire, to be able to crush our opponents mercilessly into the dust (Attitude of a Juggernaut), while at the same time we want to be revered and feel significant amongst our peers (Attitude of a Superhero). The only difference then is the path we chose to take to earn the significance each of us desires. The path you choose is completely up to you, but it comes from your values. There is no right or wrong way, only a choice to be made. What makes you feel more significant? Is it the appreciation of your talents from your peers, friends, and family (The Way of the Superhero)? Or is it complete confidence knowing that you are the best at something, and being able to prove it (The Way of the Juggernaut)?

All of what we have learned so far as in the previous lesson on how we acquire competency is still in effect in this chapter. The main purpose of this chapter is to explain why and how some people—who even though they might reach the Unconsciously Competent stage—can still be significantly inferior to others. This is because there are those in the Unconsciously Competent stage who embrace their inner Superhero or Juggernaut as previously described, and those who do not. For competitive athletes, this is a powerful distinction, and it introduces a new sort of Black Veil that we will call the Glass Ceiling. It is a strange type of veil because it only appears just when you think you have it all figured out.

Notice the new information added onto this chart from the last one. It still depicts the same four zones that represent the four stages of learning on either side of the chart. However, now we see the different Superhero and Juggernaut levels added to it. Notice that built on top of the Consciously Competent and Unconsciously Competent sections are where subsections of Juggernauts and Superheroes exists. This is no accident, because one must have considerable skill to be qualified as a Superhero or Juggernaut. In other words, just because you follow the way of the Superhero or Juggernaut, doesn't make you one. You have to earn it through a lot of hard work and training.

But first, let us describe how to use this chart. This wheel-like chart represents a road map of the learning process and our skill levels as we progress throughout our entire careers, not in days or weeks. It's an exhaustingly long process. I am merely showing it in its entirety here as a visual learning tool. We accumulate the various attributes of each of the different sections or "zones" along each path as we mature in our mogul skiing career. Since most everyone will start reading this book at some point or another already in their mogul skiing career, one must first determine where one currently stands on the map. If one studies the map well and reads all the subtexts, one will be able to fairly accurately judge where one stands.

To begin with, one would first have to determine if their chosen path to success follows the Way of the Superhero or the Way of the Juggernaut. If you decide that your chosen goals more closely resemble the Way of the Superhero, then your path would be to the left-hand side of the chart, whereas if you are an aspiring Juggernaut, your path would be towards the right side. The theoretical beginning (for those with zero skills) for both paths is right in the center, at the bottom of the circle. This is the most ignorant and skill-less section of the chart, and is one of only two times on the chart where both sides are completely equal. However, almost nobody would really start here because most people reading this book (hopefully) has some skill and knowledge of mogul skiing. Therefore, it is only there as a reference. Now let me explain to you the differences between Superheroes and Juggernauts.

JUGGERNAUTS

> *"Success is my only mofo option, failure's not."*
> *-"Lose Yourself"* by Eminem

There are three distinct levels to being a Juggernaut. However, there are two distinct types of Juggernauts as well. The predominant and most easy to identify is the extroverted Juggernaut. The second and more difficult one to identify is the secretive-introverted kind. The former will attempt to crush everyone in an overtly dominant manner. The latter will attempt to conceal all of his means and methods to assure the greatest impact upon delivery of his strategic moves. It is also commonplace for a Juggernaut to use either of these strategies for different purposes. However, no matter the type of Juggernaut, they all tend to be very polarized (black or white) in their methods. Either they will attempt overt methods of dominance, or fly under the radar in complete secrecy, so to speak. In contrast, Superheroes will attempt a middle-of-the-road strategy and attempt to fit in more. Juggernauts can't help but strive for complete dominance.

If you are unsure about whether or not someone is a Juggernaut "flying under the radar" by attempting to fit in, or an actual Superhero, all you have to do is listen for clues in other categories of their life. If they boast about previous successes at completely dominating at something (anything), you are most likely looking at a cloaked Juggernaut. As mentioned before, there are several integral meters or "gauges" of Juggernauts. Three to be exact:

> JUGGERNAUT LEVEL 1 (JL1): Entry Level Juggernaut that has broken through the glass ceiling by cultivating the Way of the Juggernaut. These individuals are often contenders at the regional level.
>
> JUGGERNAUT LEVEL 2 (JL2): Second in skill, only to a Juggernaut Level 3. These individuals dominate their particular skill on a national stage, save for the JL3.
>
> JUGGERNAUT LEVEL 3 (JL3): Highest skill level Juggernaut there is. This person dominates their particular skill on a world stage often without dispute. It represents the ultimate realization of dominance that all Juggernauts aspire to.

JUGGERNAUT LEVEL 3

This is the very best person in the world at a given skill, trait, or sport. Outside of a major upset, the Level 3 Juggernaut is the person who wins every time. If Superman is undoubtedly the ultimate Superhero Level 3, then Darkseid (a god-like super villain from Superman's universe) is the Ultimate Level 3 Juggernaut. You can tell a Level 3 Juggernaut by the way they seem to break all the rules and still win. Using the fictional characters from above, Superman can fly at an incredible speed. In one movie, he flew so fast around the Earth that he reversed its direction of rotation. I don't know how fast that was, but it was pretty fast. He circumnavigated the globe many times per second. Now that is fast! It is hard to compete with. Darkseid, on the other hand, has the ability to teleport himself anywhere in the universe instantly. So comparatively, it doesn't matter how fast Superman really is. If they were to race, Darkseid would win every time, because he "breaks the rules." In other words, Superman is bound by the rule that he must physically travel from point A to point B. Darkseid does not restrict himself to those rules. He just "appears" at point B, wherever that may be.

Therefore, the defining trait of a Level 3 Juggernaut is their insurmountability on a world stage. They are insurmountable for one of two reasons: Either they are unfathomable, or physically advanced. This means that either their true nature or reason for their effectiveness eludes us, or there is a physiological difference, a physical advantage, that no one else has. Unfathomability can be either a little known secret applied in new ways, such as the Relax strategy from the New Mogul Method, or any number of psychological advantages.

One of the best known physical advantages in modern sports is Michael Phelps. Mechanically, he is built superiorly for swimming. Not only is he tall, but his wingspan is disproportionately large to his body size. Not only that, he is also double jointed in the elbows and knees, which gives him a mechanical advantage to every stroke. Furthermore, his size-14 feet reportedly bend 15° farther at the ankle than most other elite swimmers, turning his feet into virtual flippers. All of which combined to propel the athlete to an unprecedented 23 Olympic gold medals. Sure he worked incredibly hard and trained incredibly hard, but then again, so does everybody at the Olympic level. However, the determining mechanism for Phelps' Juggernaut-like Olympic domination that spanned two decades was his mechanical advantage. At least in my humble opinion.

EXAMPLES OF LEVEL 3 JUGGERNAUTS:

FICTIONAL CHARACTERS		
Darkseid	Juggernaut	Apocalypse

REALM OF DOMINANCE		
God-like powers	Unstoppable force	Consolidation of abilities

REAL PEOPLE			
Muhammad Ali	Ronda Rousey	Michael Phelps	Lindsey Vonn

REALM OF DOMINANCE			
Boxing	Mixed Martial Arts	Swimming	Alpine Racing

REAL PEOPLE			
Jim Thorpe	Dale Begg-Smith	Nikola Tesla	Mikael Kingsbury

REALM OF DOMINANCE			
Professional Football, Baseball, Basketball, & Olympic Champion	Mogul Skiing	Inventor	Mogul Skiing

JUGGERNAUT LEVEL 2

These are the major contenders for the sport, a small elite group of athletes that follow the Way of the Juggernaut, who have a reasonable chance of winning any competition. Similar to a Level 3 Juggernaut, a Level 2 Juggernaut is nearly insurmountable, except on a national level stage rather than a world-wide stage. While, they may be a little less consistent than a Level 3 Juggernaut, they are still a major force to be reckoned with. Unlike the Level 3 Juggernaut, where there is just one, there are usually several Level 2 Juggernauts per nation. In a mogul competition, there are usually about 5-7 Juggernauts who are true contenders in a national level competition.

Level 2 Juggernauts, as well as Level 2 Superheroes, are what make up the majority of National and World Cup Team members. They are also the next in line to become the next Level 3 Juggernaut. In the absence of the Level 3 Juggernaut, the best Level 2 Juggernaut present will likely have the most skill at any given competition. In a solid state of flow, a Level 2 Juggernaut can defeat a Level 3 Juggernaut. It is not common, but it does happen. However, it is more likely to happen then a Level 3 Superhero defeating a Level 3 Juggernaut. (To understand how a Level 3 Superhero can defeat a Level 3 Juggernaut, see "Leap of Faith" in the section on **Flow** later in this chapter).

Another potential giveaway that you are dealing with a Juggernaut is they tend to have a natural aversion to pandering, so it is rare to get any sort of compliment from one. But when you do get one, it can hold tremendous weight, because it is no small feat to get meaningful attention from a Juggernaut. Like anyone, Juggernauts can be trained to use pandering, but even if they can see the benefit in using it, they tend to use it very frugally. Even when they do give small compliments, they tend to only be objective in nature. For example, if someone had a bad competition, they might say to them: "It's okay, you'll do better next time," or "It was a tough course, don't worry about it." These sort of compliments are in stark contrast to the sort of compliments that a Superhero would give to the same person: "Hey, you were looking great out there!" or "Wow that top air was so amazing, I just didn't even see the rest of your run!" Can you see the difference? Superheroes tend to take to the skills of stroking other people's egos like fish to water. This distinction is important to understand; because Juggernauts are so egotistical and void of the idiosyncrasies of pandering, they are easy targets to be enchanted by it. This sort of manipulation can easily penetrate the otherwise impervious social armor that Juggernauts are renown for. They can more readily believe the lavish compliments bestowed upon them by the silver-tongued individuals as truth, because of their highly developed self-confidence. Superheroes frequently use this chink in the Juggernauts armor against them in a myriad of ways. So if you are one, be careful.

In the comic book realm, Ironman (Tony Stark) would be a good example of an extroverted Level 2 Juggernaut. Self-absorbed, egotistical, talented, and wildly successful, he spends most of his time alone, improving himself or working on something that he thinks nobody else can understand. Then he overtly boasts of how amazing he is to anyone who will listen to him in public. He is an overpowering extrovert, and tends to steamroll everyone else in the room—then he retreats back into some personal interest, project, or endeavor without giving anyone a chance to sway his impulses. His impulses are to dominate everyone in conversation, business, law, or fist fighting with his Ironman armor. Whatever it takes to gain complete control. However, considering the other heavyweights in his fictional universe, he will never be able to defeat a Level 3 Juggernaut one-on-one. But his skill, intellect, and renown is way-up-there. Therefore, it is plausible that he could figure out a way to oust the reigning Level 3 Juggernaut, which makes him a perfect Archetype for a Level 2 Juggernaut.

Batman would be another perfect example of a Level 2 Juggernaut. He's self-absorbed and driven by his own purpose. The difference between Batman and Ironman is that Batman is an introvert and very secretive in nature. He represents the more insidious type of Juggernaut nature. Batman is secret about everything and covers his tracks in everything he does, similar to a magician. In contrast to Tony Stark (Ironman) who makes it public knowledge that he is Ironman, Bruce Wayne (Batman) keeps his identity a closely guarded secret. Batman's cultivated strengths are ambush, misdirection, fear, and the unknown. Whereas Ironman wants you to know everything about him because it is how he uses intimidation and subjugates you, in Batman's mind, the less you know about him, the better. He thinks that makes him unfathomable. These are all dead giveaways that he follows the Way of the Juggernaut. Fear and intimidation are two of the biggest weapons of the Juggernaut. This is the same for real life Level 2 Juggernauts as well—although real-life Juggernauts may not be as archetypal as these fictional examples.

If you would like a good example of a real-life Juggernaut, go see the movie "Molly's Game." It's about a former mogul skier, Molly Bloom, who took over the world of high-rolling poker by force. One will notice immediately at the beginning of the movie how the character playing Molly (Jessica Chastain) bombards the audience with brilliant facts, figures, images and mind boggling struggles as smugly and "matter of factly" as possible. As if to say, "There, and what do you have that compares to that?" There's no mistaking this narration is meant to boast not only how skilled she was, but how much struggle she had to go through in her life. All of which was crafted to steamroll the audience with pure awe, which is 100% congruent with the way real life Juggernauts talk and operate. Later in the movie she completely takes over the world of high-stakes underground poker. In true Juggernaut form, she doesn't just take over —she blows the walls and roof off the entire operation. Because "good" wasn't good enough for her. She wanted to dominate in every single aspect of the game. By doing so she took the entire thing to a whole new level.

The entire movie was expertly done, and provides us with many insights as to what a juggernaut mindset truly looks like. She is extremely dominant, uncompromising, talented, and carves out a whole new path by "breaking the rules." She trained harder than everyone else (i.e. her boss) in the way she taught herself poker. She broke through the Black Veil of Objectivity almost immediately, simply by realizing she didn't know enough. Then without a second thought, or care in the world of what anyone else thought, she started studying everything she could get her hands on about poker, and flew through the learning process at breakneck speed. "Molly's Game" provides a very good glimpse into the way a true Juggernaut behaves.

EXAMPLES OF LEVEL 2 JUGGERNAUTS:

FICTIONAL CHARACTERS		
Ironman	Wolverine	Batman
REALM OF DOMINANCE		
Extrovert: Intimidation, Intellect, Domination	Introvert: Decimation and Fury/Wrath	Introvert: Fear and Preparation
REAL PEOPLE		
Theodore Roosevelt	Molly Bloom	
REALM OF DOMINANCE		
Statesman	Mogul Skiing	

JUGGERNAUT LEVEL 1

These are the fledgling Juggernauts who compete at a very high level regionally. Anyone who has broken through the glass ceiling by utilizing the Way of the Juggernaut is classified as a Level 1 Juggernaut. Level 1 Juggernauts tend to win many events at a regional level, but lack the consistency and skills of Level 2 and 3 Juggernauts. There are usually several Level 1 Juggernauts at any given regional competition. Their personalities are usually abrasive, withdrawn, self-absorbed, and are abnormally hard on themselves. Many times, they are socially withdrawn, and they feel that their time is better spent training than with others. This gives them greater skills earlier in their careers, which gives them a technical advantage over those that follow the Way of the Superhero. Additionally, Juggernauts tend to "live in their heads" more. Meaning they tend to think about their training and the proper movements, even when they are not training, a great deal more than Superheroes do. Remember, Superheroes tend to have thoughts of others and the meaning of social interactions, whereas Juggernauts tend not to be bothered by such things. That brain power is continuously focused on improving their skills, and committing those to muscle memory by constantly visualizing. If they are in a social situation, Juggernauts also tend to stifle group synergy. They tend to see it as a threat to their dominance. What's more surprising is that they are naturally inclined to stifle synergistic attempts that are intended to benefit them directly. They do this because they feel safer and more comfortable dominating the group if everyone works alone. They may do this intentionally or simply out of reflex. If they are an extroverted Juggernaut, they will often try to dominate the conversation so that no one else even gets a chance to talk. Synergy can be seen as a personal threat to a Juggernaut.

When training, it is important for a Juggernaut to find a training partner who is also one. Juggernauts train well together, because they can exist together in a constant state of competition with each other. They can push each other beyond the ability that they are able to push themselves, because of their innate need to be better than each other. This training, in fact, benefits both of them, but usually one will advance in abilities beyond the capability of the other. When this happens, it is important to "trade up" for a better Juggernaut, and then work with them until you surpass them as well. The best type of teachers/coaches for Juggernauts are Level 3 Juggernauts. This is because they will infuse them with a higher level of skill at a faster rate than a Level 3 Superhero will. They tend to hold back less information, because they really don't care if they hurt your feelings, and that is how Juggernauts like to absorb information: As fast as possible, regardless of how it makes them feel.

Additionally, Level 3 Juggernauts have access to higher level skills than Level 3 Superheroes, and they are more likely to be willing to share that information. This is because, after a Level 3 Juggernaut's competitive career, they find it most ego-rewarding to provide the most highly-tuned skill set to their athletes than anyone else is capable of. I like to think about it with this analogy: "They will condescendingly throw Thor's Hammer at your feet, just to see if you can pick it up." This way, you at least have exposure to it and a chance to give it a try. Superheroes don't have access to Thor's Hammer, so they can't throw it at your feet, even if they wanted to. Plus, the condescending nature of such an act will seem distasteful to a Superhero. However, fledgling Juggernauts crave such a chance.

Level 2 Juggernauts, by definition, dominate the national stage. At the very least, they are true contenders at that level. This is pretty black and white, but there is another way to know when one has graduated from a Level 1 to a Level 2 Juggernaut. It happens when other people start to talk about the athlete as a formidable opponent. It often happens in spite of the juggernaut's best wishes to keep his skills cloaked. People tend to edify Juggernauts disdainfully, more like as a warning than anything else. When a Juggernaut cannot go anywhere in the country and not have knowledge of her accomplishments precede her despite her best efforts to conceal them, then she is a Level 2 Juggernaut.

As an interesting footnote: Introverted Juggernauts tend to like to merge into peripheral sports when this starts to happen, because they crave the advantages of "flying under the radar." They also tend to do well in those other sports as well, but every time their reputation gets dragged out into the light, they tend to slip away into the shadows of a different sport. Because of this, one of the fairly familiar attributes of a Juggernaut is they have many sports that they play.

"A superhero movie is only as great as its villains."
-Chadwick Boseman

"Most of the things that we consider evil are only lacking in social niceties."
-Ed Bloom

SUPERHEROES

"When you are up in life,
Your friends get to know who you are.
When you are down in life,
You get to know who your friends are."
-Unknown

There are three distinct levels to being a Superhero, and just like Juggernauts, there are two distinct types. The first is the type that promotes themselves by uplifting everyone around them at the same time. They are the ones who try to make sure everyone feels included. They have a history of helping others through volunteering, philanthropy, creating institutions, and truly being there for their friends and family. They tend to have a silver tongue, as well as a whole lot of spirit, and people are drawn to them. They are natural born leaders. The second and more underhanded version is the type that works to raise themselves, and possibly their friends up, by tearing other people down. The first kind is more rare, and are true treasures wherever they exist. The second is harder to identify. Similar to introverted Juggernauts, they too work in secret. Their major weapons are of the "cloak and dagger" variety. They work to uncover information about others so that they can use it as ammunition to use against them. These are the types who start rumors, bear false witness, and can turn one's friends against them. They divide, create, and monitor social boundaries to their own benefit, as well as those whom they care about. When they use insults or are demeaning, they usually do it in a very tactful way. The best way I have ever heard it put is that when they will stab you in the back, they do it with a velvet glove on their hand. They work on tearing down others, by ruining their reputation, undermining their accomplishments, and influencing as many people to their way of thinking as possible.

The two types of Superheroes can be very difficult to distinguish from each other. Both of them are at home in social situations and have almost identical mannerisms and demeanors. Also, it is important to know that both versions of the Superhero personality type can and do exist in all Superheroes. It is just a matter of which tactics they think is most applicable to a given situation. Although they can (and do) use both strategies, most of them choose to use one or the other the majority of the time. However, all of them tend to think that they are doing what is best for themselves, and (usually) their friends. Where Juggernauts tend to be polarized, Superheroes are not. Everything is a sort of gray area to them. They tend to like debate, arguments, and anything that has subjective leeway. What both archetypes of Superheroes have in common is that they do much of their work through, and with, others. They are naturally inclined to be pandering, unlike Juggernauts. In doing so, they can simultaneously raise the spirits of those to whom they pander, and cover their tracks by removing suspicion if they are up to "no good." Whereas Juggernauts tend to like to work alone, Superheroes tend to work as a pack. Because of this, they are very well suited for team sports. They crave and feed of synergy and/or drama. As mentioned before, there are several integral meters or "gauges" of Superheroes. There are three of them:

SUPERHERO LEVEL 1 (SH1): Entry Level Superhero that has broken through the glass ceiling by cultivating the Way of the Superhero. These individuals are often contenders at the regional level.

SUPERHERO LEVEL 2 (SH2): Very high performing athletes, which make up the majority of athletes on the National stage. They are contenders at a national level and may see some worldwide exposure.

SUPERHERO LEVEL 3 (SH3): Highest skill level Superhero there is. These persons are contenders on the world stage. They have the highest renown of anybody, with extremely high-level skills.

SUPERHERO LEVEL 3

The very best athletes in the world that retain their compassion for others as they cultivate their sport. They don't usually dominate their sport, but they are always contenders, usually finishing very close to the top. They might not take first on the world stage all the time, but they will consistently get top 5. Unlike a Level 3 Juggernaut, there can be several Level 3 Superheroes on the world stage. People love to hear about them, and can relate to their upbringing and hardships. They are the first to give back to the community and volunteer when they are needed. When they compete, they tend to do it for others as much as themselves. They are always thinking of others, as well as wondering what others are thinking of them. They crave public attention, public places, and the ebb and flow of all kinds of relationships. They tend to be more interested in savoring the present moment than in planning or reflection like Juggernauts prefer.

They will often trade gym and training time for when other people need them, or for fun-filled events such as parties. This is what gives them an advantage over Juggernauts as far as networking and renown goes. They tend to have a lot of friends, and a massive fan following that dwarfs that of Juggernauts. They are the crowd favorites, and can effectively use the crowd in their favor to sway the judges' opinions. If they are in a team sport, they know how to elevate the entire morale of the team to win the game even in the face of seemingly impossible odds. They are extremely likeable people and tend to go out of their way to make you feel good about yourself. They are people you tend to root for even if you have never met them before. They tend to try to lift people up and make the world a better place, which can also be seen in their personal lives.

EXAMPLES OF LEVEL 3 SUPERHEROES:

FICTIONAL CHARACTERS				
Superman	Professor Xavier	Magneto	The Flash	Wonder Woman
REALM OF DOMINANCE				
Main purpose is to help other people	Main purpose is to help all the people to live together in harmony	Main purpose is to help other mutants	Speed/Help others	Main purpose is to help her people
REAL PEOPLE				
Micky Mantle	Apolo Ohno	Drew Brees	Jonny Moseley	
REALM OF DOMINANCE				
Baseball	Speed Skating	Football	Mogul Skiing	

SUPERHERO LEVEL 2

These athletes follow the same general personality archetype as the great ones above, albeit a bit diminished. They are the best examples of those that follow the Way of the Superhero on a national level stage. There are quite a few of them, and this group tends to outnumber the Level 3 Superheroes and Level 2 and 3 Juggernauts combined. They tend to make up the majority of the World Cup and National Level Competitors. They are true contenders at national level competitions and solid World Cup competitors. They like the limelight and can usually be found networking and making new friends. They like to be the center of attention, although they can be a little insecure at times. They care what others think of them and have a carefully cultivated persona that they want people to see. They don't like when people probe that persona with too many questions. They tend to blend well into any public surrounding, and they like to judge others. They also have lots of friends and large fan bases. For as much as they take from the community, they try to give back. They are willing to help others and tend to form close bonds quickly with other people. They tend to be optimists and are naturally inclined to look for the best in any person or situation.

Robin Hood is a shining example of the Level 2 Superhero archetype. He exudes his strength as the leader of the "Merry Men." He is almost inseparable from his band of outlaws. Robin Hood is so well known amongst his men because he has the ability to see the best in them. Many of his men came from questionable backgrounds, but Robin Hood has a way of finding new recruits, finding and bringing out the best in them, and giving them a choice to be part of a greater good. The most powerful methods that he uses is his ability to accept people without judging them, or condemning their transgressions of the past, and giving them a new purpose. Additionally, he is very charming, tactful, and respectful, which goes a long way to ensure his leadership role.

However, when one is to lead men, all of that isn't really enough. People like to follow someone of great skill. Robin Hood cultivated great skill with a bow, which in his day was one of the most powerful weapons. The idea that Robin Hood is the "Best Archer" in the world may lead one to believe that he should be placed in the Juggernaut category. However, if you look further into the story, it is more likely that his skill was simply added to his character to tie the whole story together. Also, it is a fairly common strategy amongst a Superhero's synergistic core of peers to spread renown of their members. Therefore, it can be believed that his reputation was inflated to legendary proportions as a method increasing the apparent formidability of his band of thieves. If you accept this premise, then Robin Hood was more likely just a "really good" archer. Remember, all of the archery competitions that he won were hosted by King Richard, and therefore, was only at the level of a regional competition or national level at best. This nevertheless is a good lesson on just how much advantage a Superhero can gain from their renown, networking, and people skills. Robin Hood is so much a part of his entourage that you would never be able to fight him one-on-one. One would have to fight his entire gang, and together, they have "additive synergy." Due to this, he is also inseparable from his reputation because he has multiple sources around him that are quick to glorify him.

The takeaway from this is that when a Superhero is arriving at a competition their reputation will precede them, especially if they are really skilled in building prestige. Though, much of it is an illusion. Juggernauts, on the other hand, tend not to have precedence when they approach. For example, it is a commonplace for the secretive kind of Juggernaut to appear out of nowhere. Remember that is part of their strategy to increase their effectiveness, by catching you unprepared. Superheroes tend to build their renown in "hype," and want you to know them before they approach. You can tell the difference when a Juggernaut approaches, because the silence tends to be deafening.

Mystique (from the Marvel Universe) is an archetype of the more insidious kind of Superhero. Her mutant ability is the ability to "shape shift," which means that she can change her physical appearance at will to look exactly like anyone she wants. This ability gives her an upper hand as a master spy, master assassin, and all-around master of "blending in." She has successfully infiltrated places with the highest security levels, like the White House and maximum security prisons. She is extremely loyal to her close circle of friends (ex: Magneto and the Brotherhood of Mutants), and believes that what she does is for their, as well as her own, benefit. She is the ultimate cloak-and-dagger type of Superhero. She is an enchantress, a master of tact and pandering, networking, creating and maintaining social boundaries. Additionally, she has been known to spread rumors, undermining those she seeks to destroy by sabotage. She also has a master "silver tongue," which can easily influence others to do her dirty work for her if she finds it convenient. By all accounts, one of her core personality traits is that she does not "stand out." That is important to her, so that her underhanded actions can be handled in relative privacy. This is in stark contrast to the extroverted Juggernaut. Even the introverted Juggernaut tends to find it hard not to stand out during an actual competition.

EXAMPLES OF LEVEL 2 SUPERHEROES:

FICTIONAL CHARACTERS			
Robin Hood	Cyclops	Storm	Mystique
REALM OF DOMINANCE			
Sherwood Forest Take from the Rich and Give to the Poor	Marvel Universe Leader of the X-Men	For the good of all people	Marvel Universe Deceit and Cunning
REAL PEOPLE			
	Toby Dawson	Travis Cabral	
REALM OF DOMINANCE			
	Mogul Skiing	Mogul Skiing	

SUPERHERO LEVEL 1

These are the fledgling Superheroes who do well at the regional level. Anyone who has broken through the Glass Ceiling by utilizing the Way of the Superhero is classified as a Level 1 Superhero. Level 1 Superheroes tend to be more interested in having fun while doing the sport, rather than doing well in the sport. Albeit, they tend to be good at the sport as well, which creates a permanent rift in their minds. They feel a constant pull in two different directions. One, to spend increasingly more time having fun with their friends and exploring the world, and the other to train harder because they like the attention they get from being good at their sport. It is fairly common for Level 1 Superheroes to help out with events, or anywhere else they fit in. They tend to be self-conscious and think highly of how others perceive them. Socially, they tend to be exclusive and like creating social boundaries. They like fitting in and being popular. They tend to have more friends than any of the Juggernauts, but have not yet created a real fan base because they lack both the impressive physical skills required, as well as the social tact. One of the more notable giveaways of someone who follows the way of the Superhero is that they can usually be caught bursting out in quick laughter if they see someone fall or do something embarrassing. It is a combination of their empathy and deeply rooted insecurity that provokes the laughter. Some of them realize it is socially inappropriate, while others never learn to control it. Juggernauts, on the other hand, tend not to laugh at others' misfortunes. Generally, it's because they don't care as much about the social repercussions of the said event. They will see it merely as an objective happenstance, and classify it on a scale of physical pain or that particular athlete's ability to perform in their competition that day. This is another good way to tell if you are dealing with a Superhero, because lower-level Superheroes do this out of reflex, and it can take them years to suppress (if ever).

When Superheroes train, it is most beneficial to them to have another similarly skilled Superhero with whom they can train. It is best if they push each other and encourage each other. The goal being to create a synergistic bond with someone on the team that you have a lot of access to. This is the lifeblood of a true superhero, and can, in fact, make or break their career. So if you are a fledgling Superhero, just be careful who you choose to be your training partner. Make sure that the person(s) that you spend most of your time with on the team is the person most likely to help advance each other's careers. The best teacher/coach for a fledgling superhero is undoubtedly a Level 3 Superhero, because they will take greater care of your morale and your emotions than a Level 3 Juggernaut. If one expects that coaches should be pandering and tactful, try to steer clear of Juggernaut type of coaches. However, sometimes, it is necessary to endure both types for a more well-rounded training.

Although it is known that a Level 2 Superhero is one that competes and contends on a national-level stage, it is fairly difficult to distinguish the line from when one graduates from a Level 1 to a Level 2 Superhero. The easiest way to make that distinction is about the time other people start praising the athlete without being coaxed by the athlete. In other words, when people that are outside of your social group start to talk positively about you from their own accord.

> *"It takes you three seconds to decide*
> *if you are a superhero or not.*
> *I am."*
> -Hrithik Roshan

SKILL AND DIFFICULTY LEVELS

Now that we know what the different levels of Superheroes and Juggernauts are, let's learn about the difference in skill and chosen difficulty levels between the two.

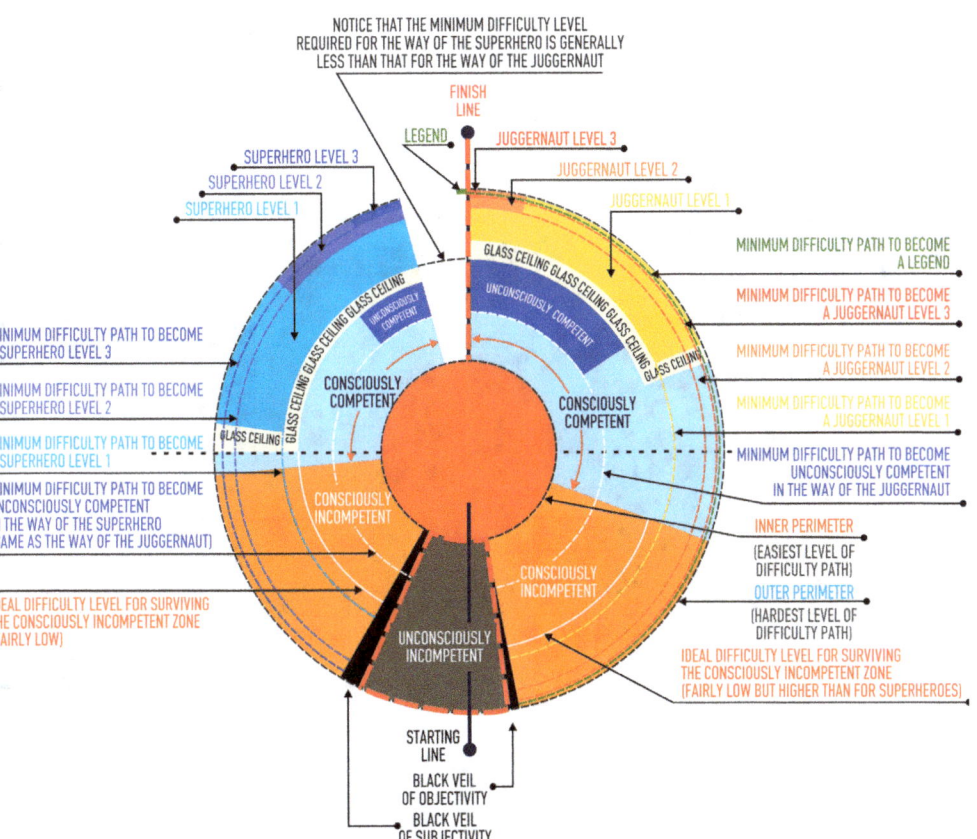

Difficulty Levels of Superheroes and Juggernaut

Notice the new dotted lines that circumnavigate the chart above. These represent different levels of difficulty: the closer to the center of the circle, the easier the difficulty level. The closer to the perimeter, the more difficult. As we progress on our learning path radially around the circle, we increase our skill level with each degree of improvement. Since the angles are more tightly packed on the inside of the perimeter (the easier side), this explains why we experience an increase in skill level more rapidly but stunt our ultimate attainable skill level by taking "the easy way out."

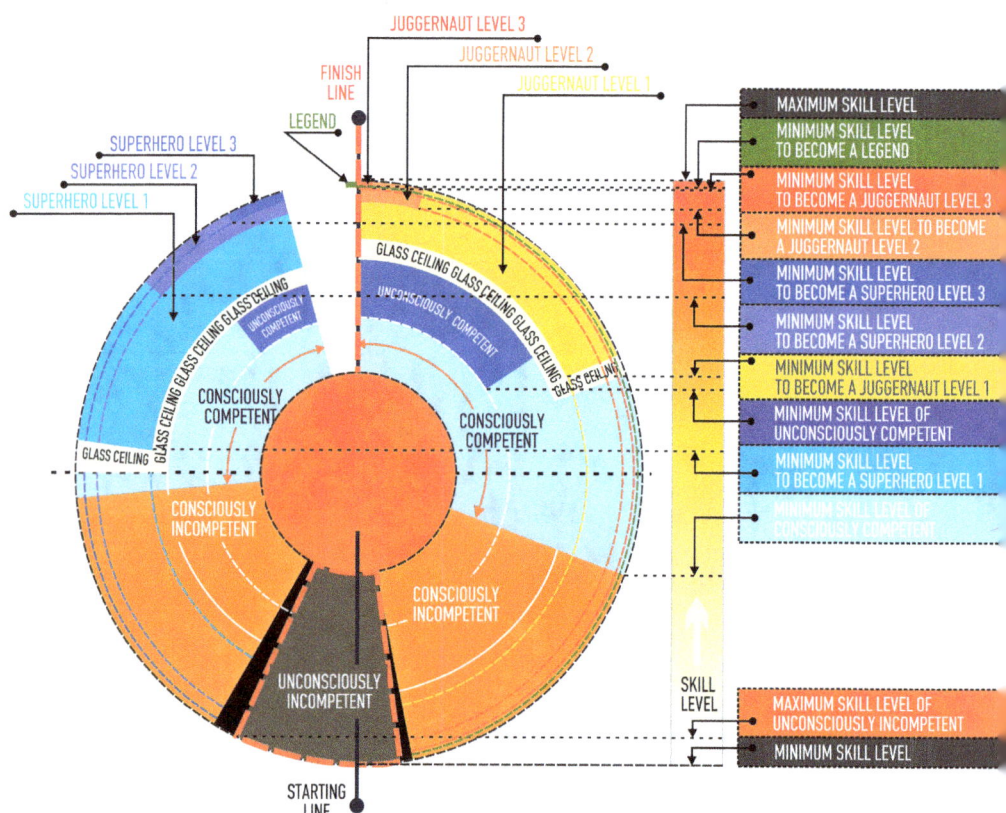

Superheroes and Juggernauts Skill Level Comparison Chart

Time invested is represented by the total length of the dotted line of the "difficulty path" that we choose to follow. Time invested and difficulty of our paths we choose is the major challenge. The more time we invest and the more difficult path we choose, the greater our theoretical skill level.

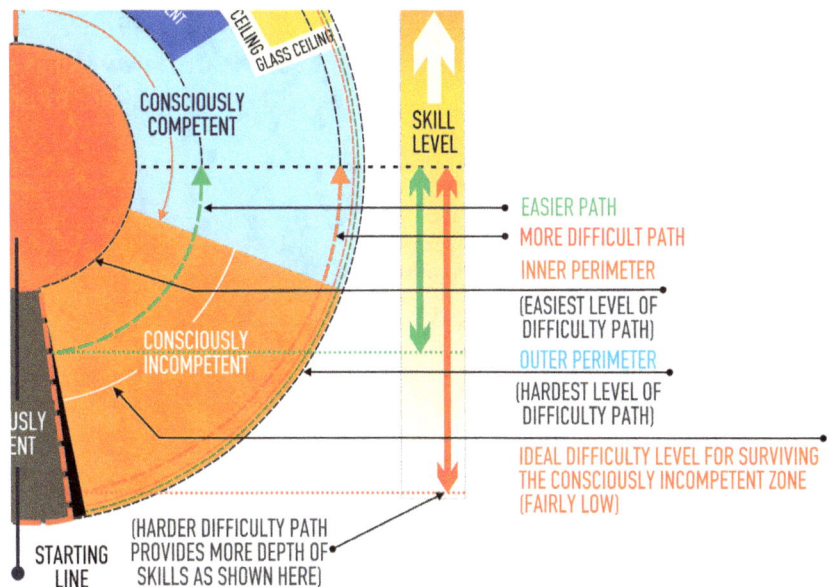

Increased Difficulty Provides Depth of Skill

This can be shown in the picture above. The solid green arrow next to the skill level graph represents the overall breadth of skills learned from someone who chooses an easier path (represented by the dotted green arrow), versus someone who chooses a more difficult path (depicted by the dotted red arrow). As you can see, the breadth of skills learned by someone who follows a more difficult path represented by the solid red arrow far outmatch the breadth of skills of the former. The tradeoff here is that the red path is much longer than the green path, since the length of the two dotted arrows represents time. In other words, the more difficult the path we choose, the slower our progression, but the more depth of skill we earn. However, it is also important to point out that the easier the path that you are on, the more difficult it will be to ramp up the difficulty at a later stage. So it is a bit of a balancing act. Consult with your coaches on just how much difficulty to take on, and when.

The graph represents how difficult it is to learn a new skill when one is just starting off. If you imagine you are following a learning curve on the perimeter of the circle, in the consciously incompetent zone, then you put in a lot of distance horizontally without much progress vertically. Since the vertical aspect represents skill, the horizontal distance you must travel (which represents no beneficial traits) to earn that skill may seem excessive. The fastest learning curve on the chart happens in the consciously competent zone because almost all effort applied to learn a new skill is directly or mostly vertically oriented, which means almost all of your efforts result in improved skill level.

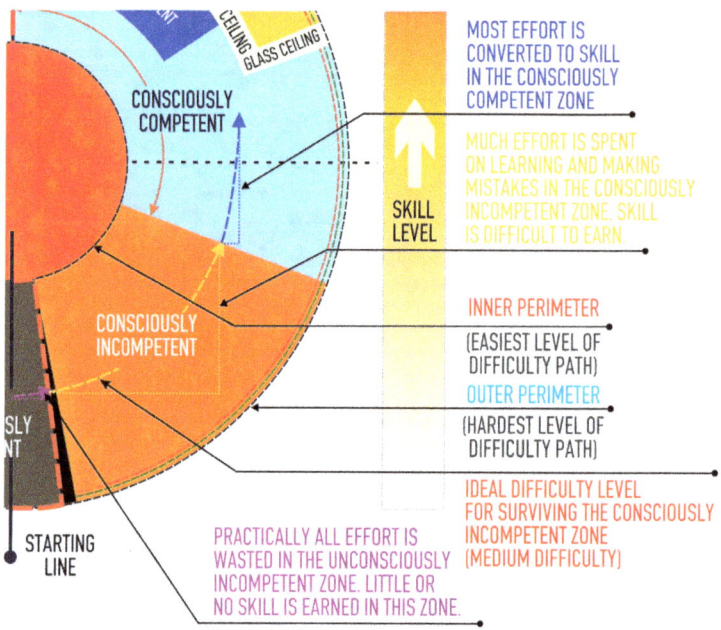

Percentage of Effort (Curved Arrow) that is Converted to Skill (Vertical Part)

It becomes reversed again as you progress up the ranks even further. The vertical component once again begins to dwindle as you are becoming one of the best in the world; new and better skills become very hard to learn, and very hard to improve on. The top of the chart on both the Way of the Superhero and the Way of the Juggernaut is the Unconsciously Competent Zone represented by span of the solid green line (next page).

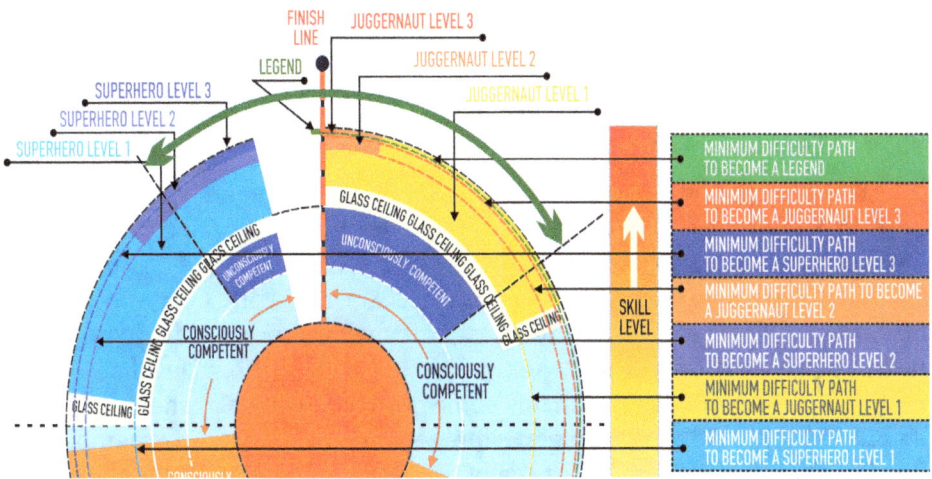

Bedrock Area for Superheroes' and Juggernauts' Skills

This zone is the bedrock for the Superhero and Juggernaut levels of ascension. Notice, however, that this zone does not go all the way to the inner perimeter of the circle. The meaning of this is because those of us who take too easy of a path will never reach this state of competency. You can become consciously competent to a high degree by being lazy, but you can never achieve unconsciously competent skills. Or at least, not in the way it is meant here.

WHEN TO INCREASE YOUR DIFFICULTY LEVEL

In mogul skiing, we want the time invested at any given difficulty level vs. the theoretical skill acquired to be as optimized as much as possible. To do that, you need to find as good a coach as you can find. However, I aim to give you some idea of which path you are going to want to follow. Mathematically, we have a solution for this: A straight line. By definition, the shortest distance between two points is a straight line. However, there are some special considerations that we will take into account later in this chapter that make the optimal path not quite a straight line.

Since increasing our skill level is so difficult in the Consciously Incompetent phase, it is important to take an easier route there. Taking too hard of a route while you are in this zone will only cause you to slide off track, and give up. This is because the sport will seem too difficult or impossible if you take too much of the difficult stuff on right away. Taking too easy of a path, however, will most likely fail to spark an interest in you, which will push you to the other side of the ridge. So there is a very narrow ridge of difficulty that you must have in your learning at this time so that you stay interested but don't get overwhelmed with the sport.

Use the opinion of a good coach to guide you through this precarious portion of your mogul skiing lessons. To find a good coach, you can contact your local mountain training center and ask if their mogul coach has any significant competitive mogul skiing experience. Former World Cup and Olympic mogul skiers are obviously the best, but they can be hard to come by. However, try not to settle for one that has less than National level accomplishments. Other ways you can find some good coaching is by checking out an online Mogul Skiing Forum and simply asking the community members there. They can be helpful—just make sure you know who you are talking to. One good forum to check out is: http://forums.mogulskiing.net/index.php. Another good site to check out is www.mogullogic.com. There you will find good video analysis by former Olympians.

When you reach the Consciously Competent stage, it is time to turn up the difficulty meter. This is the part of your learning curve where you learn the fastest, and gain the most skill. This is the stage to push yourself, conquer your fears, and lean into your boundaries. Maybe find a good friend who has the same or better skills than you, and work with each other to push one another. Motivate each other to keep doing better and more difficult tricks. Do not skimp on your training in this phase because you will pay for it later. If you take on and practice low difficulty level skills in this phase, then the next phases of Juggernauts/Superheroes will be much more difficult in contrast. Ultimately, it can be the real reason you decide to give up later on—besides the fact that these zones have a minimum difficulty level built right into them that need to be maintained.

There is a little bit of wiggle room in the lower 1 and 2 levels of The Way. These are the levels to step off the gas for a little bit. Skill accumulation is not as steep in these areas, and therefore, this is a good time to give the dangerous stuff a rest for a while, as you hone in and lock down your money-maker skills. Build confidence and results in these phases. Mogul skiing is a high-risk sport—you can't keep the difficulty high forever without something bad happening to you. This area of the chart is your breathing room. Be aware other "full-throttlers" in the unconsciously competent phase will likely not slow down in this new phase, and this is where I've seen the majority of the career-ending injuries come from. If you can be disciplined enough to back off just a tad, you will go far. At this stage in the game, it is more important to persevere so that you can still be left standing when the dust settles. It's not the time to push ourselves to our limits. With that being said, I am reminded of this quote:

> *"Persevere.*
> *Because on the road to success,*
> *there is never a crowd on the extra mile."*
> *-Charity Gibson*

Once your competition has weeded itself out, (and your "money-maker" skills are fully honed), that is the time to step on the gas again and start winning everything in sight. The Unconsciously Competent phase is wasted if it does not have a high degree of difficulty to it. But at this point in our career, we tend to stick to what we are good at. In the higher athletic realms like Levels 2 and 3 Superheroes and Juggernauts, we need to constantly keep our difficulties at an increasingly higher level just to keep pace—because if we can't do it, someone else will. Competitive sports can be like a moving treadmill. You have to keep moving (keep improving) just to retain your current level, especially in mogul skiing. This is because the sport is evolving very fast. What was good enough for World Cup 10 years ago is no longer good enough to make World Cup today.

With that in mind, it is important to realize that most high-level athletes intrinsically know this fact. Which means that if you want to eventually beat them, you not only have to improve, you have to improve faster than they are improving themselves. Similar to if you were both running on a very long treadmill, like the moving walkway at the airport. If you both run at the same speed, you will never catch the person in front of you. Sure, you will zip past the bystanders that are not on the treadmill, and that can feel empowering. But comparing yourself to others that are not in competition with you is ultimately irrelevant. In other words, even though you may be working really hard to improve yourself, it is all effort that is forfeit if you don't catch and surpass the person(s) in front of you. This will always be the case if the person you are trying to beat is working harder than you. However, it is advantageous to participate in as many mogul skiing summer camps and dry land training sessions as your pocketbook can afford. If you are getting more or better training than everyone else, it will help you close the gap on your more skilled competition during the off-season—especially if they take the summer off.

Sure, at the lower echelons of the sport, talent can play a large role in catapulting you to the forefront. But at the very upper echelons, it becomes less of a factor, because everyone that didn't have considerable talent has already been weeded out. At the pinnacle of the sport, pretty much everyone has similar talent levels. What matters up there is how efficiently you convert that talent to skill. We do that only through hard work and training. Lots of it. For instance, each level or section of this chart can take years, or even a decade or more to perfect.

The takeaway here is that the only way you will ever catch up to the athletes you want to beat is to work harder, longer, and/or learn faster than them. How hard you push yourself when compared to your friends, family, or teammates doesn't really matter. Think of them as the bystanders at the moving walkway that we just talked about; they are inconsequential. All that matters is whether or not you are improving faster than (catching up to) the person that you want to surpass one day. Ultimately, however, they may even retire before you ever catch them, but chasing them will teach you the speed that you need to run so that others behind you can't catch you, either.

> *"I chased the devil named Flash,*
> *and pursuing him has made all the difference.*
> *It has made me a better man."*
> -Michael Mead

Furthermore, level 3 Superheroes and Juggernauts have the highest difficulty levels and they need them to be there. If you are good enough to win everything by dialing it back a notch, then do so. But these are the culmination areas of your career, so you can't skimp on them. With all that being said, we can approximate the best-fit learning path for both Superheroes (Blue Arrow) and Juggernauts (Red Arrow) below.

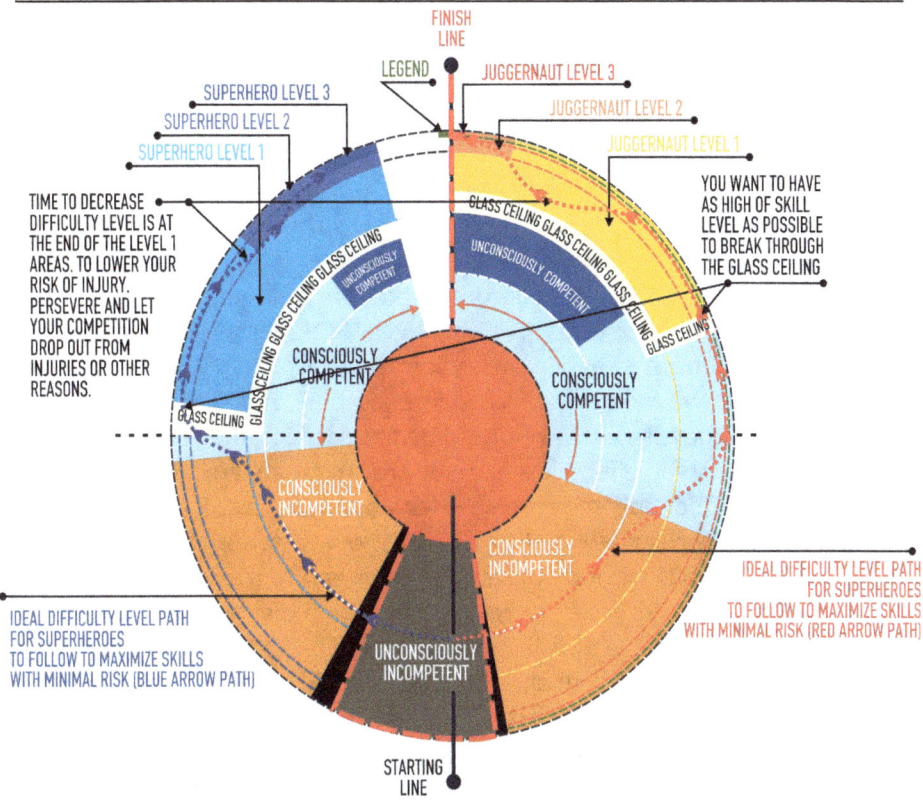

When to Increase or Decrease Difficulty Levels as for Superheroes and Juggernauts

BREAKING THOUGH THE GLASS CEILING/HERO STORY

As you have probably noticed by now, there is an ominous white boundary surrounding the ranks of Superheroes and Juggernauts branded as the "Glass Ceiling." As we briefly discussed earlier, the Glass Ceiling is ultimately the thing that separates everyday "Joes" from being the type of person that other people look up to, admire, idolize, and like to talk about. The "Glass Ceiling" is a term used to separate the people whose best result comes only from the application of acquired physical skills, from people who harness the power of tangential and intangible skills, such as Renown and Flow, to elevate their performances to unprecedented levels. The Glass Ceiling is a real thing, and you have to break through it somehow, if you want to realize your true potential. Traditionally, people who do break through it usually do it by accident, myself included. Although, if you wait to break through the Glass Ceiling by accident, you will be much further along in your career than you need to be when you finally break through, thereby losing a lot of time where you could have utilized its benefits. In the worst case scenario, you may never break through it at all. But lucky for you, neither one of those scenarios are going to be applicable to you because I am going to explain how.

In fact, you've already learned about it. It's the Way of the Superhero or Juggernaut, which has the result of creating an avatar which is capable of a better quality of skill and accomplishments than you are. Hence the explanation of the different types and levels of Superheroes and Juggernauts. We can choose to assign our avatar to be either a fictional character or a real person we look up to. It is only their best qualities that we want to focus on, so they should have the same basic values and archetypes that we do, for them to be effective avatars for us. To create an "alter ego," you must first believe deeply in yourself. Then you must have a rock-solid idea of your goals, where and what it is you want your "alter ego" to do for you. Invent some gimmick or ritual to call your alter ego to the forefront of your consciousness, like Bo Jackson used to do with a distinct heel-toe movement. When your alter ego is in control, you need to pinpoint your focus to a very specific goal, which should be in line with your career goals, and then just let him or her at it. Lastly, it is most important to let your avatar go at the end of your competition run, or at least at the end of the day with another distinct movement or ritual. This releases him or her (and yourself) from too much prolonged focus and effort, and allows you to be yourself once again at the end of the day. After all, even Superman needs to take his cape off and just be Clark Kent for a while. On the mogul course, however, you can let your alter ego do all the purely goal-driven accomplishments for you.

In order to help you further grasp the concept of an alter ego, you need to think about, develop, and write down your hero story. Your hero story is where your avatar gets its power. It is the key to breaking through the Glass Ceiling that separates Superheroes and Juggernauts from everyone else. You need to have it in order to become a successful mogul skier. This story is what you base your avatar on. It is the story of all the obstacles and tribulations that you have overcome in your life that has brought you to where you are today. Additionally, it explains the purpose for which you did those things, and has built right into it the ideal person that you are trying to be. In short, it is the story of triumph over your inner and outer demons.

At first, only your closest friends will know your hero story, but you must take care that you guide them ever so carefully to recognize and remember the points in your life that were the most difficult for you as they truly were. Gradually, you will have to tell your hero story as a self-promoter of sorts to everyone else, in order to build your renown. As more and more people know your hero story—which, by the way, will be validated by people checking the facts behind your back—and as you become a more and more successful mogul skier, other people will begin to tell your hero story for you. As more people tell your hero story, they build you up. The more people build you up, the more renown you earn. The more renown you have, the easier it is to progress up the ranks in the Way of the Superhero or the Way of the Juggernaut. Hero stories are so powerful because they utilized the power of admiration; the power of someone else doing your bragging for you.

Renown is a big part of becoming successful, so much so that it can have more importance at the higher levels than actual skill does. It is true that the more skill you earn, the more renown you earn, but they are not proportional. You don't earn as much renown just from skill as you might think. The real lion's share of your renown comes from self-promotion. At least at first. Once you have become a Level 1 Superhero or Juggernaut, you need to get your name on the table and into the conscious awareness of everyone else as often as you can. The reason for this is so that they are forced into taking your claims into consideration when they are forming their opinions about who is good in the sport. If you can make wild claims that turn out to be true, or can back them up when you are called upon to prove it, this can skyrocket your renown.

However, the opposite is true if you turn out to be a fraud. Once other people see you as a fraud who makes fraudulent or skewed claims, it can be very hard to rebuild your reputation, if ever. So don't be that guy or girl! Only tell the truth about what you can do, and be able to back it up. However, it is generally acceptable to present your skills for consideration in the most positive way possible. The relationship between skill and renown can be seen in our graph, if we look at it from the front, rather than from the top. Since the graph I created is actually a 3D model, this is quite easy to do (see picture to the right).

Skill vs. Renown

Next, we will look at this 3D chart from the front view to get a better understanding of just how much of an impact your level of competency has on your renown. Notice first just how much higher the renown is for Superheroes and Juggernauts than it is for people all the way up at the unconsciously competent level. Look at just how much renown is gained by those able to break through the Glass Ceiling (shown in white).

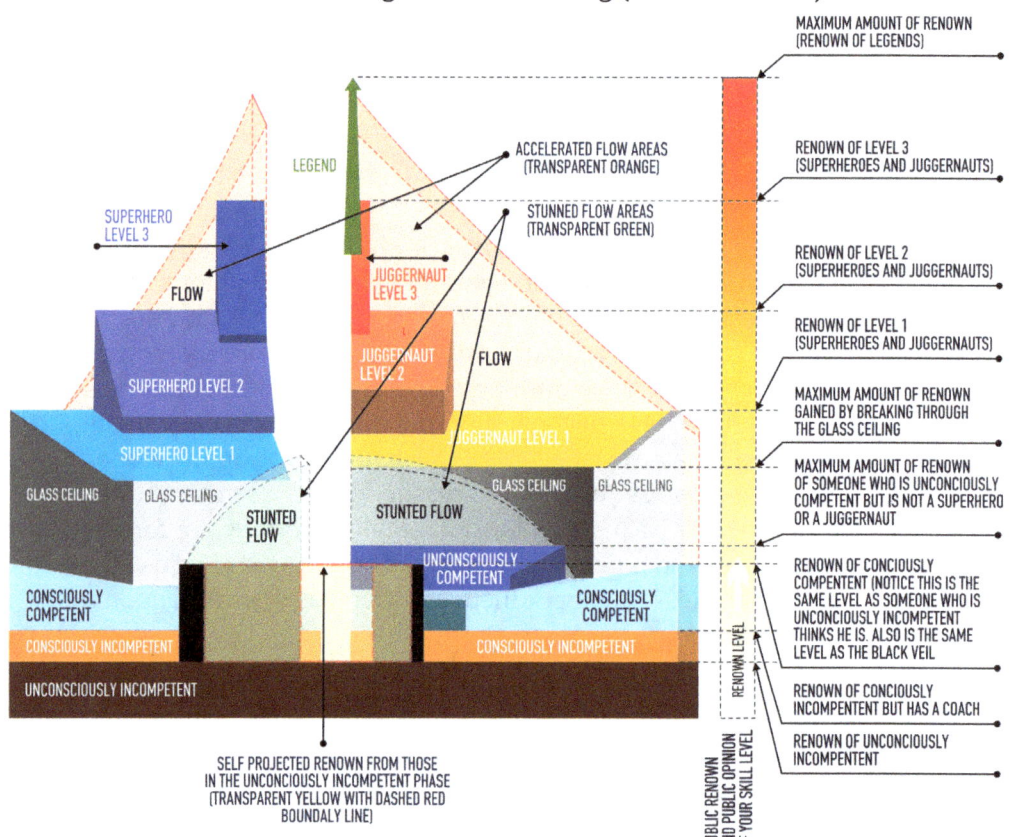

Your Public Renown and Public Opinion of your Skill Level

Notice how quickly one can gain renown as public opinion of your skill level as opposed to how slowly it takes to gain that skill level. Renown does, in fact, increase all the way up to the level of Legend, but not as much as you might think. This is because in our small world of mogul skiing, the few athletes that the public knows retain a large amount of public conversation on the sport. So even if you are a Level 1 on this chart, and you feel that you don't have much value or self-worth when compared to the

Level 2's and 3's skill level, it is beneficial to take a step back and look at this chart and become aware that the public might have more renown for you at your current skill level than you might be aware of. The public will tend to think of you as a "Top Shelf" skier just by the pure fact that you are a competitive mogul skier and you broke through the Glass Ceiling. Renown is fickle, but as long as you give people something to distribute about your skiing—and as long as you keep it positive and keep doing well—then people will love to talk about you, and your renown will skyrocket, even if you're not the most skilled mogul skier.

> *"The participant's perspectives are clouded,
> while the bystander's views are clear."*
> *-Chinese proverb*

> *"Sometimes I can feel my bones straining under the weight
> of all the lives I'm not living."*
> *-Jonathan Safran Foer*

CHAPTER 17
LEGENDS, FLOW, AND DOING THE IMPOSS1BLE

"It always seems impossible until it's done."
-Nelson Mandela

FLOW

Take a look now in the heart of the chart and at the very top. You should see semi-transparent green and orange areas. These are the intangible skill levels only achievable through a state of "Flow." Flow is that state of optimal consciousness that we both feel our best and perform our best. It is also commonly called "the zone." Most athletes are familiar with the zone or flow, regardless of the name they call it by. In a state of flow, you tend to be aware of how difficult a goal is, but you are detached from that difficulty. Everything seems possible, and time seems to slow down or even stop. The "how" of how to do something seems less important, as it just sort of occurs naturally without thinking. All that we feel is a state of knowing that it will work. The state of flow has been the holy grail of athletes since the advent of sports. However, it can be seriously stunted unless you break through the Glass Ceiling. This stunted state of flow is depicted as the semi-transparent green area (see below).

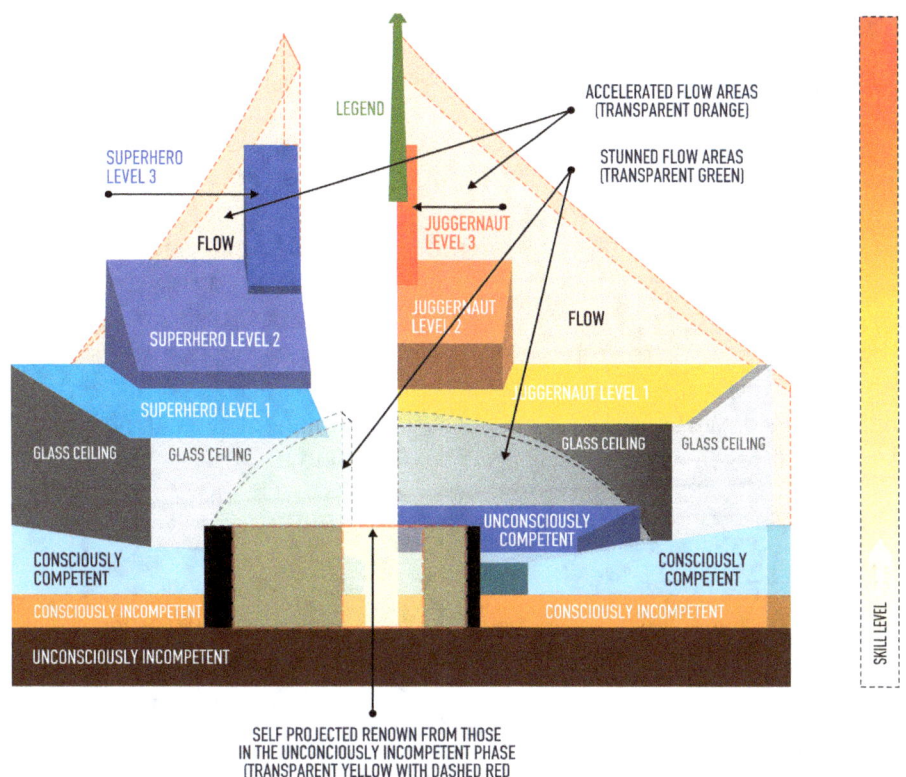

Accelerated and Stunted Flow States

Even so, these stunted flow states can still, in fact, induce the momentum one needs in order to break through the Glass Ceiling, if only accidentally, but it is rare. That is why the very tops of these flow states are higher than the Glass Ceiling levels (which are depicted in white). On the bright side, notice how much more impact the state of flow has on renown and skill level for those people who have broken through the Glass Ceiling (depicted as the semi-transparent orange areas). Look at the picture above to see just how much more public renown people on the flow curve of the chart have. In addition to their already high renown level of public opinion, those people performing in high states of flow have the best renown amongst their peers (other mogul skiers). This is because, amongst other athletes, the unexplainable results associated with flow are coveted the most. Renown is depicted as the smaller white-to-red gradient scale, next to the Skill Level scale below, named "Renown from Athletes" (below). It is named this because athletes from just about any sport can see and recognize true states of flow, even in sports that are not their own. What's more, the level of renown you get when you are in a state of flow as a Level 2 or 3 is literally off the charts of the "Skill Level" scale.

By having this high skill level and consistently exceedingly high levels of performance enhanced by states of flow, we can now see the renown from within the ranks of mogul skiers themselves. Notice that the most renown goes to the athletes who demonstrate skill levels and performances that are literally off the charts, even when compared to legends. The people that perform at these levels are the true treasures of our sport, revered from within the ranks of mogul skiing. But notice that one doesn't necessarily even have to be a Level 2 or 3. One can be a Level 1 Juggernaut and still lay down some performances that are higher than even Legends' known skill level, while in a state of flow (see below).

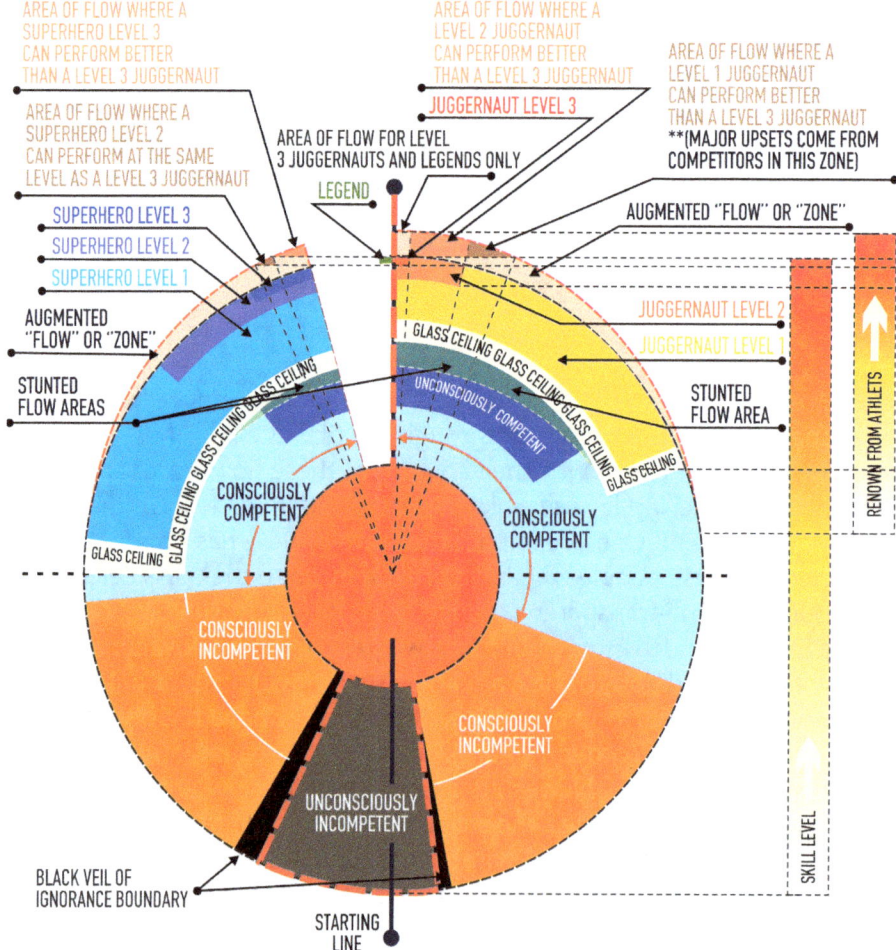

Renown From Athletes Comes from Flow

DOING THE IMPOSSIBLE

This is the part of our lesson that gets really interesting. Now we will be discussing not only how and why major upsets happen, but how to predict the probability that they will.

Notice at the top of this chart that there are several areas of the Flow Zones shaded. These areas represent the times when less skilled athletes can not only perform better than Level 3 Juggernauts and Superheroes, but also Legends! These areas of performance are the times when we can boggle the minds of not only the public, but other competitive mogul skiers. They represent the times and conditions that a major (or minor) upset can occur. Specifically, notice the flow area shaded in solid red above the Level 1 Juggernaut. This area predicts the chance, however small, that a Level 1 Juggernaut can perform better than Level 3 Juggernauts. It can be thought of as a "perfect storm" of consciousness that can propel young athletes to the fore-front of the sport without warning.

This also represents the "major upsets," however rare, as well as where and why we get 14-year-old Olympic champions from time to time. The rest of the special shaded areas of flow are noted on the chart and are self-explanatory. Take some time to review this chart because it is very predictive as well as explanatory.

Given an adequate display of flow, enough to properly wow the masses, your renown will circle temporarily up there around Level 3s and Legends themselves. However, it is not sustainable forever. But that is another benefit to the alter ego effect. It is supposed to keep you more focused for longer periods of time, which helps to induce the flow state. The flow state is hard to achieve, but it is possible. It may take years of training and experience to reach this level. It certainly doesn't happen overnight. From my experience, as well as the consensus of professionals in the industry such as Steven Kotler (Rise of Superman), flow is usually triggered after a prolonged or intense anger from failure. It sort of only comes to us when we really need it to, when our trials truly call for it. That is why the faces below depict anger where the flow state begins. In fact, almost all the areas of the chart can be depicted by emojis to help explain the general emotions of the people going through certain phases of their learning curve (see next page).

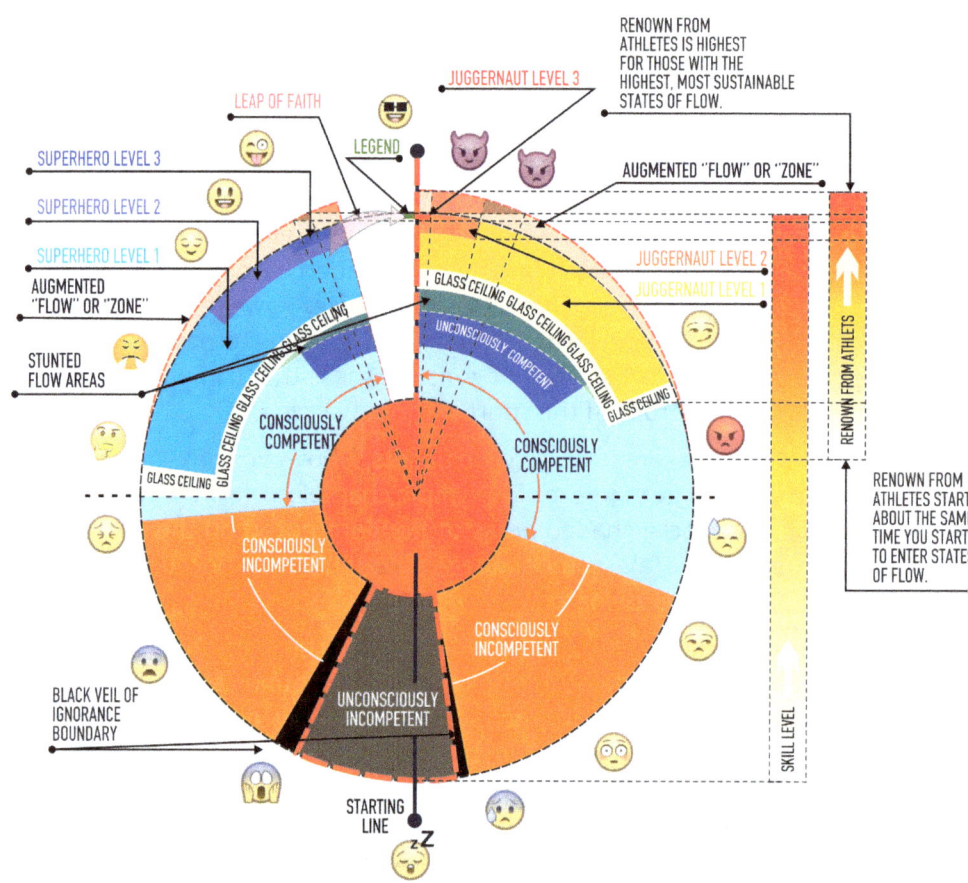

Emoji Descriptions of People at Different Stages on the Way of the Superhero and Juggernaut

LEAP OF FAITH

> *"If you had one shot, or one opportunity*
> *to seize everything you ever wanted,*
> *in one moment, would you capture it?*
> *Or just let it slip?"*
> *-"Lose Yourself" by Eminem*

After studying the chart on the previous page, you probably noticed a small new area at the top called the "Leap of Faith." For the purpose of this chart, it represents the special conditions and state of mind that those following the 'Way of the Superhero' will have to undergo if they want to be able to defeat a Level 3 Juggernaut or a Legend. It is not to say that anyone cannot utilize its overwhelmingly powerful benefits for themselves. However, for simplicity's sake, on this chart, it represents a combined perfect storm of a high level of skill, performed under a high degree of unconscious competence, augmented by a sustained level of flow, and backed by popular public renown. In team sports, it reaches its pinnacle as Team Synergy. Remember that synergy is one of the greatest weapons Superheroes have against Juggernauts. Incidentally, this is why Juggernauts tend to gravitate more towards individual sports, where synergy is more difficult to cultivate. Superheroes tend to do better in team sports because it is fertile ground for synergy. However, both types are found in multitudes in both types of sports.

The "Leap of Faith" is required for Level 3 Superheroes to defeat Level 3 Juggernauts, since by definition, the Juggernaut has the most highly cultivated skill(s). Matching skills vs. skills will most likely end in defeat for Superheroes when matched evenly against Juggernauts. A Superhero must compete with everything he has, and trust that the state of flow (and synergy, if it is a team sport) will find him before the Juggernaut can defeat him. Since the state of flow is so fickle, the Superhero usually cannot count on it to be there when he needs it. He cannot rely on it, but he needs it if he is to have a hope of defeating a Level 3 Juggernaut, or a Legend. That is why it is called a "Leap of Faith"; he has "to believe" that flow will choose him worthy when he needs it most. Even then, he usually needs the crowd's "buy-in" to sway the judges. It doesn't happen very often, but it does happen. When it does, that is the ultimate in sports victories. It is the main reason people go to the Olympics, to watch highly skilled athletes take true Leaps of Faith that trumps ultimate skill. Isn't it? It is the ultimate hero story, to defeat the ultimate Juggernaut in a highly tuned state of flow. That is why we love our Superheroes so much. It is also why Juggernauts train so relentlessly. To make sure that doesn't happen. After all, that is the only reason Juggernauts exist, isn't it? To defeat Superman? Juggernauts represent the ultimate test of a Superhero's skill. To realize this, just look at any comic book or coming of age story out there. There is always someone or something in those stories that seem impossible to defeat. But the superheroes are still somehow able to defeat their enemies. This is what the "Leap of Faith" is, as represented in fictional comic books. The public loves to see their Superhero defeat the Juggernaut, but it is because it is the typical "underdog story." However, it is important to note that true Legends and Level 3 Juggernauts don't always exist in active competition. This is because many aspiring Juggernauts break themselves or burn themselves out while trying to become a Level 3 Juggernaut. And since by definition, there can only be one Level 3 Juggernaut, they don't always exist. So there are times during our sport when Level 3 Superheroes are in fact the most skilled skiers on the mountain. When there is a true Level 3 Juggernaut, you will know it—everyone will. If you doubt that, just look at Michael Phelps. Do you think anyone doubts that he is the fastest swimmer in the world? Probably not.

The last thing of significance that is built into this chart is the difficulty to maintain any given skill level. This is important because as athletes, we need to train to not only improve our skills, but also to maintain them. The difficulty and time invested to sustain and improve any area of skill level on the graph is represented by the sloped surface of that area. The steeper the slope, the more effort, time, and dedication is required to sustain that amount of skill as a mogul skier. The hours per day that are generally required are noted per region below. You can think of it as placing a ball on any one of these surfaces. If left unattended, it will roll off one level of difficulty, to the next, to the next, and so on. But if you spin that ball really fast "uphill," it will sustain or improve its position. The faster it spins is representative of the harder you train.

Interestingly, one can imagine the same spinning ball on the upper skill levels, gradually falling from each higher level to the next lower one. This represents the "fall from grace" as the best athletes become too old, or train too little to keep up with the next generation, so their "ball" slows down, and they fall a level. Take, for example, an imaginary spinning ball on the extremely steep face of the Level 3 Juggernaut section. If it slows down even a little bit, it will fall to the Level 2 Juggernaut section. Then if it slows down just a little more, it will fall to the Level 1 Juggernaut section. Here is where it stops. Notice the flat ridge surface of the glass ceiling. It offers a buffer, and forever separates and elevates those that break through it from those who do not. The same is true for someone in the unconsciously competent section. If they put down their activity for a long enough period of time, the imaginary ball will roll onto the consciously competent section, where the individual would actually have to take a moment to think about things that he used to do unconsciously in order to do them correctly. If he then puts it down much longer after that, he will realize that he cannot do it anymore, and has relinquished himself to the bowl-like cavity at the center of the 3D chart. This may happen even to the best of us at some point in our lives; whether replaced by newer technology or the failings of our bodies, we will eventually realize that we have become consciously incompetent at something we used to be good at. However, we will never again become unconsciously incompetent once we break free of the black veil. That, I also represented in the graph below.

Anyone can understand the concept that if an athlete is pushed too hard too soon in a given sport, they will burn out, often times before learning any real skills. Conversely, if they do not take part in enough of the sport to make it interesting, or if it is too easy, they will not be invested enough in the sport to continue it. Both of these scenarios are incorporated into the model below. Remember the best-fit difficulty line for getting through the consciously incompetent phase? In the 3D model, it is actually modeled as a ridge with sloped surfaces on either side. It is intended to demonstrate that if one takes on too much difficulty in this phase of learning, they are likely to wash out. Similar to the ball analogy above, if the ball on this ridge-line titers to the outside of the circle, it will roll off the chart, which is intended to represent a washout in the sport.

A washout is a person who quits a sport, never to return again. If the imaginary ball traveling this ridgeline tips or is too far to the inside of the circle, meaning the intensity or difficulty is too easy for the individual, they are likely to become uninterested in the sport. When someone becomes uninterested in a sport, it is not the same as washing out. If someone is simply uninterested, they will do the sport with little consistency and with low difficulty levels, but not abandon it completely. This concept is represented by the interior of the circle as the bowl like concavity at its center. It depicts those individuals who have lost the motivation or interest in the sport required to improve themselves, which means they will remain forever consciously incompetent in that sport.

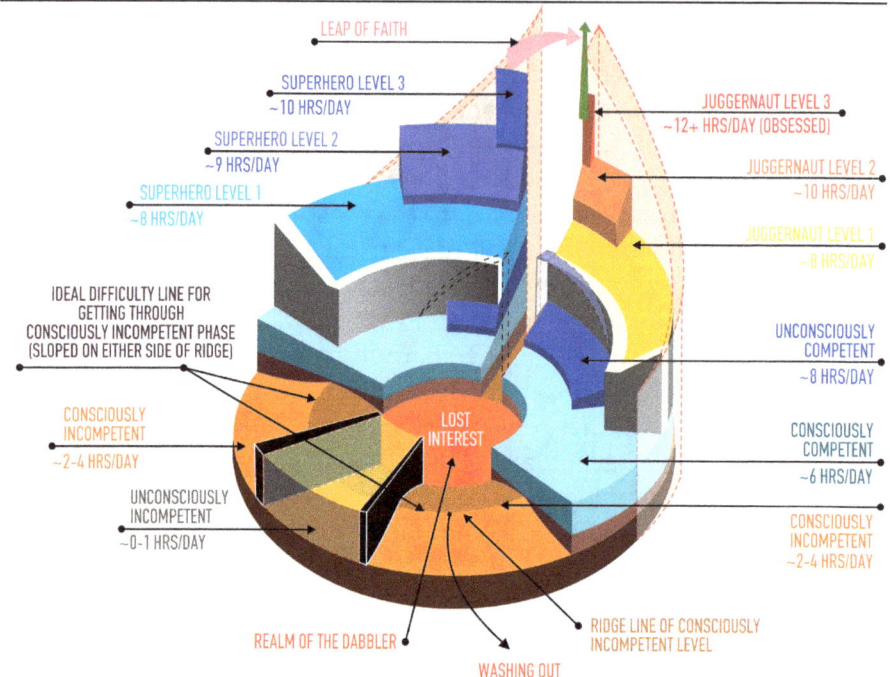

Typical Time Investments by Skill Level

Obviously, these numbers are just a general estimate. The actual number of hours trained and experience will vary by the individual. But the chart gives you a general representation of what you can expect from people at the different levels of skill. Hopefully, this chart has provided some illumination into sports psychology and the interrelated nature of certain traits of mogul skiing, skills, and the learning process in general. If nothing else, you should be able to understand the competitive process and mentalities better now. I will cover the specific tools used by Superheroes and Juggernauts and how to defeat them in the next chapter.

The last topic of discussion in this chart has to do with the difference of opinions that everyone has in a given sport. It has been my experience that it can seem contrary and confusing at times to decipher why seemingly similarly skilled athletes could have such wildly varying opinions about the sport, and others that seemed to have all the credibility in the world to voice their opinions either did not, or simply agreed with everyone. Shockingly, they were even able to agree with the ignorant at times. Next is my explanation of this phenomenon, as represented on our favorite chart.

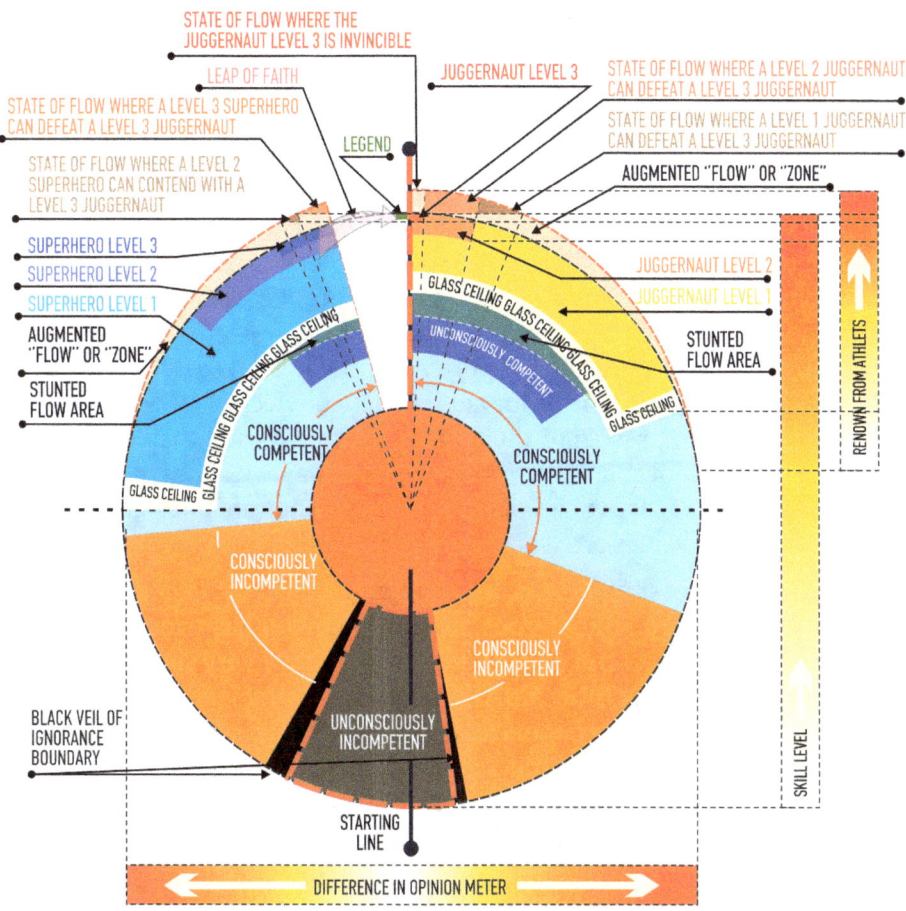

Difference in Opinion Chart

Notice the Difference in Opinion Meter that has been added to the bottom of this chart. It depicts in red the individuals that will have the greatest difference in opinions with each other, and in white with those that are likely to have similar or the same opinions. From this meter, we can predict that the individuals in the consciously competent phase on the side of the Juggernauts (right side) are going to have the most differing opinions on the whole chart from those in the consciously competent section on the Superhero side (left side). This is because they are the farthest away from each other on the graph in the horizontal direction, which is the way the Difference in Opinion Meter measures. As athletes pursue either the Way of the Juggernaut or the Way of the Superhero, and they learn how to become consciously competent via that method, they actually use their core values as the reason for their success. They feel their values and actions are justified, and this gives them confidence in their opinions.

However, what they don't see is that those on the other side of the chart feel the same way, but just have different core values that they attribute their success to. This is the point in the learning process that Juggernauts and Superheroes are most at odds with each other, and disputes are frequent. For example, they will have very different opinions on how much time is necessary for training, how important social networking and politics are, how difficult their training should be, who the best coaches are, and even the politics of the sport. All of these disagreements are simply drawn from a different set of core values to which they owe their accomplishments and assign to their egos. The real reason they disagree is because they cannot see, do not understand, or have never benefited from the different set of core values of the other side. They are unaware that the other side's core values are working just as good for them.

Using this meter as a basis, we can also predict that Legends, Level 3 Juggernauts, Level 3 Superheroes, and anyone who has even attempted a Leap of Faith (successful or not) are going to have very similar opinions with one another. This is because, at this stage in the learning process, it is the merging of all the beneficial attributes from both the Way of the Juggernaut and the Way of the Superhero. They have been around long enough and have had enough experience to both witness and appreciate the beneficial attributes of the other side. They have also taken enough action to try to acquire some of those traits and core values for themselves. Their experiences and shared learning bring them closer together and create very similar opinions in their sport—not to mention that their great skill levels also give them comradery with each other when very few other people can. Few people can understand or appreciate the highest level of mechanics in their sport for which they revere so much. Even fewer people still can actually give them the type of validation that they crave at that level, if not each other. Legends, Level 3 Juggernauts, and Level 3 Superheroes will have very similar opinions on everything from the best mechanics to use in the sport, to politics, to the best training programs to give to their students. They also have similar opinions on how good they are.

This is sometimes comical because according to the chart—and in real life—Level 3 Juggernauts, Superheroes, and Legends tend to have very similar opinions. At the very bottom of the chart, which represents the most ignorant, and at the very top of the chart which represents the most accomplished, you will see similarities. Opinions like "I am the greatest in the world," "Nobody can beat me," "I've never met anyone who I couldn't beat"; all of these will likely be a part of both individuals' "self-talk." But it goes deeper than that: opinions on politics, training requirements, etc., can also be shockingly similar. These two types of people are far removed from each other in skills, experience, and accomplishments, so it is funny to watch them agree with one another.

LEGENDS

> *"There are some fish that cannot be caught.*
> *It's not that they are faster or stronger than other fish,*
> *they're just touched by something extra."*
> *-Ed Bloom in "Big Fish"*

By now, you have probably noticed the small greenish rectangle (or greenish arrow if viewed from the front) that sits atop our wheel chart. It is perched at the very top of the chart, with the highest minimal skill level of any zone on the chart. Legends represent the "Finish Line" of this entire graph, and it is the ultimate accomplishment of any athlete to be remembered through the ages. It is the smallest zone on the chart. It is even smaller than the JL3 zone, which is meant to only represent one person. This is because not every generation creates a Legend. Even though becoming a Legend may seem more or less like the birthright of the best Juggernauts, they still have to earn it. The best superheroes can only obtain it through a Leap of Faith as discussed in the previous section. But both have to work at it.

As a reminder, this means that in order to become a 'Legend', a Level 3 Superhero would have to have some amazing accomplishment to do so—such as defeating a Level 3 Juggernaut at the Olympics, like Alex Bilodeau did, twice. Juggernauts can become Legends when they retire, die, or have an extensively long and distinguished career of domination, but it is short-lived if they never give back to their sports, their community, or the next generation of athletes. Those are the requirements that Juggernauts have to meet in order to graduate to a Legend. All of the accolades in the world aren't sufficient without those things.

Superheroes usually accomplish those things earlier on in their careers, because it is in their nature to do so. Even so, they don't have it so easy. They don't automatically become Legends when they die or retire either. They have to prove their medal; they have to show that their skills are truly worthy of remembrance. This is why they become Legends after a rigorous but successful Leap of Faith. They must demonstrate that, objectively speaking, they have at least the same skills as a JL3 in order to earn a victory over them. It is rare; however, it does happen. Superheroes may actively fan the flames of their own renown throughout their entire career, but when they die, the flames die down and only the cold hard objective facts remain. Superheroes are revered in present times, but not long after their retirement, when the hype dies down, they become outdated, much like politics and trivia.

The indomitable nature and personality of Juggernauts are usually revered, and "easier to swallow" after they die or retire. So they too are remembered as Legends—for a while, anyway. However, the cold hard facts of their accomplishments are very hard to ignore from a historic standpoint, and that is why becoming a Legend may seem like the birthright of a JL3. However, they have to have enough media presence, a strong enough social network, and have given back to the people or the next generation enough, for them not to disappear from public memory completely. In other words, they need to adopt the attributes of the Superheroes in order to become a true Legend.

In summary, a Legend is the merging of the beneficial attributes from a SH3 with those of a JL3. That is what makes a Legend better than either a SH3 or a JL3. They are a hybrid of both. It is a learned attribute, not an inherent one. There are those that become Legends via the Way of the Superhero, and there are others that become Legends via the Way of the Juggernaut. Below, I list the best examples I could find of each one, with explanations on how they became Legends.

FICTIONAL LEGEND	SKILL/REALM OF DOMINANCE	BECAME A LEGEND VIA:
Jean Grey/The Phoenix	Telekinesis/Telepathy/Phoenix Force	The Way of the Juggernaut

Jean Grey (from the Marvel Universe) is a great fictional example of what it means to be a Legend. As one of the lead members and integral parts of the X-Men, she is a very powerful yet mother-like figure to her team. Her telepathy and mind reading capabilities allow her (or make her) feel more compassion for everyone in the world, and she strives to use her powers to help as many people as she can. That is her Level 3 Superhero side. However, there is another even more powerful figure that lives deep within her: the Phoenix. The Phoenix is a mighty cosmic being that lives inside Jean. The Phoenix is so powerful in fact, in the 2016 film, X-Men: Apocalypse, Jean Grey as "The Phoenix" literally vaporizes the all-powerful mutant known as Apocalypse, when the entire rest of the mutant team combined were no match for him. The Phoenix inside Jean Grey represents the Level 3 Juggernaut side of her. The combination of both a Level 3 Superhero and a Level 3 Juggernaut inside one person is a Legend as defined in this book. Therefore, Jean Grey is one of the best examples I could find to represent the fictional Legend in this section because she exemplifies only the best attributes from her two sides. Although, since many of us were not born with split personalities or internal dormant cosmic beings living inside of us, we also have to look to the real world for examples of what it takes to become a Legend:

REAL WORLD LEGEND	SKILL/REALM OF DOMINANCE	BECAME A LEGEND VIA:
Miyamoto Musashi	Warrior	The Way of the Juggernaut
Alexandre Bilodeau	Mogul Skiing	The Way of the Superhero

BECOMING A LEGEND VIA THE WAY OF THE JUGGERNAUT

"When the tiger comes down from the mountain to the plains, it is bullied by the dogs."
-Chinese Proverb

Miyamoto Musashi - Musashi lived his life as probably the most fantastic example of a Level 3 Juggernaut that I have ever uncovered. Unlike our western legends such as Achilles, there is no divinity attributed to him.

He was simply a great warrior. Additionally, the real-life accounts of his accomplishments are numerous and correlated.

Miyamoto Musashi (Self Portrait)

He was a Japanese swordsman who lived from 1584 to 1645, according to Wikipedia. In this point in Japan's history, members of the samurai class dueled regularly in order to establish their worth. A samurai who killed 10 men in duels could demand far greater sums than a samurai who only killed one man in a duel. Musashi won his first duel when he was 13 years old against an armed samurai. The young Musashi charged at the samurai against his uncle's wishes with a quarterstaff (a bo, as it is commonly known). The samurai attacked with a wakazashi (traditional Japanese Samurai sword), but Musashi threw him to the ground and struck him hard between the eyes when he tried to get up. He then proceeded to beat him to death with his wooden stick. And that was just the beginning.

He fought over 60 duels in his life and was never defeated. Not accounting for the hundreds of lives he took in the six major battles he was engaged in. What is perhaps most impressive about these battles was that he wasn't always on the winning side, yet he always survived unharmed. It is also known that he survived multiple ambushes of skilled warriors of ten men or more, including one that was a rigged duel which had a hidden force of archers, musketeers, and swordsmen. If that wasn't enough, he single-handedly destroyed the Yoshioka School (the foremost of eight major schools of martial arts in Kyoto, Japan at the time) by killing all of its masters and prominent students. His skill was so great that in most of his 60 duels, he only used a simple wooden sword, or in one case, a bo he carved from a boat oar. It is important to point out, however, that he never restricted what weapon his foe was allowed to use, and usually only dueled the Grand Master from a number of different Martial Arts Schools. Musashi dominated the world of fighting so much in those days, he actually evolved naturally into a living legend. The quote that proved to me that Musashi had evolved from a Level 3 Juggernaut into a Living Legend by way of the Juggernaut was:

> *"When I reached thirty (years old), I looked back on my past. The previous victories were not due to my having mastered strategy. Perhaps it was a natural ability, or the order of heaven, or that other schools' strategy was inferior. After that, I studied morning and evening searching for the principle, and came to realize the Way of strategy when I was fifty."*
> *-Musashi, Book of Five Rings*

The takeaway here is that a man can be a Level 3 Juggernaut or Superhero without actually knowing how or why. When one truly reflects on the discrepancies that brought consistent victory, the reasons can become blurry and subjective. One of the defining characteristics of a Legend is that those individuals have taken the time to truly boil down all of the facts to reveal the real reasons that they are or were consistently victorious. Few young people, especially Juggernauts, can sidestep their egos long enough to systematically and objectively categorize the differences that allowed them to win so often. They attribute it all to their own greatness, rather than to the difference in the details of their skills or physical advantages, as compared to those they defeated. Even the great Musashi didn't realize that he could improve from a Level 3 Juggernaut to a Legend by doing so, until he was 30 years old. It took him the next 20 years of his life to boil down his perfect strategy into comprehensible parts. When he did, that is when he became a living Legend as described in this book, the finest example of one that my research has ever uncovered. Additionally, in true Legend form, he did his part by giving back to the world by teaching what he learned in the forms of his two books:

1. THE BOOK OF FIVE RINGS
2. DOKKODO ("THE WAY OF SELF-RELIANCE")

Musashi's most archetypal quote as a Level 3 Juggernaut:

> *"The path that leads to truth*
> *is littered with the bodies of the ignorant."*
> *-Miyamoto Musashi, The Book of Five Rings*

BECOMING A LEGEND VIA THE WAY OF THE SUPERHERO

"You can't relate to a superhero, to a superman, but you can identify with a real man who in times of crisis draws forth some extraordinary quality from within himself and triumphs but only after a struggle."
-Timothy Dalton

Iurii Osadchi / Shutterstock.com

Alexandre Bilodeau

Alexandre Bilodeau - Alex is one of those exceedingly rare individuals who seem to have a dual mindset of both the Juggernauts and Superheroes. This is the embodiment of what a Legend is. They have both the beneficial traits of a Juggernaut, as well as those as a Superhero, and they use them synergistically together. Bilodeau is so well-rounded in his traits that it can be difficult to determine whether his ascension to the pinnacle of mogul skiing was via the Way of the Superhero or the Way of Juggernaut. However, if you apply my filters described in the previous sections, he is a natural Superhero.

There are several attributes that Bilodeau has that one could use to convincingly classify him as a Juggernaut, rather than a Superhero. For example, it is clear that he is an extremely competitive person in every aspect of his life. One may point out that his excessive competitiveness is a trait of a Juggernaut. However, anyone who has competed for a long time will tell you that everyone at the upper levels of the sport are extremely competitive. How they deal with it, however, is different. Winning is a drug. If you do it a lot, you become addicted to it. When you are addicted to something, you go to excessive lengths to acquire it. Both Superheroes and Juggernauts can become addicted to winning, and therefore, either can be extremely competitive.

So if Alex is actually a Superhero, where did his Juggernaut-type skills come from? When someone is actually able to merge together the skills of a Juggernaut and Superhero, there usually has to be a really good reason for it. Alex's reason is his brother, Frederic, who suffers from cerebral palsy. Frederic played a big part in Alex's adoption of his Juggernaut traits. He states in a video on his philanthropy page that it was out of respect for his brother that he drove himself so hard to go after and realize his dreams.

Alexandre and Frederic Bilodeau

Surely, he had a constant reminder of how fortunate he was to even be able to go after his dreams as a mogul skier. In another interview in the mogul skiing documentary, "Bumps" by Zach Hoffman, Bilodeau goes on to say that he wouldn't have the same skills, the same abilities or the same determination, if it weren't for his brother and the people around him all through his life.

"Even if it's raining outside, or minus 40 (degrees) and I'm like, 'Oh my God I don't want to go train today. It wouldn't be a big difference skipping one day,'" Bilodeau said in an interview before the 2014 Olympics. "But looking at my brother, to be able to give him that chance of being in my body for just one day, and going to the Olympics, he would jump in my shoes and go out there and run a marathon. So I'm like 'OK, let's stick to the plan, let's go.'" It is obvious that he feels a responsibility to Frederic to push himself. "Most of his dreams are not realistic, and when I think about it, I'm like 'where are my limits?' I have to remember that," Bilodeau explained. "And out of respect to my brother, I have to go after those dreams and do all within my power to try to make it happen." His overtly laser focus on skills, abilities, and determination are the signature characteristics of a Juggernaut.

That aside, if you listen to everything else Alex says, and look into his lifestyle and how he treats others, you can easily see that he is a naturally born Superhero. Bilodeau simply cares for other people way too much to be a true Juggernaut. However, his adopted Juggernaut traits, driven and inspired by his disabled brother, were a perfect storm that propelled him to become a living Legend far faster than even Miyamoto Musashi. Musashi had to learn and teach himself how to give back. As a Juggernaut, that sort of thing didn't come naturally to him. However, it does to Alex. It is a prerequisite of this book to give back to one's sport in order to be considered a living Legend. Regardless, if Alex ever gives back any form of documentation to mogul skiing similar is irrelevant. Every day that Alex skied and trained for his brother instead of himself, he gave back to mogul skiing. It is part of who he is, and is intrinsic to a Level 3 Superhero.

Additionally, his fundraising has raised close to a million dollars for Canadian Pediatric Health Centers, and he doesn't even take the credit for himself. He gives all the credit to his brother, who loves to be a part of something that serves the greater good, that they can work on together. Although, some people have pointed out that Alex's involvement to his brother is a publicity stunt. That is disappointing to hear, but this chapter offers a good explanation to both why they think that, and why it is untrue. The people that accuse him of that most likely follow the Way of the Juggernaut. Those type of people, if they swapped positions with Alex, may actually have tried to use Fredrick as a publicity stunt, or in whichever way they could to advance themselves and their careers. They therefore assume that Alex is doing the same thing. However, if you look closely, it is not the case. It is nice to see that Alex is able to shrug off the accusations from the Juggernauts because he knows in his heart that he is just doing what any Superhero would do: Keep his brother close, and as much a part of his life as he can. Therefore, although it is commonplace to do so, a Juggernaut should not accuse Superheroes of the Juggernaut-type transgressions, because they are pathologically different. The same holds true if the roles were reversed. Juggernauts must be judged as Juggernauts, and Superheroes must be judged as Superheroes, if we are forced to judge at all, lest we mis-condemn.

Alexandre Bilodeau was a Level 3 Superhero in the 2010 Olympics in Vancouver. In that event, we witnessed one of the greatest examples of a Leap of Faith. If you haven't seen the 2010 Olympics, I suggest you watch them on YouTube. In that event, Bilodeau had tip-top skill, found his state of flow, and had such a huge amount of public renown and popularity that was enough to just nudge out the Level 3 Juggernaut at that time, Dale Begg-Smith. It is known that Bilodeau had worked with a sports psychologist to increase his ability to control his relaxed state of flow. That flow, combined with his extraordinary level of skill, was enough to match the skills of the Juggernaut. Yet it is this author's personal opinion that popular sentiment is what ultimately pushed him into the winning spot. Not only that, but if you saw the facial expressions of Begg-Smith, it is quite obvious that he thought the same thing.

If that wasn't enough, this Legend also edged out a different Level 3 Juggernaut in the 2014 Olympics at Sochi: The most winningest mogul skier in history, to be exact, Mikael Kingsbury. In doing so, Bilodeau secured the most successful Olympic mogul skiing career in history, with back-to-back gold medals.

Then, after the 2014 games, in true Legend form, Bilodeau displayed very mature decision deciding to ski off into the sunset with an unprecedented Olympic record. About his retirement, he stated:

*"...I feel I have done everything I could have ever done in my sport,
and that I could give to my sport.
Now I am retiring as the best skier I could have ever been."
-Alexander Bilodeau*

This demonstrates the mastery of career timing, which is also an attribute of a Legend. Furthermore, both Legends, Miyamoto Musashi and Alexander Bilodeau, also practice the Art of Lifelong Learning (Chapter 21).

Alexandre Bilodeau (center) with Michael Phelps (left)

For more information, and to help Alexandre and Frederic battle against cerebral palsy, please go to: www.Alexbilodeaufund.com

"So many of our dreams at first seem impossible,
Then they seem improbable,
And then, when we summon the will,
they soon become inevitable."
-Christopher Reeve

"At any rate, that is happiness;
to be dissolved into something complete and great."
-Willa Cather

"What would you attempt to do if you knew you could not fail?"
-Robert Schuller

"It's kind of fun to do the impossible."
-Walt Disney

CHAPTER 18
MENTAL WARCRAFT

" 'There's no harm in thinking.'
We were talking about Crazy Uncle Albert,
and whether it was right to use your brain to build weapons."
-Unknown

Rather than be a victim of mental warcraft your whole life, it is better to discuss it formally and lay it all on the table. That way, even if you choose not to partake in mental warcraft, you will at least be able to identify it and defend yourself against it when it is used against you, as most likely will be the case at some point in your life. This section is composed of some of the more subtle mind games that you will be exposed to throughout your athletic career, and offers guidance on the best way to mitigate the effects of these tools when they are used against you. It also offers insights as to the specific advantages that each one of these mental weapons has to offer, should you choose to use them. However, if you choose to use them, tread carefully. If you have no desire to learn about mental warfare, head games, or the like, please skip to the next chapter now.

FEAR AND INTIMIDATION

"Yes, I believe that the art of winning is through intimidation, and not necessarily do you have to speak about it."
-Mark Spitz, Nine-time Olympic Champion

Fear is a tool that almost all competitive mogul skiers use against each other on the mogul course. Intimidation, however, can only effectively be used by Level 3 Superheroes and Juggernauts. This is because, by definition, they are better than everyone else. However, it can be used to a certain degree by any lower level. For example, a Level 1 Superhero can be intimidated by a Level 2 Superhero or Juggernaut, but not the other way around. It does not matter if it is a Superhero or a Juggernaut intimidating a Superhero or a Juggernaut. Either one can intimidate the other, as long as one is a higher level than the other. Similarly, a Level 1 Juggernaut may intimidate a consciously competent or consciously incompetent person. However, it's about there that it stops. Unconsciously Incompetent people aren't generally intimidatable because they are ignorant to what should scare them. If you really wanted to intimidate an Unconsciously Incompetent person, you would most likely have to educate them first. Even then, results are sparsely proportional to your actual level of intimidation and can and will backfire at times. It is best to leave unconsciously incompetent people alone with their ignorance, there is nothing to gain by attacking them, and very much to lose. Besides, the black veil of ignorance can only be truly lifted by one's self. It is important to point out here that, intimidation generally does not lend itself out to be manipulated very easily.

Intimidation generally can only be actually "used" without risk of back-firing by Level 3s because they are the most vindicated. It is most often used by Level 2 and 3 Juggernauts because it marries better with their personality types and skill levels, but Level 3 Superheroes do in fact use it from time to time as well. So it is important to not only understand how and why people invariably can and will use it against you, but what to do about it, regardless of if you plan to use it yourself or not.

Speaking from my own experience, I like to use a visible lack of fear as a catalyst to instill fear or intimidation into someone else. It is not hard to scare someone who is already afraid of the said thing even more, but often times, it is beneficial to instill it in people who aren't afraid or intimidated to begin with. A good place to start is with people who pretend they are not afraid of something. If you want to intimidate these people, start by scratching the surface, if only to let them know that you know it's a facade. Something you might say is, "Icy course today, gonna be real fast," or "That first mogul after the top air is a serial killer. A real mean one. Haha." Depending on where their weaknesses and fears actually are, you can tailor each seed of fear differently.

Usually, people's reaction is a snappy comeback or just mild anger in general. They will generally think they know what is going on. But not entirely. What's more, their type of immediate reaction is irrelevant. What you look for and what you are really trying to do is to make their defenses go up, so that they get tense or worried. Being tense is the opposite of being relaxed. Now that you know how invaluable the ability to relax is, you know just how insidious this tactic is. So the first thing some people do is try to take away their relaxation, or at least make it more difficult for them to relax.

Seeding their mind with worry and doubt also impedes their ability to regain their ability to relax, even if they do actually realize that they have lost the ability to relax and try to gain it back. It is a not only a really powerful maneuver, but almost everyone uses it. Remember from Chapter 12: The Cave of the Mind how difficult it is to stop fears from leaking in? Remember how easily they can take root in your mind. It is the reason we make for the corks and plugs. It was the reason we first got rid of all of the pickaxes. Here, the opposite is true. Here, we are intentionally being the pickaxes.

Even if you never plan to use this tactic for your own personal gain, the knowledge of knowing how and why others will use it against you can make you immune to it. Knowing how it works, what is affected by it, and why they are using it, is the only vaccine against their play on your fears. If all else fails, simply remove yourself from the situation, go somewhere quiet where you can be alone, meditate using positive self-talk, and visualize you skiing a good run over and over again until it's time to actually do it.

Warning: You cannot use this method if you are afraid of the same thing yourself. If your target sees that you are actually afraid of the same thing, they will not be affected by this method the way that you intended. In fact, the poison may work in reverse, against you, just as effectively in the same way it works on other people. So be careful when trying to implant fear in others, because it is known to backfire.

HEAD GAMES

> *"To win one hundred victories in one hundred battles*
> *is not the acme of skill.*
> *To subdue the enemy without fighting is the acme of skill."*
> *-Sun Tzu, The Art of War*

One of my favorite and most consistent processes of defeating mogul skiers that were better than me began by understanding just how those mogul skiers thought of themselves. By truly understanding how others think of themselves, from taping into their "personal movies" (their hero story). Being able to accurately assess which level of Superhero or a Juggernaut they are gives us a distinct and unpredictable advantage against them. You see, great mogul skiers already know they are better than you, and all they have to do is ski their run, and they will beat you. This is in their conscious mind. However, in their "not-so-conscious mind," they are expecting you to accept this as reality as well. Therefore, if you do not act in this manner, by not accepting that they are better than you (or at least not acting like it), by skiing your full run to the best of your ability with expectation that you are going to win, it can upset the mindset and the ego of the skier that is better than you.

In other words, if you do not act as they are subconsciously expecting, their "not-so-conscious" mind will set off warning bells that something isn't right with what they were expecting, and this might upset their reality. As this happens, the only thing that they will be consciously aware of is that the cause of the warning bells originated somewhere from within you. They will most likely be unable to readily put their finger on the exact reason, but only know that the disruption and the uncomfortable feeling is somehow stemming from you. If you get this far, then you have successfully intercepted their mojo, and that is the goal. Their conscious and unconscious mind will then war with each other over, which in reality is correct. You will know when this happens because they will usually be flustered, noticeably upset, or start to brag to anyone within earshot about some skill or accomplishment that they have. They do this in order to reassure themselves that they are, in fact, still better than you. However, as long as you can upset them and remove them from their relaxed confidence, that is the best chance you have to disrupt their performance. If you can disrupt it enough, you can beat them in head-to-head competition (like duals). The confusion, mixed with the sudden onset of uncertainty, upsets their previously demonstration of confidence, and they can begin to doubt themselves. If done with the proper timing, as in just before the gate drops, it can be enough to disrupt their focus, and a mogul skier is only as good as his focus.

Now obviously, this falls deeply into the social sciences, and there are a ton of variables that you need to be familiar with for these head tricks to work. Additionally, they will not always work. However, if the mogul skier is better than you and you have no other means to beat them, you might as well give it a try. After all, you can't lose twice.

Superheroes are easier to play head games against than Juggernauts. This is because Superheroes tend to make more information about themselves public and be more influenced by other people and their actions or non-actions. Juggernauts tend to be more private and unconcerned with the "goings on" of others. However, since this tactic attacks the subconscious expectations and ego, it can work on Juggernauts as well. It's just not as effective. Additionally, Superheroes usually have very carefully manicured social identities, that they strive to uphold, so any social workings that are not in line with the social identity which they created for themselves is going to bother them. Juggernauts tend not to care much about their social identities before a competition, but may brag about it afterwards. The way a juggernaut thinks is that he or she is competing against themselves, and you and your actions are of little consequence to her. The best thing to do is to stunt a Juggernaut's bragging after the competition; call them out and don't let them brag unmitigated. It works in the long run to stunt the growth of a potential Juggernauts renown, as well as his ego and confidence. You can only destroy a Juggernaut in the long game, not the short game. Besides, you don't have to worry about playing head games with Juggernauts so much, as they tend to destroy themselves regularly without your assistance—usually by jumping too big, going too fast, or both.

THE LOOKING GLASS

> *"I do not have to be where you are to see what you see,
> to feel what you feel, to know what you know.
> Because I've been there before."*
> -Michael Mead

The Looking Glass is a tool used most often by Juggernauts to assess their opponents. However, it can, in fact, be used by any athlete of relatively high skill level against any athlete of a lower skill level. It is a powerful tool because it can be used to predict the future, namely your future actions. All athletes of a given sport follow similar learning paths—like learning to walk before you can run, but neither of these can happen before you learn to crawl. As an athlete progresses through her career and up through the ranks of her sport, she is likely going to hit more milestones along the way than she had originally planned on. Thus, ignorance is paved over with experience. As she navigates the different avenues to be the best, she will invariably arrive at the most efficient and effective means to defeat all her adversaries.

However, the road to the top of mogul skiing is never an easy one, and more often than not it is treacherous. The athletes who become the best have gotten that way because they have triumphed over many difficulties in their path. Some of these obstacles were met head-on and overpowered, while others were avoided on purpose. A select few were survived by pure luck.

In any event, by the time you get to the top, you have likely seen it all. Things that were not clear to you at the beginning will now make perfect sense. Dangers that you were not aware of in the beginning—because of the darkness of your ignorance—are brought forth into the light by your knowledge and experiences. Former obstacles cease their impedance and can be transformed into tools of intimidation.

Let me give you an example. Imagine a Level 3 Juggernaut for a moment. King of the hill. The best of the best. Has seen and done it all. She is looking down from her podium (notice elevated position from the 3D model) on the less-experienced athletes navigating the treacherous journey of skill advancement. It might seem to a JL3 that their opponents are blindfolded, bouncing from one fruitless endeavor to another, ignorantly and iteratively, since this can often be the path when you are learning new skills and training. They can see the whole picture because they themselves were once right where you are, but they have already learned how to overcome those obstacles that you are now confronted with.

With the knowledge that you are currently seeking already in hand, they can use it as a baseline by which they can assess your choices, skills, fears, troubles, worries, etc., to a surprising level of detail and accuracy. Not only that, but they can also accurately predict your probability of success, failure, your soon-to-be-had pitfalls, your shortcomings, any course corrections that you would need to take, and so on. They can accurately gauge all of that because they have been in your shoes before. It seems like they can look inside you and even see your future, and in a way, they can. The knowledge of where you are, combined with the knowledge of where you want to be, is the power of the Looking Glass. It is like a one-way mirror where the more advanced athlete sits on the side where they can see through and "into" the less advanced athletes.

On the other side of the Looking Glass, the less skilled athletes only see their reflections. In other words, they can only see and relate to the skills and traits that they have available to them currently to try to fathom the more experienced athlete, which does not work. It is like a one-way mirror that is only transparent for the more-experienced athlete looking down on the less-skilled athlete. The former don't have the skills or experience required in order to be able to comprehend the latter.

This is what is known as the Looking Glass. The presence and proper use of this tool is one of the surest and clearest signs of a highly skilled athlete. However, what is interesting here is that the lesser-skilled athletes often make the mistake of looking into the Looking Glass towards the more advanced athlete in an attempt to find their weaknesses, analyze their mistakes, vices, problems, etc. However, what they are really seeing is merely a mirror projection of their own mistakes, vices, problems, etc. This is because you cannot assess what you cannot conceive of. So your brain compensates by filling in what it doesn't know with your own attributes, and then projects them onto others. Sometimes, these are deeply rooted fears and insecurities that you might not even be consciously aware of. Many higher skilled athletes inherently know this fatal flaw and can use it to read your innermost secrets like a book, as if they were your own subconscious. It is a very creepy feeling being assessed by someone who can be so intimate with you, yet so cold and insurmountable at the same time. Beware of the Looking Glass. It is a tool that elite athletes use to great success against their narcissistic would-be challengers. Since we are all narcissistic to some degree, we all unwittingly reveal too much information about ourselves at times, which can be used against us.

The information that we leak out about our knowledge and skill level of mogul skiing usually comes out in the form of "insights" into the sport. Our own opinions about the sport, when spoken out loud, reveal our experience level, our fears, troubles, worries, and not least of which our skill level, among other things. Proudly pronounced to all that can hear, this is where higher level Superheroes and Juggernauts gain valuable information and insight into information about you that they can use to their own advantage if they need to.

People drunk on their own insights are too verbose and reveal knowledge about themselves that can be used against them. A good Juggernaut or Superhero knows this, and they always have an ear open for such rants or acknowledgments of one's fears. In other words, the insights and opinions of lesser-experienced people actually illuminate their own shortcomings, unbeknownst to them, right in front of the Juggernaut's or Superhero's perceptive eye. The lesser athlete digs himself an inescapable grave when he then begins to fabricate a world in his mind which proves the validity of his "discoveries" which are based on pure assumption, and his own fears. Then he charges right into the cold hard hands of the ungraspable Juggernaut or Superhero who never allowed her true skills to be revealed.

The Level 3 Juggernauts are the best at this. The lesser athlete usually goes away utterly defeated, bewildered, confused, disillusioned and usually crushed right down to the very spirit. This is a good sign you have competed against a juggernaut, in case you didn't know it beforehand. They invariably try to mercilessly crush your spirit. They do it suddenly, unexpectedly, and on purpose, whenever they can. Just like an ambush. This is because they want you to think twice the next time you compete against them. They will constantly work on and play to your fears and short-sightedness to instill fear and intimidation in you. This is what it feels like to fall victim to the Looking Glass. So do your best not to reveal too much information about yourself and only confide in people whom you trust. It is ill-advised to publicly announce your fears, weaknesses, or even opinions. Remember, the information they glean from your opinions can come back to haunt you, so don't give it to them. It's better to keep your mouth shut, especially when the stakes are high.

A good Juggernaut or Superhero, if actually involved in revealing conversation, will even play along until they drain every ounce of narcissistic self-insight from the lesser-skilled individual. They will pay very close attention to the specific fears that his insights are categorized around. Thus, unless you are on the top of your game, or you very much trust the individuals which whom you are expressing your opinions/fears, it is a good idea to keep them to yourself, lest they be used against you. Generally, it is the best practice to keep your fears and opinions between you and your coach. During your learning process, you should be a consumer of opinions, not a creator of them. Ask as many questions as you can from the best coaches and athletes that you can find. Refer to Chapter 19: Your Opinion Betrays You. This is just another way in which it does.

The way out from behind the wrong side of the Looking Glass is to realize that your own insights are really just your own fears and troubles projected on to others. It is not them at all. We tend to see in others what we least like about ourselves. Realize that those projections are your own demons manifesting themselves and are playing you for a sucker. You have to be extra vigilant to deal with those hidden fears. Eventually, you will become familiar with all of your fears and then when you judge others, you will not be projecting your own fears onto others, nor will you be convinced they have the same difficulties and troubles as you. Only then can you study them and actually learn the necessary information from your target to accurately assess their skills and weaknesses. When this happens, you will know that you are on the proper side of the Looking Glass.

"He doesn't give up – ever.
He is not intimidated by anything.
He just doesn't care.
You can't intimidate him."
-Keith Johnson

CHAPTER 19
YOUR OP1NION BETRAYS YOU

> *"The average person thinks he isn't."*
> -Father Larry Lorenzoni

> *"The first Principle is that you must not fool yourself,*
> *And you are the easiest person to fool."*
> -Richard P. Feynman,
> (Nobel Prize-winning physicist)

Life is all about learning. The more we learn, the more we grow. The more we grow, the more successful we can become. Learning has the inherent difficulty of not only accepting new ideas, but understanding and utilizing them to their fullest potential. Accepting a new idea is often the most difficult part of the learning process. This is because who we are is the culmination of our opinions of the past. When a new idea challenges those opinions, more often than not we reject it out of reflex. However, if the source of that new idea is someone who has achieved something that you want to achieve, and their "new idea" has anything to do with the goals that you have for yourself, it's time to abandon your own opinions and accept the new idea. It is a combined effort of trust and dedication. Trust in the one whom you choose to learn from, and in the dedication to your goals. The combination of those two things will allow you to abandon your old opinions/ideas for new ones. However, I am not suggesting you go blindly in the direction of your mentor. I like to mull over new ideas and let them marinate in my brain for a while, as Aristotle suggests: "It is the mark of an educated mind to be able to entertain a thought without accepting it."

YOUR OPINION BETRAYS YOU

As a rule, most people are good at the latter part of that statement, but are too stubborn to entertain the idea in the first place. We have a habit of believing that our current opinion is better by default, simply because it's ours. And the invading opinion is (usually) immediately vanquished by whatever opinions that we already have in its rightful place. This tends to happen weather or not we take the time to consider it or not. It is almost like any new opinion that is in contrast to any that we currently have is doomed to fail no matter how promising it is. We will even go to the ends of the earth to make up reasons why the invading opinion is wrong.

Whenever I am stubbornly resisting new ideas because of my own rigid opinions, I like to remind myself of the above quote by Aristotle. Please take a few seconds to close your eyes and make a promise to yourself that you are going to try not to judge what you read based on predisposed, rigid opinions. You will learn in this chapter that your own opinions can betray you. It is not always wise to believe your own opinions. If nothing else, take note of every time you make a judgment, and how hard it is to go even a few minutes without making a judgment. Just make an attempt to be self-aware of your own opinions as they spring into your mind.

In this chapter, I will attempt to show you how your own opinion, that very verbose voice in your head, the one with which you identify yourself, can betray the real you. And you probably don't even know it. Your very nature can betray you. Our nature as human beings is to think that our opinions matter more than anyone else's. After all, the non-stop chatter of our own inner voice by itself is more than enough to seduce us. It isn't that we can't see the faults in our own opinions—it is that most of the time, we simply don't want to. If one has the aspiration to change his life from a low state to a high state, one must undergo deep changes from within. On the road to success, the last things to change are the things that we are most personally identified with—if they change at all.

If someone was inclined to undergo a truly complete transformation, she must change everything about herself. This includes the things about herself that she most closely identifies with. After all, what else is there to most identify oneself with more than one's own thoughts and opinions? Ultimately, most people do not want or need a complete transformation, but I am only bringing it up to illustrate just how closely tied we can be to our own opinions. They can be so difficult to disidentify with that they can impede our learning process, and therefore, stunt our growth as mogul skiers.

As mogul skiers, we aspire to do many things that we cannot yet comprehend. Those of us who have achieved things that we once could not comprehend will tell you that the key to achieving it began with abandoning your own limiting opinions for someone else's who we trusted. Consciously or unconsciously, we realized that those opinions that we had would only hold us back. Therefore, we abandoned them because we wished to grow. Opinions are like a snake's skin; they protect us, help us, nourish us, but from time to time, we must shed it for a new one in order to grow. In my opinion, all opinions have a shelf life to them. The more you learn about any given topic in life, the more your opinions will change, evolve, or be completely abandoned. So don't hold on to your opinions too tightly—there is always another one to satisfy you just around the corner.

The only part of us that never truly changes is the ever-present consciousness and state of awareness that allows us to monitor our own thoughts. Therefore, you can use it to constantly monitor whether or not your opinion is betraying you at any given point. Since it is the thought patterns and opinions of successful people alone that make them successful, then why not try to mimic their thought patterns and opinions? You can do that by constantly monitoring your own opinions and thoughts. If you are truly able to mimic the thought patterns and opinions of someone who is truly successful, then what is stopping you from becoming just as successful? I am not saying that you should go out and copy everything someone you admire does, but you should learn how they view the world through their own eyes—see, look, feel, how everything they lay their eyes on is simply an opportunity waiting to be cultivated, and use that energy to enrich your own personal experience.

One of the most common betrayals of our opinions we have as humans today is judging others too harshly. We too often boil down entire statements, activities, even people into an oversimplified categorization that is shallow and harsh, based on pure assumptions. In other words, we usually categorize good or bad, black or white, based on our own narrow whirlpool of personal experience and egotistic deduction. Afterwards, we tend to seduce ourselves completely in reverse, by pure induction of our meager accomplishments, back up to through the same narrow whirlpool of personal experience, where we compliment our accomplishments too highly—thereby boosting our ego and accentuating our arrogance, until at last we arrive at the opinion that we are better than everyone else. Exactly where we started. In the meantime, we tend to miss the real lesson in the experience. We tend to miss the opinions of the truly successful altogether, because we are too busy seducing our own ego.

The opinion of the successful people is what we are truly trying to find. We must learn to quiet our minds and subdue our opinions in order to hear it. Once we teach ourselves to hear the opinions of successful people, the next difficult task is to apply it, to try it out, to hold tight to it, even when your own opinion tells us not to. Why? Well, it is because this person's opinion is proven to be successful, and yours isn't, necessarily. If you remember from the previous chapter objective vs. subjective: the opinions and methods of successful people are more vindicated than yours are, and therefore, have a higher degree of objectivity than your opinions do. In other words, their opinions are much closer to being facts than yours are. Their opinions are closer to facts, while those of us who aren't as successful, are just subjective opinions. Facts are the building blocks of their success. So can you see now why it is so much more important to trade-up your opinions for theirs? Therefore, by simple deduction, on the path to success, your opinion doesn't really matter, as long as you have a mentor that you can default to as your opinions develop into facts.

Always remember that your opinion can and will betray you from time to time. It can and will hold you back, if you let it. Your opinion is the single greatest barrier to your own success. It is like being on a boat trying to sail the open seas, tied to a mooring buoy. You will try and try and try, but even with favorable winds, you will go nowhere. In the storms, you will be in danger. We must learn to let go and to be adaptable in the turbulent seas of life. Also, be aware that there is not just one "end-all, be-all" set of opinions that we are searching for, but we must be adaptable to all opinions and opportunities in the present moment. You must follow the more successful person for some time before you can learn to trust and rely on your instincts as well.

As a note: some of us may so be bewitched by the seductiveness of our own opinions that we become drunk with self-righteousness and force our opinions on others, unprovoked. This is because we believe that if we force others to adopt our opinions and beliefs, our own opinions are more justified. However, this is not only a sign of an insecure person, but a control freak. In response to the control freaks in their lives, many people throw up "walls" to block out the negative and imposing energy, and revert to strictly relying on their own personal opinions. Both of these methods are wrong. The former tends not to adapt to the superior opinions of the successful because she is too busy imposing her own will on the world and making it up as she goes along. The latter tends not to adapt to the superior opinions because they get blocked out with all the other opinions that she is constantly getting bombarded with. Therefore, the only solution is to very carefully research and choose an individual who you want to learn from, and then put your own opinions and judgments aside and learn from them as best you can.

It often astonishes me how little space in a person's brain is taken up by successful people's opinions and their proven ways. Ideally, your task should be to be deaf to all those who are not your chosen mentors/teachers/coaches, while at the same time, listening for and hearing the opinions of your coach. Often times, it is little more than a whisper, but it will undoubtedly guide you to your own success.

WHERE OPINIONS EVOLVED FROM

Throughout human evolution, life or death decisions were frequent. Since not all people made the same choices in the same circumstances, some survived, and some didn't. The ones who survived made good decisions, which were based on:

1. GOOD TRAINING - An elder showed them the right way.

2. PERSONAL EXPERIENCE - An opinion derived from a "close call."

3. PURE LUCK - An occurrence in which one does not fully understand the reason for which they were successful. For example, if you have seen and heard many people get tracked down and eaten by lions or another type of predator, you might think, "These things (lions) can see in all directions through any object." Then one day you are paralyzed with fear as you see a hungry lion pass just yards from you, but you are downwind, so it cannot smell you. He passes, leaving you alive. You might think to yourself that it was "pure luck," when in reality, it was the fact that you were downwind of the hungry lion, camouflaged by stillness. But since you don't know this, this "pure luck" was not intentional, will not be repeatable, and therefore matters little, other than as raw data for a consistency puzzle piece as described in the "Mysterious Strangers" section in Chapter 20: How to Learn.

It wasn't until I heard a podcast from Steven Kotler (Bulletproof Radio #109) that it finally crystallized in my mind that learning and being in the zone do not conflict as I had previously thought. Rather, one gives rise to the other, if one can just learn to let go of your opinions. Let me explain. Herb Benson, M.D, a professor at Harvard Medical School, did a lot of the neurochemical studies of "flow," more commonly referred to as "the zone" in sports. And he has a four-step process of "flow" (below). I provided comments and in-depth explanations for each step listed.

1. FRUSTRATION (Struggle) - Overloading the brain until you feel like you are about to lose your mind, and then pull it back.

    Frustration is the true test of any athlete, and invariably at its core is the opinions of the athlete, holding him down and restricting his progress. You see, frustration comes from your expectations, for yourself and others, and your interpretation of the material you are trying to learn. Obviously, your opinion is betraying you. It is holding you back because if you grip firmly onto a way of thinking, a way of interpreting the world, you cannot learn something that is out of your preexisting comprehension. You have to learn to let go. You have to learn to let go of your opinions and your way of comprehending and just trust in the methods of your teachers. Getting frustrated is a great catalyst for trying something new. The faster you can do that, the faster you can try something new without having to spend the time to fully comprehend it. Thus, you can learn it faster. That is why children are the fastest learners, because they don't have a fully forged opinionated system that they are trying to cram with knowledge. Like trying to jam a square peg through a much smaller round hole. Let go of your opinion, and it will set you free so that you can finally relax. Once you relax, you can finally appreciate the present moment, and when you become grateful for this, you can finally enter the zone.

2. RELAXATION - (There's that word again!) You need enough self-control to be able to take your mind off the problem. Or otherwise, your amygdala won't allow you to get your mind off the problem. A relaxation response gives a global release of nitrous oxide, which drops all the stress hormones out of your body and forges the release of serotonin and dopamine, which induces the next step.

This step is the same as the relaxation step in my Mogul Method, except mine is initiated out of fear (Step 1 - Scare yourself). The fear response invokes a flight or fight response, and you must train yourself to persistently choose the fight response. However, there is more power to it then that. Since it is based out of real danger and necessity, your survival instincts are thereby sparked, which are needed to enter and sustain a state of "flow" in the mind. But the key to opening your mind to the flow state is to relax. You have to scare yourself, but you must also be able to push through it (fight or flight), and be okay with the risk and subdue your fears (fight response, initiated by instilling fear in yourself), and then be able to take your conscious mind off of all the variables, skiing by reflex. That is when you know you are in "flow." Continue this until the end of your top air, repeat the process for the middle section, and a third time for the bottom section.

3. FLOW - By definition, is your most productive, creative, and wildly successful mental state.

4. MEMORY LEARNING APPLICATION - You usually feel bad at this stage, because the neurochemicals required to sustain "flow" are gone. You are no longer in "flow." But it is a much-needed stage, as it allows conscious reflection, learning, and hindsight analysis of the "flow" state. All of these things help shorten the time required until the next "flow" state can begin.

There is a quote that I believe goes along with this:

"Where there is much desire to learn,
there of necessity will be much arguing...
for opinion in good men is but knowledge in the making."
-John Milton

The important thing to take away from this quote, compared and contrasted to the above breakdown of flow and my analysis of it, is that it is important to become frustrated and, perhaps, even argue. But these are ultimately hamster wheels, useful only to get your determination up to a certain level that you are willing to abandon even your own opinion and thought in the process in order to find the answer. Ultimately, to absorb the most difficult of lessons, you must abandon your most prized opinions, analysis, thoughts, and trust in the unknown, because letting go of these things is the only way to open the door to the relaxation stage. You have to enter a stage where you can consciously keep your mind completely free of thoughts. Be like a watchdog in your own mind as your own opinions and judgments keep popping up. Do not let them take you over. You don't have to follow these thoughts; just let them come in (and they will), and then let them go. See how long you can sit without having thoughts (a.k.a. meditation).

I've not only seen my own opinions (judgments) betray me, but many other athletes as well. It stalls their progression and flattens their learning curve by not letting go of their short-sighted opinions. It is a very real, very pervasive problem. This problem, unfortunately, does not go away with age—in fact, in many cases, age makes it worse. Innate self-validating opinions are rarely founded on solid facts. If you see someone who has or does something that you want to do, then you should do whatever you can to learn from that person. If his opinion is different than yours (and it probably will be), and the topic is directly or indirectly related to his area of expertise, then chances are that you are wrong, not him. The sooner you can accept that, then the sooner you can learn his secrets.

THE HUMAN BRAIN

Think of the human brain as a complex electrical circuit, in which there are many pathways that electricity can take to get to the place it wants to go. In this case, imagine it is a light bulb. There is a common myth that electricity, even though it travels at the speed of light and has a bunch of different pathways (choices) that it can take, will always take the path of least resistance. This is likened to the old cliché that "you can't teach an old dog new tricks." Meaning that once you are really used to doing something one way, you will keep doing it that way because it is the most practiced method to you. In other words, you have the least resistance to doing things the way you are used to, and you, therefore, will be resistant to training yourself to do things differently. Luckily for us, the cliché "you can't teach an old dog new tricks" is only a myth. In fact (and this is a throwback to my engineering school days), just like a complex electrical circuit, our brains will send electricity (current) down ALL paths simultaneously, but only inversely proportional to the resistance of each path.

This is to say that if there are multiple paths the current can take, and one path has 3 times the resistance, only 1/3 of the current will travel down that path. This is known as Ohms law: I = V/R

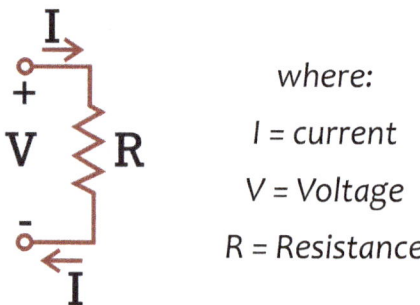

where:

I = current

V = Voltage

R = Resistance

So what does this mean for you? It means that you don't have to teach your brain an entirely new way to send its current through your body. It already has some current flowing down the correct path right now! (It has to, after all, it's a law!) It is your job to decrease your resistance on the path that your coach is trying to tell you is the best for the new skill you want to learn. So how do we do this? That's right, by getting rid of your opinions, and your unconscious thought patterns that constantly inhabit your brain. Then, the more you use this thought pattern, the stronger the synapses in your brain will get, reducing resistance even more. Only through practice, can these "good" pathways be cleaned out, and their resistances lowered. We strive to train until the desired pathways have the least resistance than the original ones, thereby becoming our new default way of doing things. Incidentally, we can modify or amplify our reflexes in the same way.

There is an analogy that goes along with this. Think of a backyard, overgrown with tall grass. It is so tall, you can't even see over the top it. In front of you, there is a well-traveled footpath that leads to a storage shed, but the path is long and meandering. The storage shed represents the place that you are trying to get to in the most efficient way possible. But the footpath zigs and zags this way and that, wrapping around some old overgrown junk and lawn furniture. It is anything but a direct route. You might know deep down know that there is a shorter physical distance to just walk straight through the tall grass, but you don't, because it will be difficult for you to push through, or maybe you are afraid of banging your shin on some hidden junk along the way. Or maybe there are snakes or something, and "oh well," maybe you'll just do it next time.

One day, your husband or wife is on the roof fixing a leak while you are meandering your way out to the shed. This time is different because they are able to give you an eagle eye perspective of where you are trying to go in the most efficient way possible. They can clearly see not only the most direct route to the storage shed and can direct you to it, but also all of the obstacles that lie in your path. They can guide you directly to the storage shed, making you aware of the hidden junk that you might bang your shin on. With their help, you can forge a new path, which will be difficult at first, but the more you take that path, the easier it will get until it is more well-traveled than your original path. That is how coaching works. Your spouse on the roof represents your coach in this example. They can see things that you can't. They can tell you to be wary of something approaching that you cannot see. All the time while keeping you on the most direct path to your destination, but you will have to trust them, abandon your opinions and fears, and you will get to your destination faster.

> *"Two things are infinite: The universe,*
> *and human stupidity;*
> *and I'm not sure about the universe."*
> *-Albert Einstein*

> *"The first step toward change is awareness.*
> *The second step is acceptance."*
> *-Nathaniel Branden*

> *"The best mind-altering drug is truth."*
> *-Jane Wagner*

> *"All that matters is the correctness of your analysis."*
> *-Jason Capital*

> *"Our heads are round, so thought can change direction."*
> *-Francis Picabia*

CHAPTER 20
HOW TO LEARN

"The greatest thing I've ever learned,
was learning how to teach myself.
And the greatest thing I ever taught myself,
was learning how I learn."
-Michael Mead

INTRODUCTION

Everyone has things that they want to be able to do, that they don't know how to currently. We usually blow them off as impossible, impractical, too time-consuming, or just too difficult to learn. However, more often than not, they are not. We degrade ourselves with negative self-talk, like "I'm just not that talented," or "I'm not smart enough to learn that," or "I'm just too stupid." The real culprit is actually that most of us, myself included, were never taught the proper way to learn. Most of us were forced to sit in a one-size-fits-all public education system and had information crammed down our throats that we weren't even interested in learning in the first place. Granted, some things we needed to learn whether we liked to or not. But the way most things were taught to us was in a one-size-fits-all method. If you could absorb the information in the way it was presented, then you were considered smart. If not, then you were considered dumb. The problem with our public schooling systems is they unintentionally brand some kids as smart, and others as dumb, based on their inflexible information delivery system, and not the students themselves. That branding—good or bad —has a tendency to stick with those kids for life, when the real problem was that they simply digest information differently, and our education system is only set up to cater to one type of student.

The people that experience difficulty in learning right off the bat for the first 18 years of their life have to overcome enormous challenges in rewriting their self-image. To rewrite their branding, they first have to learn how they learn, because it was never taught to them. This is because not everyone learns the same way. They need to discover their own style of learning, before they can ever teach themselves what they want to learn. They need to do this because our education system is not set up to do that for us. Our education system is not even set up to properly educate our most brilliant students either. Take Albert Einstein for example. The education system failed him because his mind was put together in such a way that made him slow, yet persistent in his thoughts. His learning mirrored the way he thought. He learned slow. So slow, in fact, he failed fourth grade math. He thought very abstractly, and needed difficult, time-consuming problems to chew on. He couldn't keep up with the quick repetitious math problems that were presented to him and the rest of his class. His teachers branded him as dumb! Turns out, that fourth grade math was too fast for the most famous mathematician and scientist of all time! So if you ever felt dumb, so did Albert Einstein. How is that for good company? In the next section, I will show you how-to-learn, how-you-learn. Then I will explain to you how to teach yourself, so that you can actually learn those things that you may have told yourself that you would never be able to.

Many times over my very different careers as a mogul skier, a stuntman, and an engineer, I constantly wanted to be able to do things that I couldn't. I wanted to be able to do more difficult tricks, or solve more difficult equations, for example. Some things appeared to be so far out of my comprehension that they seemed utterly impossible. If it happened to be a new physical trick, as a stuntman, for example, I couldn't always fully visualize the physical movements and the complex gyroscopic feeling that were required to be able to do that trick. Since I couldn't see the trick performed in my mind's eye, I couldn't perform the trick. There were many challenges inherent in the difficult tricks that I wanted to learn. This was because of any number of unpredictable internal and external forces that would be acting on me. As a stuntman, I had to take into consideration such things as a moving rail car suspended at a height, collapsible platforms, falling ladders, explosives, personal equipment, weapons, backpacks, and/or being set on fire. There were many numbers of combinations of multiple accessories and challenges associated with the stunt world that regular life simply didn't provide any training for. So many of those things I had to teach myself, and teach it well, so that didn't get hurt in that very dangerous environment.

On the other hand, some things (especially in mogul skiing) seem easy to comprehend, but remained nearly impossible to implement in practice. Skiing on the Glass Plate was one of those things. Another example is the concept of being able to ski the moguls at a rate which your legs move faster in full ski gear than you can move them while sprinting on dry land. Yet, mogul skiers do it all the time. Another difficult concept to grasp was being able to ski in the moguls as fast as someone straight lining it on the flats next to you. Then again, some things seemed impossible to comprehend and practice altogether, like my engineering homework. Whatever the challenges that you are faced with, regardless of how impossible they seem to learn, I have developed several methods that you can use to help you learn those impossible things.

What is important to take away from this is that things are not always easy to understand. However, even though we may not understand them, they exist anyways. Somebody somewhere has already learned them; therefore, we know it is possible. People all around us are doing things that we may not be able to comprehend on a daily basis, but that doesn't have to mean that we can't learn how to do them. Many people see where I am in life now, and assume that I have always been smart, but it is untrue. When I was young, I was a C student at best. I simply couldn't learn at the same rate as the other kids. It seemed, at times, that I needed at least twice as much time to digest the same material as the other kids, if I could do it at all. I took an extra-long time learning how to read, for example, and was almost held back in school because of it. At other times, language tasks seemed too foreign and too difficult to understand altogether. So much, in fact, that I even had to take speech impediment classes so that I could cram in more time to learn to how to read.

From my perspective at that age, school and the things I was expected to learn looked like they only had a casual relationship with reality. The impossible was handed to me on a daily basis, it seemed, and it became the norm for me. I made the effort to just keep on keeping on until I was able to do the tasks that were given to me as good or better than my peers. However, I am still a very slow reader to this day. I have great difficulty keeping up with subtitles at the movies, for example. When other people give me a short thing to read and are waiting for my reaction, most of the time, I fake-read the majority of the material for fear that they will realize how slow of a reader I am. If people know you're a slow reader, they think you are dumb, or so I thought. I didn't want anyone to think I was dumb.

By the time I hit junior high, I was an above average student, and by the time I graduated high school, I was one of the best in my class. Since I was so far below average in grade school, few would have predicted this. I had to learn everything the hard way, by simply putting in more time to study. I believe there is something innately powerful about people who learn everything the hard way. We tend to be unwavering in our determination, dedication, and are unphased by difficult things, because well, difficult tasks are the norm for us. We tend to make little of our mistakes, and the people who constantly want to belittle us. We also tend to be thankful for, and relish in, the small accomplishments much more than average people do. This is what helps us sustain ourselves during impossible tasks.

What I just described are some very powerful attributes that you might want to cultivate should you want to improve your path to success. You will be met with mistakes, have no doubts about it. The naysayers will heckle you and try to pull you down from day one, so you must learn how to cope with not making everyone happy. After all, it's not your job to make everyone happy. It's your job to make YOU happy first. Other people will never be completely satisfied with how happy you make them, anyways. When other people just want you to make them happy, that is just their way of subjugating you. They do it to enrich their own lives, not yours. Remember that.

Eventually, in everyone's life, we are confronted with an impossible task, sooner or later, that we must learn how to do. When no matter how you look at it, you may not be able to even begin to figure out where to start or how it's done. Most people will get to this point, throw their hands up in exhaustion, and exclaim (with all the violent flare that their inner prima donna has to offer) that "It's impossible!" or "It can't be done!" It is at this point that we begin.

(Please check your prima donna persona at the door.)

LEARN HOW YOU LEARN

On the road of life, you will experience more than one seemingly insurmountable obstacle. That is guaranteed. Many people will work to discourage you from conquering each of those obstacles. At times, it may seem that the hecklers and naysayers are as numerous as the snowflakes on a cold, lonely, snowy night. But you shouldn't let them make your decisions for you. You cannot let them dissuade you, either. After all, without the cold, you cannot appreciate warmth. Similarly, without the naysayers, you cannot fortify your self-confidence and independence. If you truly want to be successful in anything you choose to do in life, you must continue to learn. In the learning process we call life, problems arise that we must learn how to solve on our own. You may doubt yourself at first, but you will learn how to overcome them.

You will need to learn to become aware of what exactly it takes for you to absorb and retain information. Not what "they" say it takes for "someone" to retain information, but YOU. What do YOU require? What do YOU need? Do you need to read what you just read five or six times? What about 10 or 20 times? Do YOU need it perfectly quiet? Or do YOU need music on and/or a social environment? What do YOU need to do to your environment, or to yourself for retention to occur? Pay attention as often as you can when you do remember things. Write it down. Why was it easy for you to remember? What was special about the topic or the material or the environment that made it easy for you to remember? If one subject is easier to understand and remember than another, what similarities can be made from that subject to another more difficult one? We create parities between what we understand well, and that which we do not, in order to create a memorable link between what we know and the subject we are trying to learn. A good way to do this is in the form of a silly story or rhyme, to conjoin aspects of your less favorite subject with parts of your favorite one(s). Doing so creates a stronger link for remembering the material. Plus it's fun! You may even begin to notice you're smiling while you are studying as you come up with one silly story or rhyme which links dissimilar topics in a unique or funny way. Then you will smile again when you get your results back!

Another way many people learn is by reflection and analysis of the past. A great deal more time in my life than I care to admit has been spent analyzing my past. Reflection and analysis of the past uses the power of hindsight and your (hopefully) wiser, more experienced self that exists here in the present moment. I like to constantly scour my past experiences for any information that could give me further insight into myself, my skill, or my endeavors. Looking back over my life, I have discovered there are a variety of "tiers" or "levels," if you will, to the knowledge we acquire throughout our lives. These "levels" help us gauge the value of the knowledge we have acquired. I learned this partially because I was a pathological reflector on the past, partially through my training as an engineer, and partially from a moment of true clarity that I had. To me, it was nothing short of an epiphany. However, it is so simple that I am sure I am not the first to discover this simple realization. In the past, I have even used this method with great success, even though I did not ever consolidate the method for its true power with real clarity. In other words, it worked for me, even though I didn't know I was using it.

In explanation, I once had a girlfriend who seemed to somehow make me perform better in my athletics when she was around than if she wasn't. My performances were top-notch when she was around, regardless if we were fighting or not. That's all I knew at first. If she was around, I could comfortably count on an excellent performance. That was the first level of the knowledge; the "what" of what was going on. I didn't understand WHY I performed better, just that I DID perform better when she was around. The second level of knowledge is in the "why" or the "how" of the outcome. I discovered by reflecting specifically on those moments "why" I was able to perform at a higher level. The reason was that I was tenser than usual when she was around. My muscles were more alert, too. However, the real secret was I was forced to exhale strongly enough to release the excess tension before each trick, just to be able to perform the trick at all. The forceful exhale allowed me to combine the greater strength of tense muscles with the flexibility that comes with relaxation through a strong exhale. It may be a standard skill for some, but it was something that I was never formally trained to purposefully do. Done with the proper timing, it can be very powerful. The point, however, is that I was able to teach myself this valuable skill without any outside input simply based on reflecting on some perplexingly good results I had gotten in the past. I did this by simply drilling down into the memory and asking myself all the appropriate questions.

LEARN HOW TO TEACH YOURSELF

"If we wonder often, the gift of knowledge will come."
-Arapaho saying

Asking yourself the appropriate questions is a great way to teach yourself. You don't need to overcomplicate it, just stick with these basic questions listed below, be as thorough with your answers as you can be, and then write them down. Also, be patient with yourself. Relax and be patient. The answers will come to you eventually—although it may take up to several weeks of mulling over a difficult topic for the answer to occur to you.

1. WHY?
2. WHAT?
3. HOW?
4. WHAT IF? (FEARS VS. FEAR OF FAILURE VS. FEAR OF SUCCESS)
5. TAKE ACTION! (USUALLY NEEDS TO HAPPEN BEFORE YOU ARE TOTALLY READY)

Once you understand how YOU learn, you can then begin to teach yourself how to teach yourself. Force yourself to find a quiet room, if that is what you need, or fore yourself to read that line for the 10th time, or to ski another run when all you want to do is go in. (However, do not do any highly difficult jumps or training exercises if you are tired, because that is a good way to get yourself hurt.) These are some ways that you may begin to teach yourself. In order to do so, you must learn to develop your willpower. Willpower is based on telling yourself that you are going to do something, and then following through. After all, do you really want to be the type of person who does what he or she is told by others, but slacks and neglects what YOU told yourself to do? Of course not. You have to have more respect for yourself and what you tell yourself to do than you do for other people and their wishes. After all, only making everyone else happy is a pretty crappy way to live. Nine times out of ten, those people think less of you than you are aware of, anyways. So the first rule is to respect yourself enough to do what you say. In that way, you can truly become your own master. For you to be your own master, you have to act that way. The principles you then discover about yourself will allow you to accomplish your best possible achievements.

> "You are your own greatest teacher, your own greatest adversary,
> your own greatest pupil, and your own greatest masterpiece."
> -Unknown

This learning model (on the previous page) will create a perpetual knowledge stream that will allow you to mount the insurmountable. Let yourself be your life's work, and you will live a very fulfilling life. Give yourself what you truly want, and do not seek it out in others, because only you really know what you really want. The next section is dedicated to one method that I have used (and continue to use) with great success. However, it is not a substitute for hard work, research, practice, or patience. It is merely a catalyst to help you learn in areas where you lack a teacher. It may not work for everyone, but since it works for me, I am glad to share it with you.

The person who invented it is Jim Kwik. He is a world renowned memory and learning expert and his method for increasing the speed at which you learn anything is called **F.A.S.T** (Forget... Active... State... Teach.) I am not going to get too far into it here, but I highly suggest you go check out hi method for yourself. You can start by going to: http://jimkwik.com/ and subscribing to his email list. You will learn a lot of helpful tricks from him, I promise!

One thing I would like to point out about the learning process is that the state of our moods can have a huge impact on how fast we learn as long as how well we retain it. If your state and energy are low, then your learning is going to be low. It is the difference between a thermostat and a thermometer. A thermometer reacts and reflects to the environment whatever it might be. This is the default setting for your state, which is at the mercy of your environment. On the contrary, a cultivated state of mind is like a thermostat, which sets a standard, or sets a goal and makes the environment reflect that standard. So it is important to be aware of the fact that you don't have to be a slave to your mood. You can in fact, with practice, change your state. That is one of Jim's most important lessons. I just want to make sure that you know it IS possible. Please visit his website to find out more.

> "With great responsibility comes great power"
> -Jim Kwik

When we take great responsibility for our actions we have great power to change our lives. Those people that take responsibility for their own state and do something about it when it is below where they want it to be become very powerful in their own lives.

LOCK & KEY

"Higher levels of difficulty automatically unlock lower levels of difficulty."
-Unknown

When someone who has used what they consider a valuable (and often misunderstood) piece of information, which can be used to achieve a remarkable result, this is commonly known as a "key." "Keys" are perplexing because not only are they usually misunderstood, they are also poorly circulated due to their valuable nature. Keys are familiar amongst all professions as the cliché: "The keys to success." You can imagine a locked door with success on one side and you on the opposite side. With the proper key, you will succeed; without it, you will not. However, most consider "keys" to be uniform and transferable. In other words, they are the same and used the same way from one person to another (one key for one door).

Over the years of your training, you will inevitably come across people that have a skill that you desire, who are either unwilling or unable to teach you the said skill. I like to think of those skills as little lock boxes or locked doors that protect valuables. So for the purpose of this chapter, let us define a "lock box" as a skill, a trait, or an advantage that you seek to acquire, and a "key" as the knowledge, the opinion, or the explanation that paves the road for you to acquire what you desire. Since physical lock boxes are opened with a key, which gains you access to their valuables, it serves as a good analogy for new skills, since similarly, they can be locked away in the mind of one of your competitors. Yet they can be unlocked in surprisingly similar ways with a "key." There are only a few steps to unlocking a common physical lockbox:

1. Insert key into lock box.
2. Turn the key left.
3. If still not open, turn key to the right.
4. Pull key out.
5. Open lock box.

This is a familiar and simple method that I will use as an analogy in this section. Since there is a way to apply this simple, repeatable process to the things that we would like to learn, yet have no teacher to teach us. Since the "lock box" is usually discovered first, the main variable here is the "key." The main challenge in this analogy method is you have no idea what the key might be, or how it might look, or even exactly how to use it. The first step is to find the right "key" for your specific locked box. That's where things begin to get a bit turned upside-down, so to speak—meaning it's better to be a key collector than a box collector. Therefore, by simple deduction, your probability of solving problems (unlocking boxes) goes up when you have more keys than lock boxes! So how does one become a key collector? Where do you find these keys? Well, they are all around you for sure. You just have to generally know what you're looking for, even though you may not specifically know what it is. The more keys you can collect on topics that interest you, the more lock boxes you will be able to open on that topic without having to search for a new key every single time!

WHERE TO FIND KEYS

1. FROM PEOPLE WHO ARE BETTER THAN YOU
2. FROM PEOPLE WHO HAVE ACQUIRED WHAT YOU SEEK (NOT TO BE CONFUSED WITH PEOPLE WHO POSSESS WHAT YOU SEEK)
3. FROM WISE TEACHERS
4. FROM MYSTERIOUS STRANGERS (THE CAVEMAN METHOD)

FROM PEOPLE WHO ARE BETTER THAN YOU

You must be extremely open-minded when you go searching for the key to someone's skill who is better than you, because obviously, they know something that you don't (albeit sometimes unconsciously). To begin with, you must be aware of, and sensitive to, everything they do, whether it seems important to you or not. This is because somewhere in that person, clues to their skill(s) are sure to leak out in seemingly mundane ways. Aggregate as much information about them as you possibly can, especially anything they do or say that might be even slightly out of the ordinary. Soak it up. Regardless if you think that it really has any effect on that skill that you seek or not, write it down. Do not let your opinions get in your way. Do not judge the person that has the skill that you want to learn from your own standards. Learn to judge them from *their* own standards.

Are they content with themselves? How? Why? Ask yourself if they are they compulsive or reserved? These macro-level personality attributes can serve as a clue to unlocking their secrets. This is because these macro-level personality traits have a strong influence on everything we think, say, and do. And if you want to get inside someone's head, all you have to do is learn to think like them, even if it's not your way of thinking. Take, for example, someone who is compulsive. You may notice them rearranging the salt and pepper shakers (to get them just perfect) after using them at the dinner table. Or you may notice them at unrest when not everyone has their napkins on their laps. Compulsive people are easy to spot. Once you can clearly identify their macro personality traits, try to think like them. In this case, try to think like a compulsive person. Then ask yourself, now that you are thinking like a compulsive person, see if you can figure out as many ways as you can that that personality type would affect everything that they do relating to mogul skiing (or any endeavor you want). So if you notice that they are compulsive, you might think to yourself, well, maybe always showing up to training on time everyday rain or shine is important to them. Or perhaps training for not a minute less than the scheduled time is important to them. Perhaps this compulsive person is superstitious. Compulsive people tend to be superstitious. I knew an athlete once that was so superstitious, he created an arduous warm-up ritual. It was so painstakingly long that he had to start it well before his competition. He didn't always get it just right, and you could see it on his face when he didn't. However, when he did get his routine just right, he was a serious contender. The takeaway here is that at the heart of superstition is belief. Faith. We do ritual type of things when we are superstitious in an attempt to sway luck, fate, or the powers that be in our favor. So at the root of this is faith. Arduous ritual or not, at times this athlete had great faith in his oncoming performance. That is the important part. Great faith can be a great skill (a key) to unlocking many lesser skills (lock boxes).

So in this case (above), we took someone who was compulsive and drilled down into his way of thinking to discover what he did that might make him better than us. We went looking for a "key." What we found from our deduction of simple macro-level personality traits that leaked out during his everyday behavior is that one of his likely keys to him being better than us was his great faith. We then can take the good parts of faith as a key, while leaving the entrapping aspects of superstition on the table. Faith acts as a lubricant for skills. You have to trust all of the movements you make. You have to trust that the landing is going to be there when you are ready for it. You have to trust your skills enough to scare yourself (Step 1 from my Mogul Method). Faith, check to see if you have enough of it. At times, you may find that it is all you are missing. The following statements by world-famous personal development guru, Tony Robbins, are advantageous for you to apply to how to learn from people who are better than you.

> *"Duplicate their mental syntax."*
> *-Tony Robbins*

> *"Duplicate the beliefs of the person who can do what you want to be able to do."*
> *-Tony Robbins*

It should be pointed out that it is not always so easy to obtain a true "key," as in the example above. Many times, true "keys" stick out simply because they appear as something simply out of place, or something that might be missing, but we can't put our finger on it. At first, we don't have to. Just start by making a mental catalog of things that are out of place or missing from people who are better than you. Keep applying that template to others who are better than you. Constantly cross-reference your "keys" between people who are better than you. Use the cross-reference to see if you can spot a pattern or gain any more insight as to the possible use of the "key" that you found. In other words, now that you found a key, constantly be on the lookout for the "lockbox" it might open. If you don't know what lockbox the key you found actually unlocks, but many of the people that are better than you, display the use of that key. Then you should probably do it too, if you can. Simply by practicing a key, even without knowing what it is used for at first, will sometimes uncover its true purpose. As the self-improvement guru says:

> *"Duplicate this persons' (the person who you want to be like) physiology, posture, breathing, etc."*
> *-Tony Robbins*

Let's go back to our analogy of a physical lockbox and key for a moment. It is plain to see that just by looking at some random key, one usually cannot deduce what kind of lock box it will open. Much less often will it open the specific lockbox that you want opened. You will likely have to try it out in multiple lock boxes before you will find the right one. But with practice, you can get a pretty good idea of what kind of key you're looking for, and by extension, if you already have a key, what kind of lock it will open. Here I am referring to an actual physical lock and key, not skills and their acquisition. However, the two are tangentially related. Once you have acquired many keys, you will have a better idea of which lock boxes to start looking for, thereby enhancing your probability of opening similar boxes greater than before.

In sports if you already know how to jump, and have a good "air sense" (key), then learning a new trick (lock box) will be easy for you. It is like a snowball effect. Once you start to figure out how to do it, and the more you do it, the easier it becomes. Before you know it, you may be opening lock boxes like the great Harry Houdini, and everyone will be amazed at your relative ease to solving difficult problems and acquiring amazing skills.

However, this is not always the case with the acquisition of successful traits. The same "door" cannot always be opened by different people with the same key. This is due to the interpretation of the key and its meaning. Everyone interprets things a little differently, learns a little differently, and the keys are fickle (see the "Learn How You Learn" section in this chapter). They depend highly on the person that is holding them, so even though you may hold the key that you need, it will not open the door you want it to, unless your understanding and interpretation of the keys are accurate. Then you must fall into harmony with your application of the key. In other words, you must learn to be able to teach yourself how to make the precious bit of information relatable to your own life experience and the acquisition of your own goals. This can be related to the famous philosophical quote by Confucius:

> *"To know, and not do, is to not yet know."*
> *-Confucius*

FROM WISE TEACHERS

> *"He who asks a question is a fool for five minutes;*
> *He who does not ask remains a fool forever."*
> *-Chinese proverb*

When someone has used what they consider a valuable piece of information—called a "key" (to success) to unlocking a certain secret or rarely circulated bit of information inside their profession—they are unlikely to share it with anyone (especially their rivals). Only great coaches and wise teachers have the capacity to acquire and disseminate as much of this information as they are capable, because there is no conflict of interest. I find it important to point out that great coaches, more often than not, are ones who are retired from competition altogether. This is because the competitiveness of elite athletes tends to create "secret-ism" of their best methods. Even Olympians and world champions can be guilty of withholding vital keys (the true secrets to their success) from their pupils. And rightfully so. After all, if you were winning world level events because you knew something that no one else did, would you want that information getting out? No, of course, you wouldn't.

However, the problem is that many athletes gravitate to Olympians and world champions for the keys to success. This is somewhat misguided. Although they may have the best technique, and perhaps even the best knowledge of the sport, they are less likely to share that information with you than someone who is retired. If you get a chance to be coached by Olympians and world champions, don't do it to learn any secret. You are better off just to learn from their behaviors and the way they carry themselves. Experience how they move, breathe, act, react, etc. That is the priceless information that you can get from environmental exposure to Olympians and world champions. Just understand that great competitors often refuse to show all their cards. This is because they are usually coaching a fairly broad spectrum of talented athletes. Many times, they will want to control the flow of knowledge, so that it is to their own advantage as well. I assure you, this happens a lot and the proof is in their resume. If they are consistent at beating everyone, then they are likely using every possible competitive advantage to do so. They may even be intentionally withholding information that might get your skiing to the next level, just in an attempt to slow down your learning process (depending on how far along you are in your training). I've seen it happen personally and I've even been guilty of it, so you should just be aware of this.

However, what the best athletes don't know—and only you know now that you have read "The Invincible Mogul Skier"—is that the breakthrough knowledge required for improving one's skills varies slightly from athlete to athlete. This is because knowledge is only as good as it is applicable. Every person applies knowledge differently. In other words, more often than not, just knowing the key to a great mogul skier's success isn't enough. There must be a conversion process of that knowledge, so that it can become applicable to you personally, in the flavor that YOU learn. That is the great mystery most people do not understand. One may read many autobiographies and know the key for those great persons' success, but they rarely induce the metamorphosis of those keys so that the knowledge becomes absorbable in their own practice and daily applications. The metamorphosis of knowledge is chock-full of pitfalls and should be done only under careful supervision by a knowledgeable coach as often as possible. This is because many times the knowledge doesn't mean what you want it to mean. At times, you will be blinded by your own fears and ignorance. Nothing corrupts knowledge more wholly than fear and ignorance, so tread carefully.

Wise teachers and coaches often try to deliver keys to you in an augmented tone of voice. It should be the focus of the student to realize when these secrets are unveiled by the "piercingness" of their delivery. Your job is to realize that a real "key" has been dropped upon you, and that although you may have no attachment to it, understand it poorly or incorrectly, or even if you disagree with it, it is your job to pick it up and carry it with you everywhere you go. Why? Because this little golden nugget of words has somehow, or in some way, been used to create some kind of breakthrough for one or more people. Potentially great people. It is likely that this key has made a difficult obstacle surmountable for someone who is more skilled than you. You can imagine it as a key that unlocked an unbreakable door on the path that a very successful person followed. A door, which incidentally, now stands stoutly in front of you, locked.

Now it is important to realize that these great "keys" will most likely not "click" with you right away. In other words, the right key will not open the right door for you right away. That is why good coaches will keep dropping it as many times as you need to hear it, so that it will stick with you. That is the importance of great mentors because they take great pains to make sure that the really important information sticks with you. However, it is still your responsibility to be ever persistent in the pursuit of the TRUE meaning and use of the key, until you can understand, value, treasure, and effectively use the secret of the key in the same way (or better) than the great one that dropped (or taught you) the said key (secret). It is your job as a student to learn to spot when these keys are dropped, pick them up where they fall, and write them down in your journal (so you don't forget them). Then just allow the true meaning of the secret to present itself to you in its own time, as you become a smarter, deeper, more well-rounded athlete. Never throw away (disregard) keys. Never convince yourself that you understand a secret thoroughly enough. If you do either of those things, you are retarding your capacity for greatness.

> *"A teacher affects eternity;*
> *He can never tell where his influence stops."*
> *-Henry Adams*

5 RULES FOR FINDING A WISE TEACHER

1. Avoid someone who reminds you of a courteous waiter.
2. Seek someone who scares you a little.
3. Find someone who gives succinct, clear directions.
4. Seek someone who loves teaching fundamentals.
5. All other things being equal, pick the older person.

VIBING FROM OTHERS

> *"If you want to find the secrets of the universe*
> *think in terms of energy, frequency and vibration."*
> *-Nikola Tesla*

When I see a key inadvertently dropped by a successful person, I am unlikely to know the true meaning of the key right away, just like most people. All I know is that it is important to that person, and therefore, might also be important to me. I just don't know how presently. Especially if it has to do with mogul skiing. Therefore, in order to try to understand the true meaning of the key, I will tend to try to vibe the information that I need from that person.

One of my most precious keys that I ever picked up in my life was dropped by one of the most talented mogul skiers I ever met. I picked up the key at first because I simply thought it was slightly strange. Somewhat irregular. I didn't know what or it's true meaning, but I picked up the key like I always did. I figured the truth would become apparent to me someday if the key was any good. And boy, was it good. The athlete that I am referring to has since passed away, but in his short career, he was easily one of the best Level 2 Superheroes I ever met, with a serious bid into becoming a Level 3 Superhero. He was loved by everybody, and his broad skills rivaled the best Juggernauts. He had the entire package, well on his way to becoming a Legend. A truly spectacular skier to watch. I knew this skier well, since we were on the same team together. The vast majority of the time, he liked to listen to gangster rap, and it was pretty hardcore most of the time.

One day at a competition in Telluride, CO, I noticed he was listening to very soft music. It must have been very relaxing music because he was visibly "jiving" very slowly and softly with the music. What was strange was all I heard him playing all day was hardcore gangster rap any other time in the day. Only when he was in the start gate, was he jiving this way. Completely relaxed. He won the competition that day. That image of him so relaxed on such a difficult course was burned permanently into my memory. That was the key as I picked it up in its raw form. Luckily for me, and now all of you reading this book, he inadvertently dropped this particular key to his success. There was something special in this change of music; it was surely a key, and I set out to find out what it was. Luckily for my readers, I was there to pick it up, dust it off, and hack into its true meaning.

For fear that I would be ridiculed or led astray if I approached him directly about his dramatic transformation in the starting gate, I decided to vibe the true meaning of the mellow music from him. It is necessary to point out that at the time, I was one of the fastest mogul skiers anywhere in the country, and he was one of very few that could ever match my speed. However, my method involved me getting very aggressive at the top of the course. I used that initial anger to overcome my fears so that I could "get up to speed." It is where the Step 1: Scare Yourself of my Mogul Method was born. I thought of my aggression at the top of the course as my true secret to my speed. Yet, here was a man that, with a completely different approach, could match my speed. Plus, he was far more consistent at posting good results than I was. So I was determined to figure out the true meaning of this key.

I tried many different logical interpolations in my mind to uncover the secret, but all of them failed. I only succeeded once I vibed the true meaning from him using the steps I describe below. But basically, I imagined myself in his shoes, with his past experiences, with his usual gangster rap blaring in my ears. At first, it was actually pretty easy, because I myself listened to pretty heavy metal music when I skied as well. It is what helped me to ski aggressively, fearlessly, and focused. But then, I started imagining listening to that soft music at the top of the course and my mind just sort of stopped. The skill level, the effort, the difficulty of the mogul course, and the "loosey-goosey" body relaxation just didn't seem to want to be crammed together into one thought in my mind. They didn't mesh at all. So I followed him closely at the start of the next competition, and from a short distance, but in such a way that he couldn't see me, I copied his every body movement before his competition run, and even after he started. In doing so, I could feel what was going on. He was using his relaxation to quell the power movements, transpose the mogul impacts, and to calm his nerves. All in that one instance, the power of RELAXING clicked for me. It is what ties together strength, flexibility, and speed!

Ultimately, the epiphany I had vibed from him that day played one of the greatest roles, not only to me becoming a faster skier, but a much more consistent one. Not to mention one of the biggest reasons I wanted to write this book: So that I could teach it to as many people as possible. It is also why it is such a prolific and reoccurring theme of this book. Relaxation holds the key to so much untapped potential; it is unreal. Much of this book is built around the power of relaxation, if it is harnessed properly. I owe so much to that Level 2 Superhero who, God rest his soul, seems to still be speaking to all of us from beyond the grave in this book.

Now that we know how important of a tool vibing can be, let me show you how to do it properly. To do this, it takes some considerable knowledge of how the person thinks, but much of that information is actually pretty easy to assume. I like to think of it like the person is just a pattern of waves or vibrations of thoughts, if you will. Then, all you have to do is set your mind to "tune in" to those waves. "Tuning in" to those waves is what I consider "vibing." Since real waves consist of frequency, amplitude, rhythm and time, so does my analogy below. When I do this exercise below, inadvertently dropped keys tend to just "click" for me. Granted I have had a lot more practice at this than most. Obviously, this is a little abstract; therefore, I have broken down the analogy into easy to understand definitions below. If you are ever in doubt, just act as you think the successful person would act in every single thing that you do, while keeping the key constantly in your mind and eventually the answer will hit you. This quote sums it up:

> *"It is easier to act your way into a new way of thinking,
> than to think yourself into a new way of acting."*
> -Jerry Sternin

VIBING

1. FREQUENCY = Experiences of the individual

    a. How often does this person win? Are they accustomed to it? If so, then you need to start thinking as if you were a person who consistently wins. Or else, the key will not become tangible for you.

    b. How many supporters/enemies does this person have? Who are they? What are they like? You may use this to find the source of this person's offensive and defensive strategies. Through careful analysis, you may be able to find a chink in their armor.

2. AMPLITUDE = Open (or closed) mindedness of the individual

    a. How abstract, off-the-wall, crazy far out-side-the-box is this person capable of thinking? If it's pretty out there, then you should stretch your mind to try to think like that. Otherwise, the true nature of the key may remain forever elusive to you.

    b. In contrast, are they very closed-minded, narrow, and bigoted? If so, it may be an equally great (and perhaps even uncomfortable) stretch of your thought process to try to think like these individuals. But again, if you do not take into consideration a persons' closed-mindedness, bigotry, etc. (I like to call them "blind spots"), then you may fail to pick up a key that they drop.

3. RHYTHM = Conditioning of the individual

    a. What type of propaganda are they exposed to on a constant basis?

        i. From the media
        ii. From the government
        iii. From their parents

    iv. From their friends

    v. From their religion

    vi. From their teachers, coaches, or mentors

*Repetition is the main thing to look for here. The more one repeats something, the more that something will be ingrained into their subconscious mind. This is called conditioning. You can be actively aware of, and even responsible for, your own conditioning, such as conditioning from weight training or from a mentor. But it is more common to be unaware of your own conditioning because many of the people and organizations above have their own agendas that do not benefit you.

> *"Unthinking respect for authority*
> *is the greatest enemy of truth."*
> *-Albert Einstein*

  b. It is important to note that many people are not consciously aware of their own conditioning, and will defend that their conditioned point of view viciously (refer back to Chapter 19: Your Opinion Betrays You), even to the point of inner dialog and backward rationalization with themselves. Because the alternative (believing that outside forces control their conscious and unconscious decisions and actions) is just too scary for them to believe, they choose not to. Take a minute right now to take out a pen and paper and write down ten ways that you are conditioned to act by the group of people listed above. In other words, if none of these things existed, in what ways are you likely to act differently? Or would you act exactly the same? Remember, if you answered "exactly the same" you may be so conditioned, you are defending that conditioning.

4. TIME - It is extremely important to keep in mind that the above are just tools you can use to try to get on the same wavelength as someone. But people are infinitely complex, and almost always there are multiple combinations of the above variables in any given thought process, and they will vary with time—mostly based on the individual's emotional state—so tread carefully.

Now, please take caution here, because I have seen too many times a student picking up a key, believing they understand it, but then turn to their friends and say: "I get it, but it's not really THAT important, you know?" or "It just doesn't affect me the same way it affects him, you know?" These are some of the most detrimental thought patterns an athlete can have. If you are not as "excited" as the person who dropped the key was about it, you must ask yourself, WHY AM I NOT AS EXCITED ABOUT THIS PIECE OF KNOWLEDGE AS THEY ARE? The answer is because you don't understand the secret to the same DEPTH that they do. It is merely your job to pick it up like a caveman would any shiny object and start searching for its deeper meaning. I have had the quickest luck by waiting until my waves and vibrations of thought (as discussed above) are exactly similar to the moment when the "great person" dropped the key. Because from a coaches' point of view, the key DOES apply to you with exactly the amount of energy in which it was dropped, or else the coach wouldn't have dropped it.

MYSTERIOUS STRANGERS (THE CAVEMAN METHOD)

Next, I'll explain an easy-to-digest, easy-to-remember method for learning something that you cannot yet comprehend. The concept is admittedly a little abstract, but nevertheless effective. However, it does require an open mind. To learn something you cannot yet comprehend, you must first humble yourself and set aside all that you think you know. I like to pretend that I am a caveman in the modern world. I make pretend in this way because I find it very humbling and opens my mind to be filled with wonder. A caveman placed in our society wouldn't have any of the education, culture, or biases that we have, and therefore, is a great model for humbling one's self.

A caveman that one day found himself in a modern society would most likely try to emulate the people around him. He would do so shamelessly if he had to, in order to cope and survive. It serves as a great model for opening one's mind, so that one can better mimic those whom they want to be like. We can do this in order to learn things that we cannot yet comprehend.

To simplify things, let us make believe a situation where a modern person meets a caveman (we are the caveman). The modern person with all his high technology and modern clothing would appear odd and mysterious to the caveman. Yet the caveman would quickly realize how much more the modern person knows. He would base this assumption on his observations of the high technology and clothing of the modern man. Lacking a similar language, the caveman would not be able to ask the modern man all the questions he is sure to have. Therefore, because of his own perceived deficit, and in an attempt to satisfy his curiosity, the caveman would start to mimic the mysterious stranger's every move in the hope that some information regarding the modern man and his mysteries will become apparent, thereby answering some of his many questions. This method actually works in practice. As we mimic others, reasons for the way they act or behave a certain way tend to be unveiled. Potential benefits become apparent, and no one needs to tell us these things. Simply by mimicking another, secrets that they may wish to hide begin to leak out. That is the reason to implement the Caveman Method.

As we are pretending to be the caveman, we would conform to all of the "the mysterious stranger's" attributes. To do this, we would have to:

1. Become an expert at knowing when "keys" have accidentally been dropped, and write them down in your journal as soon as possible, verbatim.
2. Never manually metamorphose keys; it can only end up in the bastardization of the knowledge.
3. Constantly keep it in your mind, let it marinate, and ask as many questions as you possibly can to yourself, regardless of how silly you might think them to be. (You may be surprised how insightful your answers can be.)
4. Never throw away or discard keys; always keep them in a pondering state in your mind.
5. Never convince yourself that you fully comprehend any key. (Remember you are a caveman or cavewoman.)

Imagine this scenario: a modern-day adventurer comes hiking out of a cave, gets in his helicopter that is waiting nearby (naturally) and flies away—but he drops his car key on the ground before departing. Watching this whole process in awe is the last surviving caveman, sulking in the shadows. After the departure of the "sky god," he quickly trots over to the take great care in scooping up the shiny object that fell on the ground. Although the caveman might not understand what the shiny object is, or what it does, he is drawn to it out of curiosity and intuition. His intuition will then lead him to protect this object with his life, if necessary, even though he may not know why, or what it even is. His only hint is his instinct that it is a rare object, and rare things must be given protection and due process. All the caveman knows is that someone better than him valued this object, and therefore, so should he.

The takeaway here is not to imagine a caveman driving down the main street in a red convertible throwing money into the air. The takeaway is a particular feeling that resides in all of us that something we do not understand is somehow valuable and to keep it forever present in our mind, forever searching and asking questions about its true nature and for its true application. Too often I see young people ignorantly dismiss the keys to their own success because they don't take the time to let the information process in their minds. They are too impatient.

SUMMARY

It is important to keep the secret key bit of information forever in your mind until the end of time, or until the lock box which it opens appears before you, whichever comes first. Be a key collector, constantly marinating on them, saying to yourself, does it apply to this? Does it apply to that? I know it's used for this, but how does it relate to that? Where did this knowledge come from? What am I missing that I don't have? What am I not thinking of? Am I missing some information because it lies in one of my mental blind spots? Is there something else that goes with this that I need for this to work? Is there something that I don't see that I need to be able to? Or is it the significance of the "nothing" that I cannot grasp?

You will know that you have found the right lock box, and that you have opened it when answers start pouring in. More answers than you were expecting. Answers to questions you haven't even asked yet, or ones that you did not think were related. Like it did for me when I discovered the true meaning to relaxing. Be advised that sometimes, lock boxes are full of more questions than answers. This is fairly normal. This is another reason why it is so important to be a key collector. Because when this happens to you, you will likely have some keys that will actually work on those second-tier type lock boxes. The more keys you have, the faster you can open all the lock boxes. However, you will most likely never have all the ones you want.

If that doesn't work, pretend the key is like a skeleton key, and keep sticking it in every hole you can find until something clicks. This is the method of the key collector. It is the athlete's duty to actively try to find the key's true meaning, its true use, deferring their own opinions and judgments (which can cause bastardization of the key if they don't). Most of the really valuable secrets in this world are authored by incredibly deep individuals, and the depth to which a true secret penetrates is incomprehensible to the layman. Yet they are usually comprehensible and valuable to some degree to them. That is why some sayings are so famous. Because for every level you increase your intelligence, you also gain a deeper insight into the true meaning of the famous quotes true secrets. The best secrets are clichés, kicked around and mistakenly "understood" by the masses. But each time you "level up" your intelligence, a deeper meaning for the cliché will present itself. This goes on and on, greater and greater significance with each level of understanding, all the way up to the very top. Thus, the best keys are not ever forgotten, because they have value to all levels of intelligence and experience. This is the main purpose why when a key is dropped; you never want to let it go (even if you don't understand it). You never want to let it wander from your mind, because as you learn to think deeper, deeper meaning for your shiny object will present itself anew.

*"You have to know who you are to grow to your potential.
But you have to grow to know who you are."*
-John Maxwell

*"If a student doesn't ask the right questions,
A teacher cannot be responsible for his failure."*
-Vanessa Redgrave

*"The mind must be given relaxation.
It will rise improved and sharper after a good break.
Just as rich fields must not be forced,
For they will quickly lose their fertility if never given a break-
So constant work on the anvil will fracture the force of the mind.
But it regains its powers if it is set free and relaxed for a while.
Constant work gives rise to a certain kind of
dullness and feebleness in the rational soul."*
-Seneca (On Tranquility of Mind, 17.5)

*"I am always doing that which I cannot do,
in order to learn how to do it."*
-Pablo Picasso

CHAPTER 21
L1FELONG LEARN1NG

"As long as you live, keep learning how to live."
-Seneca

"Once you stop growing, you're dying."
-Albert Einstein

THE PLATEAU TRAP

"Anyone who stops learning is old,
whether at twenty or eighty.
Anyone who keeps learning stays young.
The greatest thing in life is to keep your mind young."
-Henry Ford

"Only a mediocre person is always at his best."
-W. Somerset Maugham

Beware of the plateau trap. The plateau trap is the idea of thinking that someday, once and for all, you will have everything you ever wanted, and can then "rest easy." There can be a plateau trap in any and all categories of life. The plateau trap is a highly idealized view of the world that at some point in time, what we want will actually satisfy us. That is never the case. Desire always creeps in, no matter how much we have or how much we know. That is why we must strive to always be a better version of ourselves than we were yesterday. In today's rapidly evolving workforce, and just the state of the planet in general, we can never afford to stop learning. We will miss too much. So set aside the idea that you will ever be able to subdue any aspects of your life, once and for all. Every aspect has the capacity to rise up against you again, fueled by our wants and desires. Lay down the notion that any category of your life can be completely certain, satisfied, perfect and remain that way for all time. Abandon the dream that you will ever be able to just coast or drift, or leave some portion of your life unmaintained, for it may crumble.

> *"Leisure without study is death.*
> *A tomb for the living person."*
> *-Seneca, Moral Letters, 82.4*

The essence of life is change. Change is the natural state of the universe; it cannot and will not be subdued. It will revolt against you, violently if necessary. All things must change, and so must you, so why not change for the better? If nothing else gets you, change will, and it will hurt a lot if you are stuck in your ways. So prepare for it now. Prepare yourself by practicing a life of lifelong learning. You can always be a better version of yourself today than you were yesterday, but it's up to you what that version of you will be like. Don't give up. Don't ever give up. Beware of the plateau trap, cast your eyes upwards and onwards, never be satisfied with where you are.

If you are already the best athlete in the world and you have an Olympic gold medal around your neck (like I know some of you bad-asses do, or will someday), then you can improve your intelligence, or your finances, or your enlightenment, and on and on. The world doesn't care about your ego, or how great you think you already are. It was here first, and it has seen much greater people than you come and go throughout the millennia. It demands that you give your all, that you achieve all that you came here to achieve, and then once you have done that, it expects you to give back. Giving back is just another form of ascension and evolution as a soul.

As potentially one of the greatest people who ever existed, take note of how Miyamoto Musashi intertwines lifelong learning into the requirements he places on anyone who wants to learn his strategy:

> *"This is the Way for men who want to learn my strategy:*
> *Do not think dishonestly.*
> *The Way is in training.*
> *Become acquainted with every art.*
> *Know the Ways of all professions.*
> *Distinguish between gain and loss in worldly matters.*
> *Develop intuitive judgment and understanding for everything.*
> *Perceive those things which cannot be seen.*
> *Pay attention even to trifles.*
> *Do nothing which is of no use."*
> -Miyamoto Musashi in the "Book of 5 Rings"

Musashi isn't the only Legend that exemplifies the lifelong learning way of life. The living Legend, Alexandre Bilodeau, does as well. His preferred method names sports as one of life's greatest teachers. Undoubtedly, this is heavily influenced by mogul skiing. He stated during an interview with George Stroumboulopoulos:

> *"To me, sport has been the school of life,*
> *it is where I learned my discipline that I used in school,*
> *that is where I learned how to deal with stress,*
> *that's how I've learned a lot of things."*
> -Alexandre Bilodeau
> on the George Stroumboulopoulos Tonight Show

Alex gives meaning to his powerful words when he promotes lifelong learning. But he is not the only Alex out there that promotes it. Here is another quote from a different Alex you may or may not have heard of:

> *"If you're not expanding, you're shrinking.*
> *Because somebody else is growing."*
> -Alexander the Great

Powerful words coming from a powerful person. Yet, every time I give this advice, there is always somebody that doesn't take it to heart. Every time they don't take it, usually within the same year, their business or their life or whatever else they're working on starts to show signs of falling apart.

A FINAL WORD

The world doesn't care about your self-esteem or your biased opinion of how great you would be if you had the same advantages as other people. The world expects you to accomplish something before you feel good about yourself. The road is difficult. It is filled with nasty obstacles and pitfalls. You need to be able to welcome these challenges as necessary trials and tribulations. Because in the same package as your trials comes your experience. These tests lay in front of you for the purpose of training your soul. So be careful how you treat your trials, and be mindful to never "half-ass it" through your trials, pitfalls, and difficult times, because it is upon those events where you hone your skills and where you lay the foundation for the type of person you will become. If you half-ass it through the difficult times in your life, you are essentially giving yourself "half-ass" quality, experience and skills. Treat life as if it is one big trial, one big test, and both the test administrator and test taker are essentially you. Then you will have it in the proper perspective.

> *"Wind, rain, frost, and dew.*
> *They all just teach you to be a better man."*
> *-Unknown*

Diligence is the most powerful lever that an aspiring athlete can possess. Not talent, strength, speed, and not even intelligence. As intimidating as the latter may be, they can't compete with diligence. Talent, strength, speed, and intelligence are like the mountains of the world. Awe-inspiring, breathtaking, ungraspable. Diligence, however, is like the winding rivers at their feet—twisting, turning, and even tunneling right through them at will. It may not be as exciting to watch, and it takes a great deal of time, but diligence has the power to conquer all. Some succeed because they are destined to, but most succeed because they are determined to.

It is an unspoken truth that most Olympic medalists and world champions were not the very best at any given aspect of their sport. If you were to ask them, they will tell you awe-inspiring stories of jaw-dropping feats of an individual in their sport that was better than everyone, that didn't make it to the Games for this reason or that. Do this enough times, and you will get the gist that often times the individuals that achieve the most glory didn't do so because they were the absolute best—they did so because they had the fortitude to just hang on a little bit longer than everyone else.

As a final word I would like to take the time to tell you how much I appreciate you reading this book and I hope that you have enjoyed it as much as I have had writing it for you. It is my sincerest wish that you take the lessons that you have learned in this book and put them to use in your own life. I hope that not only the mogul skills, but the hard-won life lessons that I have tried to put in to words here can help you in your life goals. I thank you for being a dedicated mogul skier and a triune athlete. A mogul skier that is refining not only their physical, but also the mental and emotional parts of themselves. An Invincible Mogul Skier.

-THE END

*"One must be careful of books, and what is inside them,
for words have the power to change us."*
-Natalie Babbit

*"Apply yourself to thinking through difficulties.
Hard times can be softened, tight squeezes widened,
And heavy loads made lighter
for those who can apply the right pressure."*
-Seneca, On Tranquility of the Mind, 10.4b

"There is no finish line."
-NIKE commercial

SPECIAL THANKS TO:

BRYON WILSON (3 Time Olympian, Olympic Medalist, Team USA)

MIKE MORSE (Olympian, Team USA)

GARTH HAGAR (Olympic Team Head Coach, Team USA)

DYLAN WALCZYK (World Cup Medalist, Team USA)

DAVID COLTURI (Red Bull Cliff Diving Series Event Champion, 2 Time National Champion, 2 Time World University Games Medalist)

RED BULL MEDIA HOUSE (For use of Red Bull Photos)
 PHOTOGRAPHERS: Balazs Gardi
 Dean Treml
 Marv Watson
 Romina Amato

FROST HOLLOW PHOTOGRAPHY
 PHOTOGRAPHER: Michael Piniewski

INDEPENDENT PHOTOGRAPHY
 PHOTOGRAPHER: George Hudnutt

NATHANIEL MEAD (PSIA Demonstration Team, for helping me pull this book together)

JOHN DOWLING (For amazing artwork)

DR. RYAN KRAMER (My A.R.T. and Chiropractic specialist. He has done more than anyone to help me heal.) 4150 Westown Pkwy, ste 201, West Des Moines, IA 50266 phone: (515)-267-9956

BIBLIOGRAPHY

Achor, Shawn. Big Potential: How Transforming the Pursuit of Success Raises Our Achievement, Happiness, and Well-Being. New York: Currency, 2018.

Bumps: A Mogul Skiing Documentary. Directed by Zac Hoffman. 2014. Truckee, CA, The High Fives Foundation. Vimeo stream.

Capital, Jason. Millionaire DNA: DNA Activation System. 2015.

Cialdini, Robert B. Influence: The Psychology of Persuasion, Revised Edition. New York: Harper Business, 2006.

Coyle, Daniel. The Culture Code: The Secrets of Highly Successful Groups. London: Random House, 2018.

Davis, Todd. Get Better: 15 Proven Practices to Build Effective Relationships at Work. New York: Simon & Schuster, 2017.

Duhigg, Charles. Smarter Faster Better: The Secrets of Being Productive in Life and Business. New York: Random House, 2016.

Durant, Will. The Story of Philosophy: The Lives and Opinions of the World's Greatest Philosophers. New York: Pocket Books, 1991.

Ferriss, Timothy. The 4-Hour Workweek: Escape 9-5, Live Anywhere, and Join the New Rich. New York: Harmony, 2009.

Foer, Jonathan Safran. Extremely Loud and Incredibly Close. Boston: Mariner Books, 2006.

Goleman, Daniel. Emotional Intelligence: Why It Can Matter More Than IQ. New York: Bantam Books, 2005.

Hager, Garth (US Mogul Team Head Coach). Interviewed by Michael L. Mead, November 7, 2015.

Herman, Todd. The Alter Ego Effect: How the World's Top Performers Use Secret Identities to Win in Sports, Business and Life. New York: HarperBusiness, 2018.

International Olympic Committee. "Freestyle Skiing Equipment and History." Accessed October 31, 2016, https://www.olympic.org/freestyle-skiing-equipment-and-history?tab=history.

Kotler, Steven. The Rise of Superman: Decoding the Science of Ultimate Human Performance. Boston: New Harvest, 2014.

Kwik, Jim. "Boost Brain Power, Upgrade Your Memory, #267." Bulletproof Radio, December 11, 2015.

Pascale, Richard, Jerry Sternin, and Monique Sternin. The Power of Positive Deviance: How Unlikely Innovators Solve the World's Toughest Problems. Boston: Harvard Business Review Press, 2010.

Ph.D, Rudolph E. Tanzi, and Deepak Chopra M.D. Super Brain: Unleashing the Explosive Power of Your Mind to Maximize Health, Happiness, and Spiritual Well-Being. New York: Harmony, 2013.

Pink, Daniel H.When: The Scientific Secrets of Perfect Timing. New York: Riverhead Books, 2018.

Plath, Sylvia. The Bell Jar. New York: Harper Perennial Modern Classics, 2005.

Robbins, Anthony. Power Talk Rules The Source of Pain and Pleasure. Robbins Research International, 1999.

———. Unlimited Power : The New Science Of Personal Achievement. Reprint edition. New York: Free Press, 1997.

Sinek, Simon, David Mead, and Peter Docker. Find Your Why: A Practical Guide for Discovering Purpose for You and Your Team. New York: Portfolio, 2017.

Strayed, Cheryl. Wild: From Lost to Found on the Pacific Crest Trail. New York: Vintage Books, 2013.

Sutton, Robert I. The Asshole Survival Guide: How to Deal with People Who Treat You Like Dirt. Boston: Houghton Mifflin Harcourt, 2017.

Tolle, Eckhart. The Power of Now: A Guide to Spiritual Enlightenment. Vancouver: Namaste Publishing, 2004.

Wilson, Bryon (Olympic Bronze Medalist). Interviewed by Michael L. Mead, June 1, 2015.

Zen. White Plains, NY: Peter Pauper Press, 2015.

APPENDIX 325

PHOTO EXPERIENCE 1: WHEN TO INITIATE UPHILL HIP DRIVE

Uphill Hip

1. Here you can see my uphill hip, as it is in its most "uphill" position. Notice in the following photos how much I drive it forward and exactly where in the turn I do it.

2. Here you can see me start to drive my uphill hip as soon as I reach the crest of the mogul.

3. Notice how with my early uphill hip drive I am able to drive through the crest of the mogul. This helps me to ski a "straighter" line in the moguls, which coincides with me not being at the "mercy" of the mogul. In other words, the shape of the rut does not dictate to me how I must exit the mogul. With good uphill hip drive, I am free to choose my own exit from each mogul, regardless of the shape of it.

4. At this point, my uphill hip is fully driven forward. My hips are square to the fall line. This is the point at which I want to initiate the Mogul Skier Hips Up Position.

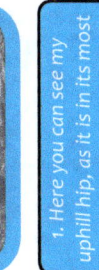

Mogul Skier Hips Up Position.

5. Here you can see me implement the Mogul Skier Hips Up position. I practice patience in this position, (also known as the Hollow Position) as I wait for the next mogul to come to me.

APPENDIX   327

PHOTO EXPERIENCE 2: HOW TO FIX MISTAKES IN REAL TIME

"Uphill Hip Drive" happens here.

1. The problem starts up here, because my center of mass is not stacked over my feet.

2. This causes me to be late on the next turn.

3. I over compensate by pushing my feet out at the next mogul, which gets me a little in the back seat.

4. Here you can see that my hips arrive to the mogul after my feet already pass it. This means that I am in the back seat. I got into this predicament because I was not patient in the previous image. I missed Step 4 of the New Mogul Method. Meaning, I pushed my feet at the mogul.

5. Here, you can see that I visually relax. This allows me get my feet back underneath me in the next step (Step 3: Relax - from the New Mogul Method.)

6. Here, I am able to do a powerful Uphill Hip drive because of my relaxation in the previous step. This allows me to get into the Hollow Position. Notice how this goes hand-in-hand with my hips being in the in the Mogul Skier Hips Up Position. I combine these attributes with being patient (Step 4: Be Patient, in the New Mogul Method). Here I wait for the mogul to come to me, rather than push my feet out at the mogul, which made me get backseat in the first place.

7. In this last image, you can see that my hips have caught up to my feet, and I am able to get stacked again (Step 2: Get Stacked of the New Mogul Method). At this point, I have successfully recovered from the bobble I made, four moguls prior.

Photograph by George Hudnutt

SUMMARY - This example is proof that the proper implementation of the New Mogul Method is not only a good way to start your run, but is also a means of recovery when you make a mistake, as seen here. The gem of this method is that it is perfectly cyclical in nature. Which means that however you may screw up, you can recover by simply starting with the appropriate step of the New Mogul Method and start the sequence over. In this example, I found myself out of balance, which means I was not stacked (Step 2). Therefore, I implemented the next step (Step 3: Relax). This allowed me to get into a position where I could force myself to Be Patient (Step 4). This allowed me to complete the cycle and arrive safely again at a nicely stacked position (Step 2).

PHOTO EXPERIENCE 3: THE POWER STORED IN YOUR SKIS

1. I am in the hollow position here. Notice how square my hips are to the fall line.

2. As soon as my tips hit the mogul, I control how much energy is stored in the ski.

3. Here, you can see that I have stored the exact amount of energy that I want in the flexion of my skis.

4. Notice that some of the snow from impact gets caught on top of my boot and skis. This is important because it will illustrate the direction of the energy transfer from this turn to the next.

5. Here, we can see that the snow that was forced on top of my skis/boots from the impact with the mogul, starts to rise as it is following a new trajectory (different from impact), as I transfer the stored energy in my ski to an upwards and sideways motion.

6. I have fully left the mogul and the same energy that I harvested from the flexion in my skis has been fully transferred to the snow that was on top of my skis.

7. Since I have much more mass than the snow, the upward and lateral movement "bonus boost" that I get from the release of the energy stored in my skis is subtle and difficult to see. It can really only be felt. But the energy transfer to the snow is mathematically the same amount of energy that I am harvesting from the mogul. Therefore, since the snow has a much smaller mass, it's physical displacement is much greater. Since it mathematically has to follow the same trajectory that my body is traveling (which came from the uncoiling of my skis), it is as good of an indication that exists to "see" the kinetic energy gained by harvesting it from my skis (The blue dotted arrows depict the movement of the snow).

APPENDIX   329

8. In this last picture, we can see the final position of the snow particles before they start to come down. The yellow arrow depicts the total lateral (left to right) displacement of the snow. The green arrow depicts the total vertical displacement of the snow. Notice how the snow both started in the same lateral position as me, and finished in the same lateral position as me on the other turn. This proves that the physics is sound. This doesn't always happen, however. Only when you harvest the energy from your skis properly does this happen! (Provided you are fortunate enough to be skiing moguls with loose snow.)

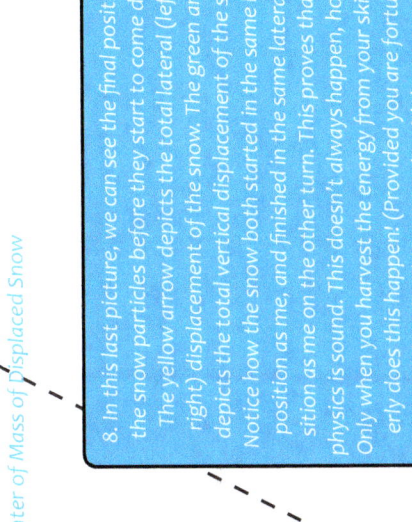

Center of Mass of Displaced Snow

9. So How Much of a "Boost" am I REALLY Gaining?:

Let's suppose the snow that got launched into the air was about 3 lbs., was lifted about 10 ft. into the air, and traveled horizontally 3 ft. Well, if that is true, and I weigh 165 lbs., then I am 55 times the weight of the snow in the picture. Therefore, my body was "boosted" upwards by 2.18 inches, and laterally by about 0.65 inches. That may not seem like a lot, but it is free energy harvested from simply skiing the moguls efficiently. Besides, when you ski the moguls very close to the crest of the mogul, as seen here, 2 inches can make a big difference! Furthermore, these skis are fairly worn out. When they were new, I could probably wrench out at least twice the amount of energy as shown here, if I wanted to. So at the high end, you could theoretically get about 4 inches of vertical and 1.5 inches of lateral "boost" if you have new, stiff skis. Awesome!

APPENDIX

Thanks for reading!
You are now an Invincible Mogul Skier!

www.ingramcontent.com/pod-product-compliance
Lightning Source LLC
Chambersburg PA
CBHW071147070526
44584CB00019B/2691